T0330317

Innovation and Intellectual Property in China

Innovation and Intellectual Property in China

Strategies, Contexts and Challenges

Edited by

Ken Shao

Professor of Law, The University of Western Australia

Xiaoqing Feng

Professor of Law, China University of Political Science and Law, Beijing, China

Edward Elgar

Cheltenham, UK • Northampton, MA, USA

Published by
Edward Elgar Publishing Limited
The Lypiatts
15 Lansdown Road
Cheltenham
Glos GL50 2JA
UK

Edward Elgar Publishing, Inc.
William Pratt House
9 Dewey Court
Northampton
Massachusetts 01060
USA

A catalogue record for this book
is available from the British Library

Library of Congress Control Number: 2014937751

This book is available electronically in the ElgarOnline.com Law Subject Collection, E-ISBN 978 1 78100 160 8

ISBN 978 1 78100 159 2

Typeset by Columns Design XML Ltd, Reading
Printed and bound in Great Britain by T.J. International Ltd, Padstow

Contents

Contributors

Dr Ziliang Deng, PhD (Nottingham), is Assistant Professor of International Business at Renmin University of China. His recent research has focused on international new ventures and innovation, and his recent papers appear in *International Business Review*, *Thunderbird International Business Review*, *Asia Pacific Journal of Management*, *Asian Business & Management*, and *Journal of Policy Modeling*.

Du Weike received his Bachelor degree in engineering from Huazhong University of Science and Technology in 2001, and Juris Master degree from Xiamen University in 2004. He was an examiner for re-examination of the Patent Re-examination Board of the State intellectual property office of China from 2004 to 2010, and has been a judge of the Supreme People's Court of China since 2010.

Professor Feng Xiaoqing, PhD in Law (Peking University), is a Professor of Law at China University of Political Science and Law (CUPL), Vice-president of Intellectual Property Law Society of China, Director of Research Center in Intangible Assets Management of CUPL, Director of intellectual property management interdisciplinary, CUPL; visiting scholar, University of British Columbia (UBC) Faculty of Law, Canada; member of Experts of Committee on case guidance work of the Supreme Court of China; Attorney at law, Beijing Tianchi Hongfan Law Firm and Arbitrator, Beijing Arbitration Commission.

Professor Seamus Grimes is Emeritus Professor of Economic Geography at the Whitaker Institute, National University of Ireland, Galway. He obtained his PhD at the University of New South Wales, and spent many years teaching geography at the National University of Ireland, Galway. His research focuses on multinational foreign investment in Ireland and China, with his current work looking at foreign R&D investment in China within the context of the new indigenous innovation policy. He has published widely in international journals.

Dr Peter S. Hofman is an Associate Professor in Corporate Social Responsibility and Corporate Governance at Nottingham University Business School China. He is also head of department of International

Business & Management at NUBS China. His research focuses on the way business–government–society interactions influence corporate strategy and on the relationship between corporate governance, corporate social responsibility and innovation. His work has been published in the *International Journal of Human Resource Management, the Asia Pacific Journal of Management, Technology Analysis and Strategic Management, Business Strategy & the Environment* and *Energy Policy*, among others.

Professor Michael Keane is Principal Research fellow at the Australian Research Council Centre of Excellence for Creative Industries and Innovation (CCI), Queensland University of Technology, Brisbane. His research interests include China's cultural and media policy, creative industries in China and East Asia, East Asian media co-productions, and East Asian cultural exports. He is author of six books and editor or co-editor of eight others.

Dr Kong Xiangjun is a member of the Adjudication Committee of the Supreme People's Court (SPC) and the Chief Judge of the Intellectual Property Division of the SPC of China. He received his LLM and LLD from China University of Politics and Law. He adjudicated many cases of great influence in both administrative and intellectual property areas, and was selected as one of the ten national outstanding young and middle-aged jurists in 2007. In 2009 and 2010, he was listed amongst the top 50 most influential people of the global intellectual property community.

Dr Alexander Newman, PhD (Nottingham), is currently a senior lecturer at Monash University in Australia. He has published widely in the areas of entrepreneurship and organizational behaviour in such journals as the *Journal of Organizational Behavior, Leadership Quarterly, Entrepreneurship, Theory and Practice, International Small Business Journal, Human Resource Management* and *Journal of Business Ethics*.

Professor Ken Shao, PhD (London), is Professor of Law at the University of Western Australia and a committee member of Australia China Business Council (ACBC). Previously he was founding director of Australia's premier Postgraduate Certificate in Chinese Law (partnered between Murdoch University and City University of Hong Kong). He publishes and researches in China's innovation economy, international intellectual property discourses, and Chinese culture and history. He has been interviewed by such media as *The Australian, the Guardian* (UK), ABC, SkyNews, and China Radio International on topical issues about China. He has published with various journals including *the WIPO Journal, Columbia Journal of Asian Law, Hong Kong Law Journal* and *Peking University Intellectual Property Law Review*.

Dr Wei Shi, Reader in Law, PhD (St John's College, University of Cambridge); Bangor University Law School, United Kingdom; Fellow of Cambridge Overseas Society, Member of the International Law Association (British Branch), Member of the Society of Legal Scholars, and Council Member of the Chinese Society of Private International Law. He specializes in the area of international trade law, international intellectual property law, intellectual property and development, and private international law in a commercial context. His work has appeared in leading international journals, such as *American Business Law Journal* and *Wisconsin International Law Journal*.

Dr Yang Lihua, PhD in Law (Renmin University of China), Associate Professor, Institute of Intellectual Property Law, China University of Political Science and Law (CUPL); research fellow, Research Center in Intangible Assets Management of CUPL. Dr Yang has presided over some important research programmes in the field of intellectual property, and published articles in the *Journal of the Copyright Society of the USA*, *Journal of World Intellectual Property*, and the like.

Professor Peter K. Yu holds the Kern Family Chair in Intellectual Property Law and is the founding director of the Intellectual Property Law Center at Drake University Law School. He has served as Wenlan Scholar Chair Professor at Zhongnan University of Economics and Law in Wuhan, China and a visiting professor of law at the University of Haifa, the University of Hong Kong, the University of Strasbourg, and Washington and Lee University. Born and raised in Hong Kong, Professor Yu is a leading expert in international intellectual property and communications law. A prolific scholar and an award-winning teacher, he is the author or editor of five books and more than 100 law review articles and book chapters. He serves as the general editor of the *WIPO Journal* published by the World Intellectual Property Organization (WIPO). Professor Yu has spoken at events organised by WIPO, the International Telecommunication Union, the UN Conference on Trade and Development (UNCTAD), the UN Educational, Scientific and Cultural Organization (UNESCO), the Chinese, US and EU governments and at leading research institutions from around the world. His lectures and presentations have spanned more than 25 countries on six continents, and his publications have appeared in Chinese and English and have been translated into Arabic, French, Hausa, Japanese, Persian, Portuguese, Spanish and Vietnamese.

Dr Zhang Zhicheng, PhD in Law (Peking University), joined China's State Intellectual Property Office (SIPO) in 1995. He was also a Visiting

Scholar in the School of Law, University of Washington (2001). He assumed his present position as Deputy Director General of the Protection and Coordination Department in 2011 and Deputy Director of the Intellectual Property Development & Research Center in April 2013. He played an important role in drafting *the National Intellectual Property Strategy of China.*

Foreword

Graham Dutfield

As a child in 1960s England, I well recall the public's association of 'Made in Japan' with poor-quality goods. 'Made in Hong Kong' gave people the same impression. This attitude was largely justified. As for the Peoples' Republic of China, nothing available at all was made there. It was a truly mysterious country. I wondered if I would ever meet a citizen of 'Red China' in my whole life.

It is astonishing how rapidly a country's image can change. Two decades later we could no longer be smug about Japan. It seemed that the future *was* Japan, an uncannily efficient land of robots, wonderful gadgets and elegant design. We had become envious and just a little fearful. In Britain whole industries gave up and shut down. Since then, though, the world economy has changed, Britain has recovered to some extent and while we continue to admire the country's consumer products we are a bit less sure about Japan.

China's image has certainly changed a lot: yesterday a nation of hermits, now (from the admittedly skewed perspective of this academic) a nation of international postgraduate students. But some prejudices are deep seated and difficult to shift. To many people, China remains the copier nation *par excellence*. An economy dedicated to knock-offs, that has prospered not by making new things but by perfecting the art of the rip-off, from the fake Rolex sold as a fake Rolex, to the fake Rolex passed off – convincingly – as the real thing.

That one human being out of every five lives in China is just one reason why China matters more than ever before. This is a country, comprising 20 per cent of us all, that has been undergoing a massive and rapid transformation which is probably unprecedented in human history. Tremendous challenges remain in this large, complex and diverse country, but many millions of people have already been lifted out of generations of poverty, with confidence that they and their children will never fall back into it. The prognosis for most of China's remaining poor, still a substantial proportion of the country's population, has never been better. The scale of these changes and their consequences and the sheer size of the country mean that what happens in China affects the whole world.

None of this is accidental. The great British scientist and scholar Joseph Needham made the English-speaking world aware as never before of China's proud history as a scientifically and technologically advanced nation. So in many ways it has already gone to where it now strives to go. It has past experience to draw upon and the confidence to know that having risen to great heights in the past, it can do so again. Second, the country has undeniably brought to an end a difficult period in its long history when first it allowed itself to decline, in part through an arrogant isolationism, and become dominated by Western powers; and then followed such errors by adopting disastrous policies based on a tragic misunderstanding of human nature and of basic economics. For China the mistakes, weaknesses and poor decisions of the past have at least provided an excellent learning experience on what to do and what *not* to do in order to improve today's China.

China may have misunderstood itself in the past but it certainly no longer has a monopoly on misrepresentation. Much has been written on China in the West and certainly not all of it is true or well informed. Indeed, much of the literature is anything but. Recent narratives do tend – correctly – to acknowledge China's remarkable progress, and there is much admiration for the country in this respect. But often they go on to make one of two highly questionable assumptions. One is that as an inherently imitative people whose economy is based on mass production of goods based on foreign specifications, low quality knock-offs and on the backs of overworked, unskilled and semi-skilled labour, its spectacular growth rates are unsustainable. Countries more culturally disposed to be creative will inevitably catch up. Of course, as economies mature economic growth rates *will* decline, and this will happen to China. Inevitably, the catcher-uppers will themselves be caught up by others. But it is unlikely to be because China is uncreative (of course it is!), but more because of increased foreign competition in both cheap mass-produced goods at one end, and high-technology goods and services at the other, and also the imperative to distribute wealth as well as to create it. Alternatively, commentators go to the other extreme and uncritically assume that China is destined to achieve global domination in a very short time.

The first assumption is of course factually incorrect, and insulting. As this book shows, China is increasingly innovative and is putting in place sound legal and regulatory institutions to replace yesterday's knock-off economy with tomorrow's innovation-based economy. There is a long way to go but considerable progress has been made. As for the second assumption, it may well happen but we really cannot be sure, besides which China is on a long journey, not a day trip. Absolutely nothing is guaranteed. You can have a population of hard-working, creative and talented people but without *continuous* good policymaking, stable government, effective institutions and open debate, none of that is sufficient. Flexibility and pragmatism are essential too. Today's effective solutions may turn out to be tomorrow's dysfunctional laws and policies. The law of intended consequences is inescapable, especially in the face of complexity. Omniscience is a fantasy, and government planners need to understand this. Predicting the future is a hazardous game. What we can say with assurance, to which this excellent and highly informative volume amply testifies, is that China's remarkable resilience and determination to strike its own path towards development is paying dividends and the future for the country is bright. Of course, we in the West are not usually well disposed towards the one-party-state system of government and doubt that such political systems can provide sufficient space for criticism and accountability. The facts remain, though, that poverty reduction has been substantial and that is something unequivocally to be admired, and that political space for open debate on economic and other issues is expanding.

What of intellectual property? As this book makes clear, one must take a holistic view when it comes to fostering innovation. Intellectual property rights are very important but they comprise just a few items on a lengthy menu of legal, regulatory and policy forms intended to enhance, organize and exploit the creativity of the human mind for the benefit of the nation and ultimately, one would like to think, humankind in general. Nonetheless, the way that they are designed – and here I talk not just of statutory law, but the institutions and the whole legal and regulatory structure – has major economic and social implications, especially for developing countries which are largely importers of legal norms, of copyright, patents, trademarks etc. that evolved in Europe over more than three centuries. As the African access to medicines debate of the late 1990s and early 2000s shows, the stakes can be enormously high. Developing countries like China have had to transplant internationally agreed norms wholesale without much opportunity to assess their likely impacts on economic growth and human welfare.

Another point to make is that we in the West must now dispense completely with the arrogant notion that China is nothing more than a pirate nation, one of the three members (along with India and Brazil) of a group denounced by a self-righteous Washington lobbyist as 'the axis of IP evil'. Undoubtedly considerable enforcement problems remain but

China has made a lot of progress in a short time, partly in response to external pressures but also because transitional economies becoming more *domestically* innovative cannot afford to let uncontrolled piracy continue. An article in *The Economist* noted in 2001 that 'countries tend to clamour for strong patents once they have an industry to protect'. The same goes for copyright, trademarks and industrial designs.

I have a few words to say also about culture and intellectual property. It is often assumed that non-Western cultures have no need for, or even understanding of, property concepts in the context of knowledge, technologies, cultural works and goodwill. Therefore intellectual property rights, because of their Western origins, belong to Western culture and are thus alien to populations such as the Chinese and Indians (as they are said to be to indigenous peoples like the Maori of New Zealand and the Inuit in the Arctic). This argument has been used politically in strategies that I personally have some sympathy for. But to suggest they have no relevance or utility is incorrect and one must simply let go of convenient untruths. As Ken Shao's work demonstrates, China has a long history of intellectual property jurisprudence and no doubt many other nations and non-Western people and populations do too.

A final observation on intellectual property is that Chinese enterprises are often associated with filing poor quality patent and utility model applications. There is probably a great deal of truth in this, and the fact that the Chinese government provides incentives for firms to file applications in China and overseas may not entirely help. Quality is ultimately more important than quantity. However, this is likely to be mainly a short-term problem. The fact that more and more United States and European patents are going to Chinese firms and that the State Intellectual Property Office (SIPO) is now a well-respected institution which cooperates with leading IP offices elsewhere leads one to suppose that seeking to acquire patents whose quality falls below the international standard is becoming both more difficult and a less attractive business strategy anyway.

The unavoidable question arises of what other countries can learn from China. This is a difficult one. There is nothing typical about China as a country. It is a large developing country as are India, Brazil and Russia, its fellow BRIC members. But the similarities end there. When South Korea developed rapidly from the 1970s, it adopted many policies from its close neighbour Japan and adapted them to suit its own circumstances. The two countries are obviously quite similar culturally and while their relationship has not always been a happy one, they undoubtedly have close historical ties. Whether the Japanese model is workable in, for example, Ghana, is another matter entirely. In terms of technological catch-up with the West, China has probably gone further than those three countries and in that sense at least, it sets a good example for what can be achieved, which other countries should study to their advantage even though they will have to find their own way. To anybody wishing to learn more about the 'Chinese way' and to better understand its advantages and disadvantages, this book is an excellent place to start.

1. The cores and contexts of China's 21st-century national innovation system

Ken Shao

INTRODUCTION

China's innovation economy is something we cannot afford to overlook.[1] Fuelled by an alluring national innovation system (NIS) that strategically supports 'self-driven innovation', China is increasingly becoming (or in my expression *re-emerging* as) a global innovation enthusiast.[2] The government actively seeks the effective provision of nutrition to innovators and has clearly set its goal: by 2020, China will have a fairly

---

[1]   There are now various statistics pointing in that direction. As the *Global Innovation Index* stated in its 2012 report, 'China's performance on the key knowledge and technology outputs pillar is outpaced only by Switzerland, Sweden, Singapore, and Finland'. *See* INSEAD & WIPO, *The Global Innovation Index 2012: Stronger Innovation Linkages for Global Growth*, p. 39. In the last few years, there have been many emerging studies on China's patent statistics. For instance, the Third Asia-Pacific Innovation Conference held in October 2012 at Seoul National University had quite a few submissions on this topic.

[2]   China's re-emergence as a global innovation leader has deep historical and cultural roots. *See* Ken Shao, 'History is a Key Decoder: Why China Aims at Re-emerging as a Global Leader of Innovation', *Law in Context*, Vol. 29:1, 2013, pp. 117–132. For describing China's innovation boom, 'self-driven innovation' is arguably better than 'independent' or 'indigenous' innovation. *See* Ken Shao, 'Zizhu chuangxin and China's Self-driven Innovation: Calling for a Holistic Perspective', *Cardozo Law Review de novo*, 2013, pp. 170–71. In this book, we do not specifically distinguish the meanings of innovation, creativity, innovation economy and knowledge-based economy. In China, the term *chuangxin* (creativity or innovation) covers all these aspects.

well-established national innovation system that supports China's construction of a comprehensive well-off society.[3] Numerous challenges remain but if we are in general impressed by how China has achieved its economic miracle in the last 30 years, then we could be equally impressed by its innovation potentials – a key part of China's next-stage reform objectives.[4] And as we know, China can move fast.[5]

This book, titled *Innovation and Intellectual Property in China: Strategies, Contexts and Challenges*, is a unique response to this striking phenomenon. In this book, we attempt to discuss the contexts of and challenges to China's ongoing innovation and intellectual property (IP) strategies, which blossom under the wide spectrum of China's comprehensive national innovation system. In particular, this book represents an effort to create a platform for a number of Chinese IP authors to introduce to the English-speaking audience a variety of 'insiders' perspectives', which are followed by constructive perspectives of international authors. Importantly, 'intellectual property' in this book is not analysed from the popular, normative piracy perspective, i.e., viewing China as a leading pirate of foreign IP rights. Rather, it is discussed as a catalyst to China's innovation economy, together with other catalysts such as talent plans, funding, industrial parks and creative clusters, and government support.

There exist many confusing, misconstrued impressions of China's innovation boom, which is a result of ill-contextualized narratives of China that diffuse under broader cultural and ideological backdrops.[6] For over a century, our world has accumulated an excessive amount of plausible 'China information' that needs to be replaced by 'China knowledge'. This requires a *holistic* perspective of China, which can only

---

[3]   'Hu Jintao: Generally Complete the Construction of the National Innovation System with Chinese Characteristics by 2020', *China Daily*, 7 September 2012.

[4]   For the latest debates on this, visit http://business.sohu.com/s2013/18shqh/.

[5]   This can be seen, for instance, from China's new President Xi Jinping's recent speech delivered in China's foremost innovation park – Zhongguancun Science Park. 'Xi Jinping: Implementing Innovation Drive cannot Wait, Window-shop or Slack', *Xinhua News*, 1 October 2013.

[6]   For instance, Western critics have used the term techno-nationalism and threats to describe the nature of China's current innovation efforts. *See* Richard Wallace, 'China Eyes "Creative" Industries in Intellectual Property Push', *Elec. Eng'g Times*, 29 August 2005, p. 1.

occur in pace with de-ideologization and when an authentic micro-perspective of China's culture, history and present is adopted.[7] For example, are China's innovation efforts aggressive or *inherently* nourished by its creative cultural DNA? Where is China's reform heading? Yet, China knowledge and the holistic perspective do *not* automatically mean insiders' opinions, because China's own heritage is, too, deeply misunderstood by many Chinese. But we believe that this book's insiders' perspectives, accompanied by the international perspectives, at least can serve as a better information seafood platter for our readers' selection.

China's 30-year reform has now entered into complex deep water.[8] Solutions do not simply come from naive mimicry or irrational rejection of foreign experiences. China needs to enter into an era of 'mature self-consciousness' that has been *fundamentally* absent in China's search for its own destiny since the early 20th century. Mature self-consciousness longs for a culturally self-conscious, independent and critical thinking soul that converts essential and often buried Chinese values and legacies into an *internal* driving force for the exploration of *practically* feasible ways of China's future development. It should be rooted in an improved understanding of China's own tradition and meanwhile actively assess the pros and cons of non-Chinese experiences.[9] Many of China's current efforts, including those about an innovation economy, increasingly reflect such a trend. Only a holistic perspective, not a cold-war aftershock or a yellow peril mentality, can help foreigners understand China's future and have confidence in this.

The above will be further analysed in Chapter 1, which has a dual function. First, it will critically assess certain intriguing core components of China's national innovation system from a holistic perspective. Such assessment also benefits from discussions with various innovation park officials in Wuxi region, Jiangsu Province. Second, it will provide a brief introduction to other chapters. As a whole, this book is well organized

---

[7] For a succinct article about true China knowledge, *see* Ken Shao, 'The True China Knowledge that Australian Businessmen Should Know', *China-Australian Entrepreneurs*, September 2010, pp. 26–29. For a holistic perspective of China's innovation economy, *see* Shao, 'Zizhu chuangxin and China's Self-driven Innovation', note 2, pp. 168–94.

[8] This now represents a top agenda for the Chinese government. *See* Zhou Rui, 'Xu Shaoshi on Five Challenges to the Reform's Deep Water', *China News*, 31 May 2013.

[9] For its more detailed methodology, *see* Ken Shao, 'The Two Londons that I Love', *Chinese Scholars*, November 2008.

but it by no means amounts to 'uniform views'. Quite the contrary, the opinions and standpoints expressed by the authors are diverse. The relevant research in China is at an early stage, and there could be obvious differences in patterns and styles of writing and thinking between non-Chinese authors and their counterparts living in mainland China. As this is an edited book, the authors are solely responsible for their own works. Collectively, this book attempts to form a dynamic discussion forum of a cutting-edge topic.

1. A MULTI-LAYERED NATIONAL INNOVATION SYSTEM

It looks like China has almost suddenly come up with a multi-layered national innovation system. This includes many components such as innovation strategies and policies, implementation measures, R&D funding, talent plans, innovation parks, cultural industries, government procurement, technical standards, tax and financial services, venture capital, higher education and research institution reforms, schemes supporting new and emerging industries, technology commercialization, regional strengths, integrated planning, and of course, IP strategies and lawmaking.[10] Collectively, these components do not have exact counterparts in other countries, and are systematic and coordinated by China's ongoing legislative and institutional reforms.[11]

The term 'national innovation system (NIS)' was initially defined by Christopher Freeman, one of the most eminent researchers in innovation studies.[12] All countries, if they can, should have such a system. This is justified by the necessity of establishing a *self-determined* 'development impact assessment' (DIA) framework, which Graham Dutfield has proposed.[13] The WTO/TRIPS regime does not explicitly provision such a

---

[10] For an early study of some of these components, *see* Ken Shao, 'Patent Law, National Strategies and Policy Incentives: China's Road to a Leading Innovator', *the International Trade and Business Law Review*, 2011, Vol. 14, pp. 85–103.

[11] For understanding the systematic and coordinated nature of China's national innovation system, *see*, e.g., Ministry of Science and Technology, *2011 China Science and Technology Development Report (Chapter 2)*, Beijing: Science and Technology Documentation Press, 2012, pp. 17–34.

[12] Christopher Freeman, *Technology Policy and Economic Performance*, London: Pinter, 1987.

[13] Graham Dutfield, 'Making TRIPS Work for Developing Countries', in *Developing Countries and the WTO: Policy Approaches* (Gary P. Sampson & W.

mechanism to its member countries living at very different development stages. It is thus left to each member country to create one. Yet, many countries do not have such a system, and are not even aware of such a necessity. They rely on the globally institutionalized, highly automatic IP pipelines, believing that this alone will create prosperity.[14]

For decades, China's market economy has been growing at high GDP rates, thanks to cheap labour, manufacturing and the world export market behind. Without playing a significant role in global innovation, does China seem to be eating its fill? There can be different answers to this question. A conventional argument is that China, through its labour-manufacturing model, connects itself with global trade and thus has dramatically developed its economy. This argument omits the keyword: the 'value chain' of the global trade, an inherent characteristic of the global market. Overall, Chinese manufacturers survive at the bottom of the chain. For instance, Apple controls 51.8 per cent of its profit in its entire value chain while its Chinese manufacturers only get 1 per cent.[15] As a world-leading economist Alan Deardorff has stated, welfare effect in developing countries can be affected by global owners of maximized patent monopoly.[16]

Even worse, within that small profit range, Chinese manufacturers need to budget for everything, including cleaning up their factory sewage, which remains a fundamentally critical challenge for China. With profit-driven appetites in the small export nutshell, a dramatically improved Chinese environmental protection framework may not see an expected force, not to mention that the US industries and IP law practice discourage effective clean technology transfers to China.[17] In addition, China has so many other domestic challenges, such as wealth gap, regional imbalance, low knowledge level that contributes to overall social

---

Bradnee Chambers eds), New York: United Nations University Press, 2008, pp. 163–65.

[14] For vivid stories, *see* Peter Drahos, *The Global Governance of Knowledge: Patent Offices and their Clients*, Cambridge: Cambridge University Press, 2010, p. 336.

[15] Booz & Company, *Chinese Manufacturing Industry Brews New Pattern*, 2009, p. 3. Available at: http://www.booz.com/media/file/New_Situation_of_Chinese_Manufacturing_cn.pdf.

[16] A. V. Deardorff, 'Welfare Effects of Global Patent Protection', *Economica*, Vol. 59, 1992, p. 35.

[17] Matthew Rimmer, 'Who Owns the Sun? Patent Law and Clean Energy', *The Conversation*, 21 February 2012. Peter Drahos, 'The China–US Relationship on Climate Change, Intellectual Property and CCS: Requiem for a Species?', *WIPO Journal*, No. 1, 2009, pp. 125–32.

underdevelopment, an unhealthy economic structure, and proven institutional deficiencies. All of them are waiting to be addressed.[18] Only a knowledge-based and pro-innovation society can do a proper job.

A heartbreaking lesson learnt from the global financial crisis of 2008 (GFC) is that over-dependence on other economies should not be seen as a desirable outcome of globalization. Rather, there is always a sovereignty agenda in our globalized society. This agenda is, too, important to an innovation economy. The international IP regime tends to erode the city walls of national sovereignties. International standards, minimized trade barriers and IP harmonization work together to delude sovereignty. All of them maintain the existing global value chain, giving little flexibility to newcomers.[19] Without a strategic, self-determined national innovation system, China can only let things drift. But this is precisely not what China wants. For a long time, China has had a plan for *re-emerging* as an innovator.

In China, the term 'to construct an innovative country' or 'self-driven innovation' is more popularly known than 'national innovation system'. The milestone of modern China's national innovation system is the *Guidelines on National Medium- and Long-term Program for Science and Technology Development* (2006–2020), which is a highly systematic master plan for a comprehensive national innovation system that suits China's extremely complex economic and social transition.[20] Self-driven innovation means that Chinese enterprises perform with their own power source, depend less on external or third-party intellectual fruits, and thus increase their share in the global value chain. Self-driven innovation can and should be achieved through different means, such as home-developed patents and original cultural goods, foreign technology acquisition, share control, takeover, exclusive licences, collaborations, and marketing and branding strategies. It certainly is not a synonym of 'independent', 'indigenous' or 'self-reliance', which means entirely home-grown, often in an isolated, duplicative or handicraftsman manner.[21]

---

18   Shao, note 2, p. 188.
19   The concept of sovereignty in national IP law and policy making is elaborated on by Peter Drahos. *See* Drahos, note 14, p. 4.
20   This was issued by the Ministry of Science and Technology of the People's Republic of China on 9 February 2006. Available at: http://www.gov.cn/jrzg/2006-02/09/content_183787.htm. For its implementation policies, *see* http://www.gov.cn/ztzl/kjfzgh/.
21   SIPO Director Tian Lipu has defined it as 'belonging to oneself, human created and new'. SIPO, 'SIPO Director Tian Lipu on the Important Role of

The US government has expressed its concerns over China's 'indigenous' innovation, in particular the Chinese policies on setting new technical standards and government procurement. In a lengthy investigation report by the US International Trade Commission, which criticizes China's self-driven innovation policies, it appears that the writers were reluctant to not view the China–US relationship as simply one between 'one of the world's most innovative countries' and 'a globally dynamic manufacturing base'. China's self-driven innovation is thus viewed as a major challenge to the US commercial interest in China.[22] But soon the US turned to recognize that the two nations 'share an interest in seeing China emerge as a prosperous technological innovator.'[23] This is an appropriate gesture because all countries have the right to become innovators.[24]

As I have elaborated on in a 2012 paper, a 'holistic perspective' of China can dramatically reduce foreign concerns. Overall, a holistic perspective requires putting *today's* China through a stretched lens and under micro-level contexts, which should include the above-mentioned international frameworks, domestic problems and solutions that are the major focus of this book and, very essentially, undistorted views of Chinese culture, both historical and present. I wrote:

> A holistic perspective of China's self-driven innovation needs to start with a proper understanding of history. Holding our historical treasure map, we will not stop at the Cold War or the China-West conflicts in the nineteenth and twentieth centuries. Rather, our precise destination is where China's self-driven innovation and Chinese *high-end* cultural DNA converge. Here is where my holistic perspective of China's history of innovation, creativity, and intellectual property – which is widely ignored in Western, and even Chinese, communities – is located.[25]

Patent System', available at: http://www.gov.cn/zwhd/2006-01/09/content_151769.htm.

[22] US International Trade Commission, *China: Intellectual Property Infringement, Indigenous Innovation Policies, and Frameworks for Measuring the Effects on the US Economy*, USITC Publication 4199, 2010, p. xiv.

[23] Statement of Philip I. Levy, 'China's Indigenous Innovation Trade and Investment Policies: How Great a Threat?', *The 112th Congress Hearing*, 2011, p. 53.

[24] China is not alone. For national innovation systems of the BRICS, *see* José Eduardo Cassiolato *et al.*, *BRICS and Development Alternative: Innovation Systems and Policies*, London: Anthem Press, 2009.

[25] Shao, note 2, p. 172.

Only by understanding the firm roots of *respecting* creativity and innovation in the Chinese cultural DNA, can we view China's self-driven innovation boom *today* as *inherently* natural, peaceful and useful for making China better under critical international and domestic conditions. Thus, a holistic perspective can create a more tolerant and mutually beneficial environment for both domestic and foreign stakeholders in China's innovation waves.[26] It can also shift our focus from ideologized concerns to possible improvements of China's innovation system. In contemporary China's complex social and economic transition, constantly portraying China's national innovation system with plausible terms such as techno-nationalism, threats or even yellow peril might talk down an otherwise fairly healthy situation.[27]

2. CORE COMPONENTS AND THEIR CONTEXTS

China's multi-layered national innovation system is generated in external and internal contexts under which there are specific needs and challenges facing China. In my view, a good way of understanding this is to contextualize each core component of China's national innovation system, e.g., funding policies, industrial preferences, talent plans, innovation parks, IP strategies, and integrated planning in a particular *sequence*. This section now proceeds to provide a contextualized analysis of four core components of China's national innovation system.

Surprisingly, the very first agenda is probably not IP. Many may doubt China's innovation capacity because they believe China has a very weak record on IP protection. But a knowledge-based economy is much more than IP, not to mention that the international IP regime is not automatically supportive of innovation growth in developing countries. China has since 2006 become a global top spender of R&D funding and there has been much discussion on this.[28] This enables me to move to the next immediate question: once the money is put on the table, who is going to innovate?

---

[26]   China's innovation policies are not insensitive to non-Chinese interests. For examples, *see* Richard P. Suttmeier, 'A New Technonationalism?: China and the Development of Technical Standards', *Commc'Ns. of the Acm*, 2005, Vol. 48, p. 37.

[27]   Shao, note 2, p. 181.

[28]   For a brief overview, *see* 'China's R&D Investment 2nd in the World: Report', *China Daily*, 15 November 2011.

2.1 Talent Plans

Who is going to innovate in China? This very first challenge is hardly attended to by Western IP scholars. In *the 2012 China Business Climate Survey* conducted by the American Chamber of Commerce in China, human resource constraints received a 43 per cent dissatisfaction rate, which topped the entire survey questions, including that of IP infringement. The survey concluded: '[f]inding qualified talent – both at the managerial level and below – is a major concern ... This year AmCham China members ranked management-level human resources constraints as their top business challenge.'[29] This high dissatisfaction rate with China's human resource quality should not lead to a totally irrelevant concern that a large proportion of China's poorly educated population may pose uncertainties to world stability. Rather, a cultural-historical perspective can shed some light on it. Chinese culture by its nature used to be highly civilized and based on education and knowledge. For complex external and internal reasons, China's quality of human resources has sharply declined in the last few centuries. The Cultural Revolution (1966–1976), in particular, drastically damaged China's education foundation. When Deng Xiaoping re-opened China's door, China had an exploded, poorly educated population that was only suitable for labour-intensive manufacturing in the then well-established global trade network dominated by key players such as the US and Western Europe.[30] However, the reformist government believes in Deng's famous saying: 'science and technology are the number one productivity'.[31] For China, a civilization based on knowledge and talents, the labour-intensive model, which had never been Deng's goal, can only be an interim anomaly.

Reconstructing China's human resource foundation is as difficult as building the Great Wall. China has spent 30 years on preparation work. This includes re-establishing foundation areas of scientific research, higher education reforms, sending students back overseas and so on. The Strategy of Rejuvenating China with Science and Education (the RCSE

---

[29]   The American Chamber of Commerce in the People's Republic of China, *2012 China Business Climate Survey Report*, p. 11.

[30]   For these external and internal factors, *see* Ken Shao, *History is a Key Decoder*, pp. 124–125.

[31]   Deng Xiaoping, *Selected Works of Deng Xiaoping*, Vol. 3, Beijing: Renmin Press, 1993, p. 274.

Strategy) was created in 1995, representing a major milestone in post-1978 China's human resource rebound.[32] So far, there have been various talent plans created to suit China's needs. One of the early policies is the Hundred, Thousand and Ten Thousand Talents Project.[33] In 2010 the Chinese government issued *the National Medium and Long-Term Guideline of Talent Development Plan 2010–2020* (the Talent Development Plan).[34] It covers comprehensive aspects of stimulating the knowledge-based economy by properly rewarding all kinds of talents and innovative efforts.[35] In an early study of China's innovation economy, I mentioned that the Talent Development Plan is designed to become a final resolution of bringing China back to a knowledge-based state.[36]

For the last 30 years, a major talent strategy for China has been encouraging Chinese students and scholars to study abroad. The reason is very clear: for decades China had been left far behind by developed countries and learning from them is one of the most feasible ways to catch up. The latest research shows that for over 30 years China has sent 2.24 million students overseas, of which 36.5 per cent have returned.[37] A fundamental dilemma facing international students in developed countries is the accessibility of career-enhancing training and work experience that take years to build up.[38] Thus, China could not be too impatient to bring its 'expats' back before the harvest season comes.

In 2008 China launched a massive overseas talent scheme – the Thousand Talents Program. Developed by Li Yuanchao, former head of the Central Committee's Organization Department, the Program creates a multi-layered strong incentive system for attracting senior and junior Chinese talents working in overseas institutions and companies to return

---

[32]   Xinhua Official Data, 'The Strategy of Rejuvenating China with Science and Education', *Xinhua Net*, 9 February 2003.

[33]   *See* http://guoqing.china.com.cn/zwxx/2013-02/13/content_27947430.htm.

[34]   For the official copy, *see* http://www.gov.cn/jrzg/2010-06/06/content_1621777.htm.

[35]   For a brief discussion, *see* Wang Huiyao, 'China's National Talent Plan: Key Measures and Objectives', 1 May 2011. Available at: http://ssrn.com/abstract=1828162.

[36]   Shao, note 10, p. 96.

[37]   For details, *see* Wang Huiyao, *Annual Report on the Development of China's Study Abroad (2012)*, Beijing: Social Sciences Academic Press, 2012.

[38]   Some of the language and engagement problems are identified, for instance, in Jane Burdett & Joanna Crossman, 'Engaging International Students: An Analysis of the Australian Universities Quality Agency (AUQA) Reports', *Quality Assurance in Education*, 2012, Vol. 20:3, pp. 207–22.

to China.[39] Certainly, in a globally free market, China is free to release policy incentives that attract its expats to return. Despite the 'not-quite-sure' feelings among many overseas Chinese expats, the 'war for talent' is emerging between China and key international innovators.[40]

The 15th-century English patent privilege was devised to introduce existing technologies from more developed states in Europe.[41] China today lives in an entirely different world, in which patent laws are no longer territorial or imitation tolerant. What England used to do is today defined as piracy. The US immigration schemes are appealing to foreign talents but their Chinese counterparts are not.[42] Resources such as substantial financial rewards, housing benefit and access to opportunities arising from China's economic boom are the real incentives. By providing strong incentives, the Chinese government clearly understands that overseas Chinese talents may bring back knowledge, experience and technology that meet international standards.[43] From this comparative perspective, the Thousand Talents Program precisely hits the point.

Other incentive programmes attracting overseas returnees and domestic talents include the 530 Project of Wuxi City, Jiangsu Province and its rivals in neighbouring cities and other competitive regions. These projects aim at providing different categories of substantial seed funding to Chinese domestic high-tech and cultural projects that are at an early stage of commercialization.[44] Recent noteworthy progress can be found in the Nanjing Nine Principles issued in 2012 in Nanjing city, the capital of

---

[39]   The Program's official website is http://www.1000plan.org/. For its policy background, *see* http://news.xinhuanet.com/newscenter/2009-01/07/content_1062 0815.htm.

[40]   The term 'war for talent' is borrowed from Ed Michaels *et al.*, *The War for Talent*, Boston: Harvard Business School Press, 2001. It is called the 'brain gain' in David Zweig & Huiyao Wang, 'Can China Bring Back the Best?', *The China Quarterly*, 2013, Vol. 215, p. 590.

[41]   P. J. Federico, 'Origin and Early History of Patents', *JPOS* Vol. XI-7, 1929, p. 293.

[42]   For how migrants support the US innovation economy, *see* the Partnership for a New American Economy, *The Role of Foreign Workers in the Innovation Economy*, 20 November 2012.

[43]   Surveys indicate that a high proportion of domestic Chinese welcome those overseas returnees who can contribute to China's development. *See* Yang Heqing & Cheng Yian, 'The Empirical Analysis of Evaluating the Implement Effect of Introduction Overseas High-level Talents Policy', *Science & Technology Progress Policy*, 2013, Vol. 16:30, p. 108.

[44]   For a discussion, *see* Shao, 'Patent Law, National Strategies and Policy Incentives', p. 101. The 530 Project is now completed and upgraded to post-sale supporting schemes. But in other surrounding cities such as Yixing, projects such

Jiangsu Province, one of China's most developed provinces adjacent to Shanghai. This policy aims to relieve employees (including both domestic talents and overseas returnees) in Nanjing-based universities, research institutions and companies, as well as university students, from their normal workload so they can engage in commercial activities meeting their innovative specialties. These activities will count towards their promotion assessments or course credits. This further allows the distribution of up to 95 per cent of the profit of employment inventions to the employee-inventors in universities, research institutions and companies, and allows patents to account for up to 70 per cent of a company's equity.[45] These policies all reflect a philosophy of upgraded, dynamic and after-scaffolding support that aims to give talents elevated platforms for contributing in the real 'battlefields'. The *Implementation Plan for the Hundred, Thousand and Ten Thousand Talents Project* issued in early 2013 represents the latest example of this philosophy.[46]

A key objective of China's government reform in recent years has been to improve the capacity of government services. Local governments in developed regions have made genuine efforts to upgrade their infrastructure and experience in serving talents' projects and needs. Suzhou City next to Shanghai is one of China's richest cities. Suzhou has established a coordinated, supportive and well-funded implementation platform for serving talents. In 2011 Suzhou's talent funding was about US$150 million. Some appointees of the Thousand Talents Program have quickly stimulated the establishment of hundreds of upstream and downstream companies for Suzhou in just a few years. In 2011 the total sales created by companies established by overseas returnees in Suzhou reached US$1.17 billion.[47]

There are of course many problems and challenges. Despite continued efforts in reforming China's education, funding and scientific systems, China needs to further improve its overall environment – including funding distribution and salaries – for talents to deliver their creative contributions.[48] The remaining problems continue to fuel significant

---

as the Talent Program for the Pottery Capital still remain to serve the same function.

[45]   'Nanjing Issued Sci-Tech Nine Principles to Stimulate Innovative Undertaking', *China Youth Daily*, 1 February 2012.

[46]   *See* http://guoqing.china.com.cn/zwxx/2013-02/13/content_27947430.htm.

[47]   'Suzhou's Pro-1000-Plan Policies and Positive Interactions between Talents and Industries', *Chinese Talents*, 2012, No. 12, pp. 36–37.

[48]   For existing problems, *see* the State Council, *Report on the Allocation and Use of the State Fiscal Sci-Tech Fund*, 22 October 2013, available at:

outflows of Chinese human resources to developed countries.[49] Studies show that talent plans in China's less-developed regions are not very attractive.[50] Overall, appointees of the Thousand Talents Program mainly contribute to research rather than entrepreneurial activities.[51] However, these challenges may *not* represent a crisis. Talent outflow, if being viewed as future talent reserves, may create long-term international linkages for the Chinese economy. China's institutional deficiencies may be of real concern for returnees but further reforms are under way and those who have successfully returned may contribute to institutional improvement.[52] In fact, economic studies indicate a positive net effect of the Thousand Talents Program.[53]

Concerns over regional gaps on attracting talents do not really make sense.[54] The effect of talent plans, including their industrial effect such as shown in Suzhou, must first be examined in developed regions which lead China's innovation economy. Less developed regions are not yet ready for a substantial inflow of talents but can start from their regional competitive potentials such as biodiversity, labour cost and less pollution. It is noteworthy that China's new leadership is determined to improve regional and urban–rural balances in public services, such as education and health care, in China's next-stage urbanization.[55] This, together with other factors such as regional competitive potential and more affordable

---

http://www.mof.gov.cn/zhengwuxinxi/caizhengxinwen/201310/t20131023_10021 04.html. For improved outcomes, *see* Zhang Xuehua, 'A Review of the National Innovation Index Report 2012', *Xinhua News*, available at: http://news. xinhuanet.com/2013-09/29/c_125470157.htm.

[49] 'China Struggles to Retain Talents', *China Daily*, 30 July 2013.

[50] Shen Yueqing & Zhu Junwen, 'The Provincial Comparative Analysis of Global Experts Import Policies in China', a China Social Science Youth Fund research project (no. 10CRK004), working paper, 2011.

[51] Yang & Cheng, 'The Empirical Analysis of Evaluating the Implement Effect of Introduction Overseas High-level Talents Policy', p. 109.

[52] Shao, note 2, p. 189.

[53] Yang & Cheng, 'The Empirical Analysis of Evaluating the Implement Effect of Introduction Overseas High-level Talents Policy', pp. 109–11.

[54] Chinese provinces and major cities all have their own ambitious and competing talent plans. For details, *see* Shen & Zhu, 'The Provincial Comparative Analysis of Global Experts Import Policies in China' (No. 10CRK004).

[55] Urbanization was China's ninth most important reform measure in 2013. For a recent discussion, *see* http://cppcc.people.com.cn/n/2013/0530/c34948-21665862.html.

housing prices, will eventually see more talents flowing to less developed regions. Chengdu Tianfu Software Park in Sichuan Province is a classic example.[56]

The challenges to China's talent plans and the overarching national innovation system are *ultimately* a human resource issue. The quality of Chinese human resource limits the capacity of China's political, legal, institutional, economic and educational reforms.[57] For instance, the extent to which the environment for talents to innovate can be improved is often subject to the local human resource quality in venture capital management, government service and market development capacities. Thus, human resource is *both* the core crux of, and the core solution to, China's overall transitional reforms as well as its innovation-based economy.

2.2   Innovation Parks and Industrial Preferences

In addition to supporting academic researches, China's talent plans encourage talents to lead industrial development of intellectual fruits. The above-discussed Nanjing Nine Principle and Wuxi's 530 Project are efforts that focus on how to motivate innovators to commercialize their knowledge fruits. This can be further demonstrated by the crucial roles that China's innovation parks and policy-driven industrial preferences play under the national innovation system.

Modern Chinese economy has an established position in the global value chain discussed in Part One of this chapter: a labour-intensive and export-driven manufacturing model. This unsustainable model, to a great extent, has already lost its chance in competing in existing high-tech industries owned by developed nations. China thus has to turn to key and emerging industries, such as biotechnology, new materials, new energies and LED technologies, in that all countries arguably stand at the same scratch line.[58] This understanding is fully reflected in *the Decision on Speeding up the Cultivation and Development of Strategic Emerging*

---

[56]   For details, visit its official website: http://www.tianfusoftwarepark.com/.
[57]   Shao, note 2, p. 187.
[58]   The Emerging Industrial Centers of China Investment Association runs an information-rich website on China's new and emerging industries: www.eicoci-a.com. For a latest study of China's role in green energy, *see* Joanna I. Lewis, *Green Innovation in China: China's Wind Power Industry and the Global Transition to a Low-Carbon Economy*, New York: Columbia University Press, 2012.

Industries (2010) issued by the State Council.[59] Government support such as reward, tax and procurement are not a Chinese invention.[60] They are justifiable due to the high uncertainties of these industries.[61] Since recent years, many of these emerging industries have been fostered and supported in China's leading innovation parks and creative clusters where domestic and overseas Chinese talents engage other components of the national innovation system, such as R&D funding, venture capital investment, tax and financial services, government procurement, and the creation of technical standards.

The construction of innovation parks is a striking phenomenon in China's recent progress of modernization.[62] Back to the 1990s, China started to build innovation incubators in many cities but these early-stage practices were different from the innovation parks that have appeared in recent years. As have been mentioned, China's innovation parks engage with various new policies that are part of the national innovation system and have diverse functions aiming to suit the needs of companies developing at different stages. Incubators remain a part of innovation parks, but not the central part. Now in many cities innovation parks are up and running but those in developed regions attract more experienced management personnel and thus possess greater capacities of supporting innovation and technology commercialization.[63]

In various leading innovation parks, the government's initial scaffolding is crucial but companies are required by policies to fly by themselves

---

[59]   For its official copy, *see* http://www.gov.cn/zwgk/2010-10/18/content_ 1724848.htm.
[60]   For instance, South Korea's technical standard-setting is viewed by OECD as a powerful driving force for innovation. OECD, *Reviews of Innovation Policy: Korea*, 2009, p. 244. For the government's supporting roles, *see* Zhou Yingchun, 'The Effect of Government on the Developing Emerging Industries of Strategic Importance', *Forum on Science and Technology in China*, No.1, 2011, pp. 20–24.
[61]   Li Xiaohua, 'Policy Orientations and Characteristics of Strategic Emerging Industries', *Macroeconomics*, No.9, 2010, pp. 20–26.
[62]   For a distinctive study, *see* Michael Keane, *Created in China: The Great New Leap Forward*, London: Routledge, 2007.
[63]   Chih-Hai Yang *et al.*, 'Why Does Regional Innovative Capability Vary so Substantially in China?', *Journal of Technology Innovation*, 2012, Vol. 20:2, pp. 239–255.

after certain stages.[64] In provinces such as Jiangsu and Zhejiang, many innovation parks have their own on-site governments. This strategic deployment aims to improve the accessibility of government services to the knowledge-based companies in the parks. These governments are formed by different offices that try to provide all-in-one support.[65] The context of the above needs to be considered: that is, the quality of government service in China remains as a known area of deficiency, which has been identified as a fundamental target of the next-stage reform by China's new leadership group.[66]

The planning and designing of innovation parks represent another essential feature of China's innovation system. New-generation Chinese cities and innovation parks embrace an elegant, bright and Chinese-humanistic philosophy of design. Innovation parks, often close to universities, industrial parks and/or scenic areas, are designed to be inspiring, grand and energy-boosting spaces for work, living and entertainment combined. In recent years, many parks have built quality apartments and houses exclusively for talents working in the parks. Cities such as Hangzhou and Suzhou, which have substantially inherited Chinese high-end tradition, are good examples of harmonizing natural environment, Chinese culture and innovation parks for stimulating creativities and pleasing busy minds.[67] Studies show that high-level planning and designing of China's innovation parks have proven positive impacts on attracting talents to work and thus form a cumulative power of gathering more people.[68]

---

[64]   For a study on this, *see* Fangzhu Zhanga & Fulong Wua, 'Fostering Indigenous Innovation Capacities: The Development of Biotechnology in Shanghai's Zhangjiang High-Tech Park', *Urban Geography*, Vol. 33:5, 2012, pp. 728–755.

[65]   As being found on my fieldwork to various innovation parks in China.

[66]   For instance, the government holds decision-making power over 18 000 administrative approval items. A recent news report shows that government officials attribute this phenomenon to poorly designed government-industry relationships. The planned economy era and its poor human resources are clearly the cause. *See* 'China Still Has 18,000 Administrative Approval Items', *Beijing Youth Daily*, A03, 20 October 2013.

[67]   For instance, *see* Sun Shijie *et al.*, 'A Case Study of the Design of Taihu Technology Industrial Park in Suzhou', *Huazhong Architecture*, 2013, No. 8, pp. 100–105.

[68]   Hu Bei *et al.*, 'Study on the Effect of Hi-tech Industry Clusters' Characteristics on Talents Attractiveness', *R & D Management*, Vol. 21:1, 2009, pp. 51–57.

It is not surprising that China's innovation parks play a vital role in implementing innovation policies. For instance, in Zhongguancun Science Park, China's foremost innovation park located in Beijing, there are more than 5000 enterprises with at least 15 000 overseas returnees. The number of listed companies in it adds up to 224. It also accommodates 67 state-level laboratories, 27 national engineering research centres, 28 national engineering and technological research centres, 24 university S&T parks and 29 overseas student pioneer parks. Zhongguancun enterprises have formulated 86 important international standards like TD-SCDMA, McWill and IGRS. In 2012, the gross income of companies in Zhongguancun was US$407 billion.[69] Most of these successful companies focus on emerging industries.

To further boost China's emerging industries, in mid-2012 the State Council issued *the Development Plan of the Strategic Emerging Industries during the 12th Five-Year Plan*. A noteworthy focus of the Plan is environment protection technology, which so far has not been rapidly developed for treating China's critical air, water and soil pollution. Another very important focus is to improve financial and banking services for innovation companies, which remain a major area of institutional deficiency. The improvement includes dynamic models for short-term financing, medium-term note, growth enterprise markets, private funding, etc.[70]

This new Plan is expected to create an improved financial environment additional to the existing R&D funding and reward schemes, in that access to bank loans is a major challenge for China's innovative companies, which usually start small. As a 2011 survey conducted by China's Ministry of Industry and Information Technology shows, only 15 per cent of Chinese light industrial SMEs obtained a bank loan in 2011.[71] These companies also face big challenges from China's venture capital sectors, in which the lack of qualified fund managers has been identified by various studies as a major bottleneck.[72] To implement the Plan, in August 2012, China issued a detailed policy that has established a State Sci-tech Finance Innovation Centre for providing a synergized financial

---

[69] Data obtained from Zhongguancun Science Park's official website: http://www.zgc.gov.cn.

[70] For its official release, *see* http://www.gov.cn/zwgk/2012-07/20/content_2187770.htm.

[71] Liu Shiping, 'Solving the Loan Difficulties for SMEs: How Long Will We Wait?', *Xinhua News*, 23 April, 2012.

[72] Shao, note 2, p. 190.

service to innovative companies in Zhongguancun Science Park.[73] Financial reform in China must be prudential and a Zhongguancun-based pilot
centre is a practically feasible solution.[74]

However, whether China's pro-emerging industry policies will, in Peter
Drahos's words, 'be capable of making the jump into the patent-walled
gardens of innovation' occupied by multinational companies remains
uncertain,[75] although several Chinese industries such as its IT industry
have emerged to lead the Chinese market.[76] A substantial analysis
conducted by the Research and Information System for Developing
Countries (RIS) in 2009 warned developing countries of the potential
patent barriers, in particular in biofuel and wind energy sectors.[77] An
OECD survey in 2008 showed that Brazil, India, China and Russia
collectively only own about 6 per cent of renewable energy patents, while
the EU, the US and Japan own almost 80 per cent.[78]. Although China's
PV industry occupies 50 per cent of the world market, it mainly
specializes in PV module manufacturing, earning only 8-10 per cent in
the global PV value chain.[79] Statistics show that China's car industry is
predominately controlled by foreign core technologies.[80] This situation
has eased the US concerns as American companies 'appear to have

---

[73]   The policy is available at its official website: http://www.zgc.gov.cn/
zcfg10/bjs/88140.htm.

[74]   The same philosophy applies to China (Shanghai) Pilot Free Trade Zone,
which was established on 29 September 2013. The Zone, focusing on financial
reforms, may be one of China's most significant economic developments in over
three decades. *See* Tom Phillips, 'Shanghai free trade zone launched in major
economic pilot scheme', *The Telegraph*, 29 September 2013.

[75]   Peter Drahos, *The Global Governance of Knowledge*, Ken Shao and Nan
Zhang (trans.), Beijing: Intellectual Property Press, p. 3.

[76]   Yu Jiang & Chen Kaihua, 'Current Situation and Challenge of Technological Innovations in Chinese Strategic Emerging Industries', *Studies in
Science of Science*, 2012, Vol. 30, No.5, p. 693.

[77]   K.Ravi Srinivas, *Climate Change, Technology Transfer and Intellectual
Property Rights*, RIS Discussion Papers, RIS-DP No.153, 2009.

[78]   OECD, *Compendium of Patent Statistics 2008*, Paris: OECD, 2008, p. 21.

[79]   Liu Chengkun, 'The China–Europe Hidden War in PV Industries', *Time
Weekly*, 9 August 2012. Chinese PV firms file many patents, but of low technical
and commercial value. *See* Arnaud de la Tour *et al.*, 'Innovation and international
technology transfer: The case of the Chinese photovoltaic industry', *Energy
Policy*, Vol. 39, 2011, pp. 761–770.

[80]   Yu & Chen, *Current Situation and Challenge of Technological Innovations in Chinese Strategic Emerging Industries*, p. 693.

continued to expand production of vehicles in China'.[81] For competition purposes, minimizing China's profit in the global value chain is a desirable effect for multinational companies.[82]

These external challenges are deeply linked to the established international environment of IP gambling and can interact with domestic challenges, especially human resource constraints that lead to inexperienced investment mindsets, institutional deficiencies and limited capacity of financial service.[83] For instance, as the *China Sustainable Development Strategy Report 2011* has warned, most Chinese provinces list clean energy as a key development area, which can easily lead to overproduction and resource waste.[84] This risk is caused by real inexperience in understanding regional specialties, local technological capacities, supply and demand, and market return and risks.[85] It can also lead to real estate speculation, given China's increasing urbanization. The interaction between external and internal factors might also have pushed China to a 'treasure hunting' approach. Innovation parks and their funding schemes, for instance, rely on a speculation that the government will be able to pick up some successful or landmark high-tech companies from those selected. While China may have sufficient funding capacity to sustain all these risks, given the complex internal and external factors discussed in this chapter and elsewhere, it remains uncertain whether this government-oriented approach can generate desirable results.

2.3 IP Strategies

IP strategies play a crucial role to the above-mentioned core components of China's national innovation system. Until very recently, however, discussions concerning IP in China had been dedicated to the violations

---

[81] United States International Trade Commission, *China: Effects of Intellectual Property Infringement and Indigenous Innovation Policies on the U.S. Economy*, Chapter 5, pp. 5–33.

[82] *See* Chapter Ten for more details.

[83] These internal challenges were identified, for instance, at the latest Development Forum of China's Strategic Emerging Industries 2013: http://finance.sina.com.cn/focus/2013zgzlxxxcyfzlt/.

[84] China Academy of Science, *China Sustainable Development Strategy Report 2011*, Beijing: Science Press, 2011, p. 12.

[85] For a detailed study, *see* Liu Tie & Wang Jiuyun, 'A Study on Excessive Convergence in the Choice of Regional Strategic Emerging Industries', *China Soft Science*, No.2, 2012, pp. 115–27.

of foreign interests.[86] Harvard Law Professor William Alford's work on China's history of IP has lead – to borrow Peter Yu's words – 'a whole generation' of Western IP scholars to believe that IP protection and China simply do not match.[87] This psychology-driven reluctance has contributed little to the recognition, as observed by Richard P. Suttmeier, a pioneer in the research of China's innovation economy, that in China 'there have been many changes in ... a variety of legal and institutional steps ... taken to protect intellectual property'.[88]

Suttmeier's observation was made two years after China issued its National Intellectual Property Strategy Outline 2008 (hereafter the IP Outline),[89] and can be supported by more recent statistics. In the American Chamber of Commerce in China's *AmCham-China Business Climate Survey* (2011), IP violation is not a more severe problem than others. Human resources constraints, as previously stated, is. Overall, the dissatisfaction rates for IP, protectionism, corruption, bureaucracy, contract enforcement difficulties and other challenges are close to each other.[90] This finding can be further supported by a conclusion in *the 2011 American Business in China White Paper*: 'We are pleased that 2010 closed with IPR highlighted as a Chinese government priority and recognize that the special IPR campaign has been active and well-conceived.'[91]

---

[86] For two recent exceptions, *see* Andrea Wechsler, 'Intellectual Property Law in the People's Republic of China: A Powerful Economic Tool for Innovation and Development', *China–EU Law Journal*, Vol. 1, 2011, pp. 3–54; Emily Gische, 'Repercussions of China's High-Tech Rise: Protection and Enforcement of Intellectual Property Rights in China', *Hastings Law Journal*, No. 63, 2011–2012, pp. 1393–1415.

[87] Peter K. Yu, 'Intellectual Property and Asian Values', *Marq. Intell. Prop. L. Rev.*, No. 16, 2012, p. 341. William P. Alford, *To Steal a Book Is an Elegant Offense: Intellectual Property Law in Chinese Civilization*, Stanford: Stanford University Press, 1995. I have written a number of papers to criticize Alford's claim. *See, e.g.*, Ken Shao, 'Chinese Culture and Intellectual Property: Let's Realize that we do not Know It', *The WIPO Journal*, Vol. 4.1, 2012, pp. 103–110.

[88] Richard P. Suttmeier, 'Will China Protect Intellectual Property? New Developments in Counterfeiting, Piracy, and Forced Technology Transfer', *the US Congressional-Executive Commission on China Hearing*, 22 September, 2010, p. 2.

[89] *See* Chapter Two for details.

[90] The American Chamber of Commerce in China, *AmCham-China Business Climate Survey*, 2011, p. 11.

[91] The American Chamber of Commerce in China, *American Business in China 2011 White Paper*, p. 80.

The above is not the focus of this chapter. The focus is China's use of IP strategies in boosting its domestic innovation economy, which will be further discussed in Chapters Two and Five. The *IP Outline* is a state-level strategic deployment that was a result of four years of hard work of the Leading Group of the National IP Strategy Formulation Working Group chaired by former Vice Premier Wu Yi.[92] The term 'strategy' in China's own context means the highest-level planning. China understands that as compared to tangible properties, IP is an essential part of public policies that must consider domestic conditions in a changing global environment.[93] IP laws and policies thus must support China's overall development sailing under the flag of the national innovation system.

Since the promulgation of the *IP Outline*, China has seen the establishment of local IP strategies, implementation measures, continued IP law-making and various supporting infrastructures and actions for an improved environment for innovation. Since 2008, China has amended and created about 54 IP-related laws and policies; most Chinese provinces, major cities and key industries now have specific IP strategies; IP offices exercise coordinating networks together with various departments and commercial sectors (including innovation parks), and their human resources have been improved, thanks to multi-layered education and training programs.[94] There are now many studies on China's patent surge and its globally leading status, though the quality of these patents may need further assessments.[95]

In a recent study, Xuan-Thao Nguyen concluded that quantitative and qualitative researches demonstrate that over 95 per cent of the IP litigations in China are brought by Chinese firms and China is quickly moving to a strong IP regime, a phenomenon that is not really seen by

---

[92] The official website of China's National Intellectual Property Strategy is http://www.nipso.cn/.

[93] Wu Handong, 'The International Environment and Domestic Context of the Implementation of the Intellectual Property Strategy', *Law Science*, 2012, No. 2, p. 3.

[94] To understand how China operates its high-level, forward-looking IP strategies in the light of its national innovation system, *see* SIPO Director Tian Lipu, 'The Implementation of Intellectual Property Strategies Strongly Supports the Construction of an Innovative Country', *China IP News*, 4 September 2013, available at: http://www.nipso.cn/onews.asp?id=18761.

[95] For example, *see* Mark Liang, 'Chinese Patent Quality: Running the Numbers and Possible Remedies', *The John Marshall Review of Intellectual Property Law*, 2012, Vol. 11:3, pp. 478–509.

the Western normative – or as I stated earlier – 'Alford-style' thinking.[96]
From 2008 to 2013, Chinese courts have accepted over 245 000 IP civil
cases with an annual increase of 37.6 per cent. This number does not
include that of administrative measures and criminal enforcements.[97] As
Chapter Five will show, the IP judicial interpretations and polices issued
by China's Supreme People's Court demonstrate a high-level understanding of IP's roles in China's overall development.

As we have already shown, China's IP strategies operate under the
national innovation system and thus must consider domestic conditions in
a changing global environment. China is aware of the danger of unreasonable global IP expansions. Benefiting from the interpretive flexibilities under the harmonized international IP principles and rules, China
has been able to establish stricter patentability criteria and universal prior
art pools in specific technological areas for reducing incoming junk
patents from developed countries.[98] Chinese IP courts have made efforts
to attend to different and balanced interests in China's transitional
economy.[99] In 2012, *Measures for the Compulsory Licensing for Patent
Implementation* was revised to allow China's State Intellectual Property
Office (SIPO) to issue compulsory licenses to local firms in cases of state
emergencies, unusual circumstances or in the interests of the public.[100]
That being said, it remains uncertain the extent to which China's IP
strategies can stretch legs in the packed global patent garden, especially
when regional and industrial human resource capacities of initiating and
implementing IP strategies require further improvements.[101]

To summarize, China's national innovation system is not limited to the
above-mentioned four core components. Ultimately, all components of
China's national innovation system require national, regional and
industry-specific integrated planning, which involves sophisticated
coordinating capacities across numerous sectors. All of these should be
understood in China's transforming reality that contains sharp regional
gaps and complex social conditions in a locally and globally challenging
environment.

---

[96]   Xuan-Thao Nguyen, 'The China We Hardly Know: Revealing the New
China's Intellectual Property Regime', *St. Louis University Law Journal*, Vol.
55:3, 2011, p. 773.
[97]   Tian, 'The Implementation of Intellectual Property Strategies Strongly
Supports the Construction of an Innovative Country'.
[98]   Drahos, note 14, p. 232.
[99]   *See* Chapter Five.
[100]   *See* Chapter Two.
[101]   *See* Part Four of Chapter Four for some of these challenges.

3. THE CHAPTERS

This book has ten chapters. Chapter One is contributed by the present author and offers a holistic perspective that contextualizes certain characteristics of and specific challenges to four core components of China's national innovation system, *i.e.*, talent plans, innovation parks, industrial preferences and IP strategies. These core components are analysed in a particular *sequence* relevant to China's internal and external conditions, together with other important components such as financial service, venture capital and technology commercialization. Chapter One argues that China's national innovation system takes place in unique, forward-looking backgrounds and is operated by integrated planning efforts that will be more visible in China's next-stage reforms. This contextualized and micro-level approach may help to shift the Western normative impression of China being a rampant pirate to the understanding of why and how China aims to *re-emerge* as a global innovation leader, amid numerous external and internal challenges.

Chapter Two, contributed by Dr Zhang Zhicheng, Deputy Director General, Protection and Coordination Department of SIPO, focuses on the 'roadmaps' of China's National Intellectual Property Strategy Outline 2008 (the IP Outline). It contextualizes and depicts what was in the mind of Chinese policy-makers when the IP Outline was formed, issued and implemented. One of the fundamental challenges haunting the Chinese IP policy-makers was how to make the IP Outline suitable for China's development. Chinese policy-makers face various key agendas that do not necessarily go along with each other. Knowledge-based economy, regional interests, a labour-intensive model, pollution, industrial preferences, international competitiveness and, of course, foreign requests are some of the examples.[102] Many of these challenges hardly exist in today's developed countries and thus are not straightforward for non-Mainland-Chinese readers. The method that Chinese policy-makers used in designing the IP Outline reflects an essential Chinese way of thinking: comprehensive, long-term and balanced.

Chapter Three, contributed by Associate Professor Yang Lihua, provides an outlined overview of post-1949 China's political thoughts, policies and laws concerning science, education, intellectual property and innovation. The author takes a rather Marxist approach to this. Ideological hormones do not have to be released when reading it, in that

---

[102] For details, *see* Chapter Two.

every author has the freedom to express his/her own views. However, it should be noted again that building a dynamic innovation-based economy in the global context could not have happened during China's era of planned economy, during which China had missed out on golden development opportunities after the World War II. As has been previously demonstrated, this critical challenge stimulated Deng Xiaoping's reform policies. Because there have been so many issues facing the reform agendas of Deng and his successors, political wish lists of 'rejuvenating China through knowledge' did not have a chance to generate desired outcomes during the 1980s and the 1990s, and this task still remains a real challenge today.

Chapter Four, contributed by Professor Feng Xiaoqing, opens by pointing out a crucial but widely ignored fact that China's self-driven innovation does not mean re-inventing everything but improved owner-ship of innovation fruits.[103] Chapter Four also attempts to identify various important institutional and legal challenges faced by China's innovation efforts. For instance, laws and policies are not detailed enough to provide sufficient support to key stakeholders; implementations of IP strategies are not strong in many Chinese firms. As Chapter One has demonstrated, many of these problems, to their very inherent origins, derive from China's poor human capital quality, which has been a key reform target since Deng Xiaoping's era. Readers should not misinterpret some of the problems mentioned by Chapter Four. For instance, many problems Chapter Four has identified are more evident in innovation parks and firms in less developed regions. Innovation parks in developed regions of course face challenges too but can better facilitate the understanding of China's innovation policies.

Chapter Five, contributed by Dr Kong Xiangjun, President of Intellec-tual Property Tribunal, the Supreme People's Court of China and his colleague Du Weike, is a systematic presentation of the first-hand, leading experience of China's judicial role in the IP area. The IP judicial interpretations and policies discussed in Chapter Five represent Chinese courts' high-level legal skills that attend to the details of many contro-versial IP cases. The key words of Chapter Five are 'efforts' and 'tendencies'. Statistics discussed elsewhere clearly endorse these efforts. As Chapter Five shows, there are notable tendencies that see adapting the judicial IP practice to China's transforming economy and society. This means a balanced but challenging approach for the needs of knowledge-based economy, the public interest, regional differences, social conflicts,

---

[103]   *See* Chapter Four, Introduction.

and foreign investment. It needs also to be pointed out that Chinese courts and judges have an incredibly heavy workload. Efforts must have been huge.

Chapter Six is contributed by Professor Michael Keane, the first non-Chinese scholar to write about China's creative clusters. Broadly speaking, creative clusters can be viewed as part of China's innovation park strategies but mainly focus on fostering cultural industries (also called creative industries) such as arts and media. Chapter Six draws a thoughtful analogy between the *status quo* of China's creative clusters, most of which 'remain in the first stage', and the 1990s early-generation innovation incubators in China, most of which 'inevitably failed to deliver measurable innovation and ultimately served as revenue generating sources for district governments via real estate speculation'.[104] Despite successful stories of modern China's nascent creative industries, such as those from China's increasingly original film productions, we are reminded by the delicate study of Professor Keane that there could be a long way to go for China to enhance cultural creativity. As Chapter Six also points out, it is too early to assess the effects of China's creative clusters. Such an assessment is not the aim of this book. What we can learn from Professor Keane's work is that China is yet to acquire further experience, both at institutional and human capital levels, for driving its creative industries and innovation economy.

Chapter Seven provides us with a detailed understanding of how foreign investment in China influences China's indigenous efforts in innovation. Dr Peter S. Hofman, Dr Alexander Newman and Dr Ziliang Deng used data drawn from the annual reports filed by industrial firms with the National Bureau of Statistics over the period 2005–2006 – the early development stage of China's present innovation system – to examine the main factors determining product innovation in private Chinese small and medium-sized enterprises (SMEs). One of its findings is that higher levels of foreign direct investment (FDI) in industries at the provincial level impact negatively on product innovation in SMEs, and thus the general belief that FDI creates knowledge spillovers needs to be refined. In fact, uneven allocations of financial and administrative resources occur not only between foreign and Chinese firms, but also among Chinese firms. Other studies show that in an innovation park, for instance, big companies naturally occupy more resources than small ones. One solution is to encourage different firms to explore different

---

[104] *See* Chapter Six, Introduction.

markets.[105] But this solution can be less effective in a global context, in which multinationals possess far advanced resources.

Chapter Eight, contributed by Emeritus Professor Seamus Grimes whose research interests include multinational R&D in China and China's innovation policy, represents a study of the more recent R&D activities of multinationals in China. This study benefited from his 50-hour interviews with Shanghai-based multinational R&D centres in 2009–2011. This chapter attempts to understand how multinationals have been transforming their profit models in China since the 1980s in an evolving environment that now gives China a very strong bargaining position for pushing multinationals to contribute to China's innovation output as a prerequisite for gaining greater access to China's vast market. This, as Chapter Eight argues, seems to be in contradiction with those multinationals' traditional strategies in China, which saw China as a low-cost manufacturing centre for generating maximized profit for foreign companies without the need for effective technology transfer. Multinationals may not be willing to let China and their labs and competitors in China to have access to their core IP, which is traditionally controlled by their headquarters outside of China. However, the general tendency is that multinationals are aware of the benefit of engaging innovation in China, at least at certain levels where there are many other new players to compete with. I think this highly dynamic reality reflects China's struggle in a challenging global climate of IP and innovation. China is gambling on the view that the Chinese market remains much too attractive for multinationals to relocate to other regions and the result remains to be seen.

Chapter Nine, contributed by Professor Wei Shi, and Chapter Ten, contributed by Chair Professor Peter Yu, bring us to an elevated land-scape of the international realities. Benefiting from a delicate examination of various economic and empirical studies of the functions of IP in national development, Chapter Nine insightfully points out that 'IPR can either ... promote or hinder economic growth, depending on how it is oriented on the "ladder of development", and ... developed countries are attempting to "hide the secrets of their success" and "kick away the ladder"'. The hidden secrets are 'tolerant' or weak IP laws and policies that had been strategically used by many developed nations for their development needs. These strategies had been part of their innovation

---

[105]   Wu Bing *et al.*, 'An Empirical Study of High-tech Industrial Entre-preneurial Networks, Performance and Environment: Analysis of National Soft-ware Parks', *Nankai Business Review*, 2009, Vol. 3, pp. 84–93.

plans and may explain why nations such as the US and Japan are leading the world's innovation economy.[106] This, again, reminds us of one of the core arguments in Chapter One: the first agenda of China's innovation system is probably not IP, but others such as talent plans, emerging industries, funding and financial services.

Unfortunately, through international IP law harmonization, the development ladder has been largely kicked away by developed countries. As Chapter Ten points out, although the TRIPS Agreement had to include certain flexibilities and transitional measures to help countries 'buy time' to update their intellectual property systems, each country's capacity to strategically use these flexibilities is different and can be limited by TRIPS-plus bilateral and multilateral agreements – such as the *Anti-Counterfeiting Trade Agreement* (ACTA) – that restrict how the TRIPS Agreement is implemented in developing countries. Together with other tactics such as a networked operation of patent offices, the TRIPS-plus magic will worsen the kick-away effect.[107] It seems that China is better positioned than many other developing countries. In addition to using IP strategies for a more development-friendly environment, China has been able to start its innovation engine by other powerful means, including pushing multinationals to innovate within China. However, to what extent China's other means can overcome the kick-away effect of global IP powers remain uncertain.

CONCLUSION

China aims to return as a global innovation leader in the near future. Overall, China has now put in place a multi-layered and forward-looking national innovation system. In it, talents and human resources, which remain a fundamental challenge for China, are a major target of China's innovation policies. China invites quality talents to contribute to the country's innovation efforts, in particular to the commercialization of knowledge fruits in internationally key and emerging industries. Many of these commercial projects are supported by well-designed, intellectually stimulating innovation parks in China's developed regions. Improved domestic IP systems, together with other mechanisms, aim to provide support to innovation as well as various other interests in China's transforming economy. Making all of these happen is not easy for China,

---

[106] *See* Chapter Nine, Parts One and Two.
[107] For how powerful patent offices involve in this, *see* Drahos, note 14.

a country with huge regional gaps and complex social conditions across its vast population. Integrated planning capacities thus form another key target of China's national innovation system.

The above efforts are accompanied by many critical challenges, which have existed and continue to develop in both domestic and international contexts. China's policy designing and implementation capacities are yet to be upgraded to facilitate better market-oriented conditions for innovative and creative industries, closer academic-industrial linkages, more efficient funding assessments and allocation pipelines, and improved commercialization of intellectual fruits. Many of these are identified as key obstacles to China's innovation capacity in a recent State Council policy release in 2012.[108] On top of it is the critical international environment where powerful companies have put up fairly strong IP garden fences for late comers.

It is important to note that this chapter as well as the entire book is not necessarily a study of the *outcomes* of China's innovation policies and laws, which are too new to be substantially tested. Certainly, there is a time gap between the grant of patents and their successful commercialization, not to mention that many nascent Chinese patents may not be high quality. The effect of education and talent plans can be long-term. Cultural industries continue to suffer from overall creative malnutrition. Institutional reforms represent a major challenge and must be accelerated to improve government efficiency in supporting knowledge-based companies in both developed and less developed regions in China. All of these will take years to get evaluated. But if we apply a holistic perspective of understanding China's self-driven innovation, then we could be positive about the future.

Overall, a holistic perspective requires putting China's striking innovation phenomenon into micro-level contexts, which should include the above-mentioned international frameworks, domestic challenges and solutions that are the major focus of this book and, very essentially, undistorted views of Chinese culture, history and present. This approach suggests that China's *re-emergence* as a global innovation leader is natural, can be peaceful and should be seen as mutually beneficial. Global interdependence 'does not relieve the need for re-generation by

---

[108]   The State Council, *The Opinion on Deepening Institutional Reforms of Science and Technology and Fastening the Construction of National Innovation System*, 23 September 2012. Available at: http://www.gov.cn/jrzg/2012-09/23/content_2231413.htm.

one's own efforts but enhances it'.[109] To put it another way, the right to develop is a fundamental right for any nation and China is simply doing what has to be done.

[109] David Kerr, 'Has China Abandoned Self-Reliance?', *Rev. Of Int'L Pol. Econ.*, 2007, Vol. 14, p. 102.

2. Roadmaps of China's *National Intellectual Property Strategy Outline*

Zhang Zhicheng[*]

INTRODUCTION

In 2004, headed by the State Intellectual Property Office (SIPO), the government of the People's Republic of China began to design the nation's national intellectual property (IP) strategy. At that time, China had been a World Trade Organization (WTO) member for about three years. Trade rules under the WTO institution had started to have an impact on China. Increasingly, Chinese enterprises were drawn into international IP lawsuits, in particular in or with developed countries such as the US and the EU members. Some countries frequently lodged legal actions against China under the WTO's dispute resolution mechanism.[1] This made more and more people and companies in China realize that IP is a key element in global economic competition and plays a very important role in a nation's development. By 2004 a modern IP system complying with the relevant international standards had been fairly well established in China. But ironically, there were only a limited number of people and entities in China that were qualified in handling IP affairs.[2] Improving China's domestic IP implementation system was still a

---

[*] The author wishes to thank Professor Ken Shao for his great support for this chapter.

[1] Ding Jielin, 'Thinking on USA's Complaint to WTO Regarding China's Failure to Protect Intellectual Property Rights', *Journal of Comparative Law*, 2007, Vol. 5, p. 115.

[2] In fact, except those in IT, other Chinese companies' annual filing never exceeded 20 items. *See* Huaiwen He & Ping Zhang, 'Impact of the Intellectual Property System on Economic Growth: Country Report – China', *WIPO-JPO-UNU Joint Research Project*, online at: http://www.wipo.int/about-ip/en/studies/pdf/wipo_unu_07_china.pdf

challenge, not to mention the strategic application of an IP system in general and the WTO rules in particular. Here comes *a compliance question* that has attracted wide attention in China: how should China respond to various challenges that the WTO system puts forward to it?

In the meantime, by 2004 the Chinese economy had been travelling at high growth rates for more than 20 years, under a labour-intensive model. Severe pollution and excessive consumption of resources and energy with declining profit margins and efficiencies were afflicting the Chinese government, industries and the Chinese citizens. It was increasingly realized that industries in China must upgrade themselves in technology and innovation. This agenda started to be frequently mentioned by the central government.[3] Soon, in 2006, China formally included the top priority of improving economic efficiency and upgrading domestic technologies into a landmark policy called *The Guidelines on National Medium- and Long-term Program for Science and Technology Development (2006–2020).*[4] Experiences of many developed countries show that innovation serves as a core driving force in upgrading and restructuring market economy when such a need rises. But here comes *a practical question* for the Chinese government: in China today, how is innovation possible?

China has very close trading relationships with many WTO members. The Chinese market is glutted with well-known brands from foreign countries and multinational companies.[5] This might give domestic and international consumers diverse options. But for Chinese companies that face increased competitive market conditions in and outside of China, imitating the competitors makes it difficult to gain an advantaged position under the WTO game rules, not to mention that developing countries today no longer have certain flexibilities in IP law-making and international legal compliance that many developed countries enjoyed at their own development stages.[6] Here comes *a competition question*

---

[3]   Shen Weiguo & Chen Yichun, 'Study on the Stage Theory and Evaluation Index System of the Second Venture of China High-tech Development Zones', *Science of Science and Management of S&T*, No. 9, 2007, p. 27.

[4]   *The Guidelines on National Medium- and Long-term Program for Science and Technology Development (2006–2020)*, the Ministry of Science and Technology of the People's Republic of China, online at: http://www.most.gov.cn/kjgh/

[5]   'Rich Chinese are Partial to Foreign Brands', *China Daily*, 21 February 2008, online at: http://english.people.com.cn/90001/90776/6357694.html.

[6]   Linsu Kim, *Technology Transfer & Intellectual Property Rights: The Korean Experience*, Issues Paper No. 2, June 2003, online at http://www.iprson line.org/resources/docs/Kim%20-%20ToT%20and%20IPRs%20-%20Blue%202O2.pdf.

haunting many Chinese business communities: can Chinese companies create IP advantages over their foreign competitors?

When China was thinking about a new wave of innovation in the mid-2000s, the world was undergoing a digital revolution that was expected to change our lifestyle and how IP is regulated and managed. The subject matter in all IP laws has now been expanded continuously, resulting in obstacles to the accessibility of information, knowledge and health. This puts forward *a fundamental question* for IP itself: what should China and its business communities do to balance the private interest in the knowledge economy and the public interest in education and medical services?

The above questions to a great extent represent recent challenges faced by China in the context of its new role in the WTO trading system. They are not only relevant to foreign investment in China, but also to a variety of complex internal factors that China cannot ignore. To address these questions in China's own contexts, the government had started to formulate China's national IP strategy suitable for the nation's specific needs. In the rest of this chapter, I will discuss the formulation of the People's Republic of China's *National Intellectual Property Strategy Outline* (hereafter *IP Outline*) and its contents, implementations, achievements and challenges.

1. AN OVERVIEW

China has a very long history. In ancient times, China had long enjoyed technology superiority that other countries and regions did not experience.[7] IP law was not a popular choice for all ancient civilizations. In the absence of IP law, the ancient Chinese valued technology and knowledge in different ways. For example, Zhuang Tse (c. 369–286 BC), one of the most important Chinese thinkers in antiquity, recorded in his book a deal of know-how transaction: a businessman bought a prescription for treating chapped skin from a family and made use of it in the army.[8] This means technologies were commercially valuable and tradable.

---

[7]   For a landmark study, *see* Joseph Needham, *Science and Civilisation in China: General Conclusions and Reflections*, Cambridge: Cambridge University Press, 2004.

[8]   Zhuang Tse, *Zhuang Tse*, Beijing: Zhonghua Shuju, 2010, p. 12.

A copyright system similar to its modern concept emerged in the Song Dynasty (960–1279 AD).[9] It can be argued that the decline of the Song civilization as a consequence of the invasion of Genghis Khan contributed to the decline of Chinese legal institutions, which might include the copyright system.[10] The Opium War of 1840 forced the Qing Dynasty (1644–1911) to face an unprecedented and Western challenge of modernization.[11] As part of its overall reform process, the Qing government established modern legal systems for protecting trademark, patent and copyright invented by the Europeans as a result of Europe's process of modernization.[12] However, China had been involved in consecutive wars and uncertainties and it was not until the 1980s that China (excluding Taiwan, Hong Kong and Macao) started to use its IP laws under its reformist policy.[13]

Over the last 30 years, China has signed all important international IP treaties. IP law-making and international regulatory compliance in contemporary China were therefore completed in a very short period of

---

[9]   For a detailed and interdisciplinary analysis, *see* Ke Shao, 'Alien to Copyright?: A Reconsideration of the Chinese Historical Episodes of Copyright', 4 *Intellectual Property Quarterly* (2005), pp. 400–31. For some of these records, *see* Zhou Lin & Li Mingshan, *Historical Materials for the Studies of China's Copyright History,* Beijing: Zhongguo Fangzheng chubanshe, 1999, pp. 2–3.

[10]   Copyright still existed during the Mongol time but there also existed harsh publishing censorship. For a discussion, *see* Shao, 'Alien to Copyright?: A Reconsideration of the Chinese Historical Episodes of Copyright', pp. 427, 409. The Song had highly developed legal institutions to protect private rights. For the example of land and property transaction, *see* Lu Hong & Chen Ligen 'On manifested Real Right in the Process of the Song Dynasty's Land Transaction', *Journal of Nanjing Agricultural University*, 2008, Vol. 8:2, pp. 92–98.

[11]   The Opium War was the war initiated by Britain against the Manchu Qing for maintaining the British export of opium to China. The Qing lost the war and were forced to sign unequal treaties. For further reading, *see* La Kai-yin & Cindy Yik-yi Chu (eds), *A Reappraisal of the Opium War,* Hong Kong: The Chinese University Press, 2003.

[12]   Xu Haiyan, 'Comparison of the Chinese and Japanese Patent Systems', in SIPO (ed.) *Patent Law Research,* Beijing: Intellectual Property Press, 2011, p. 33.

[13]   The Trademark Law of the People's Republic of China was established in 1982. The Patent Law of the People's Republic of China was established in 1984. The Copyright Law of the People's Republic of China was established in 1990.

time.[14] However, given the fact that reformist China's opening-up economy operates predominately under a labour-intensive model, only a small number of Chinese people and companies understand the new challenges put forward by the globalized IP regime. The most urgent matter for a government at the dawn of the 21st century, as said by the World Intellectual Property Organization (WIPO), was to develop infrastructures and capacities for supporting knowledge creators to protect and exploit their intellectual fruits in the form of IP strategies.[15] This was believed to be a core part of a national IP strategy, but not the only thing.

In the 2000s, IP had increasingly become more important for China to engage in further development and international competition. The Chinese economy very much depends on industries and global trade. This means strengthened IP protection and improved innovation capacity are critical to China's future. Also, considering the huge diverse needs across China's vast land, China's development may be hindered without developing technology self-sufficiency because China's capacity for buying advanced technology in the international market is yet to be developed.[16] In 2006 China issued *The Guidelines on National Medium- and Long-term Program for Science and Technology Development (2006–2020)*. This plan announced China's willingness and strategies to become an innovation country. To reach this objective, China has significantly increased its R&D investment, which soon outperformed Japan and the UK.[17]

As the Boston Consulting Group's five-phase IP development theory indicates (see Figure 2.1), a country may improve its IP protection following its growth of exports and R&D spending.[18] With significant increases in R&D spending, China is likely to reach Phase 3 and benefit

---

[14]   For China and the many international IP treaties and conventions it has so far joined, *see* the PRC's Ministry of Commerce, 'China's Accession to International Conventions for the Protection of IPR and its Participation in International Negotiation about IPR', online at: http://tfs.mofcom.gov.cn/article/cj/200503/20050300030517.shtml

[15]   An IP strategy is a set of measures formulated and implemented by a government to encourage and facilitate effective creation, development and management of intellectual property. *See* WIPO, *National IP Strategies*, online at: http://www.wipo.int/ip-development/en/strategies/national_ip_strategies.html

[16]   Yi Jiming, 'Background of the Intellectual Property Strategy's Formulation and Implementation', *Science Technology and Law*, 2013, Vol. 104:4, p. 67.

[17]   James Wilsdon, 'China: the Next Science Superpower?' *Engineering and Technology*, 2007, Vol. 2:1, p. 28.

[18]   David C. Michael, Collins Qian, Vladislav Boutenko *et al*, *Beyond the Great Wall: Intellectual Property Strategies for Chinese Companies*, Boston

from IP protection. The consequence is that more intellectual property rights (IPRs) will be produced and more right holders will actively seek legal protection. The consensus of IP protection will appear in the society and the government will allocate more resources to the implementation of IP laws.

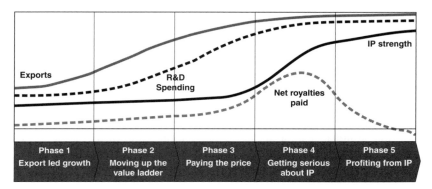

Figure 2.1   The five phases of IP development

But the reality demands more solutions than IP law-making and R&D spending. As a huge developing country, China has complex challenges that require the government to exercise high-level problem-solving skills.[19] For instance, in 2011 the per capita income of Beijing residents reached 12 000 USD. By comparison, people living in China's western regions, such as Guizhou province and Yunnan province, still have very low incomes.[20] This shows very different stages of economic, social and educational development across China and, in turn, very different needs in access to knowledge, technology and the innovation economy. How to satisfy the varied demands while implementing a unified IP system in different regions of China is clearly a strategic issue for the Chinese government to address when designing its cross-century national-level, comprehensive IP strategies.

This development dilemma is not the only issue which China has to address. In 2001 China joined the WTO as a developing country and as a

Consulting Group, 2007, online at: https://www.bcgperspectives.com/content/articles/future_strategy_globalization_beyond_the_great_wall/

[19]   This point is also mentioned in Chapter 1 of this book.

[20]   Zhang Shaolei, 'China's Average GDP in Provinces and Cities', *Finance China*, 7 February 2012, online at http://finance.china.com.cn/news/gnjj/2012 0207/516239.shtml

consequence is required to comply with the Agreement on Trade Related Aspects of Intellectual Property Rights (TRIPS) when sharing the advantages of global free trade. That means IP law-making of a WTO member country is no longer a purely domestic affair. To comply with TRIPS, China's IP laws have been revised extensively following China's accession to the WTO. For example, during the US–China negotiations for joining the WTO, China expanded its patent law's protection scope for medicines when many Chinese people still could not access basic medical treatment.[21] As a developing county, China has to keep a balance between the demand from developed countries such as the US and China's own needs in varied domestic conditions. Moreover, those revised laws bring about more investment into public resources for stricter IP enforcement.

In this context, China initiated the formulation of its national IP strategy in 2008.

2. FORMULATION OF CHINA'S IP STRATEGY

In 2004 the State Council of China made the decision to formulate a national IP strategy. Vice Prime Minister Wu Yi headed the Leading Group of the National IP Strategy Formulation Working Group (hereafter the Leading Group), which was composed of more than 20 ministerial governmental agencies. The Leading Group also set up an office in SIPO for coordination purposes.[22] To make sure that the forthcoming national IP strategy meets China's specific and varied needs, the Leading Group invited hundreds of experts to carry out a study on 20 research projects, including theoretical and macro-level problems in IP, patent strategy, trademark strategy, copyright strategy, IP law-making, IP management, and key stakeholders of IP.[23]

---

[21]   Yang Jun, 'Research on the System of the International Coordinating Mechanism from Perspective of the Conflict between the Patent and the Public Health', Doctoral Dissertation, East China University of Political Science and Law, 2006, p. 174.

[22]   The General Office of the State Council, 'Circular of the General Office of the State Council on Establishing the Leading Group for the Work concerning Formulating the Strategy for National Intellectual Property Right', online at: http://www.chinalaw.gov.cn/article/english/Regulations/Laws/200603/200603000 48057.shtml Date of Implementation: 8 January 2008.

[23]   'The National IP Strategy', *SIPO Official News*, 11 June 2008, online at: http://www.sipo.gov.cn/ztzl/ywzt/zscqzl/zlmt/200804/t20080424_392534.html

According to WIPO, IP strategy is a set of measures formulated and implemented by a government to encourage and facilitate effective creation, development and management of IP. It should outline how to develop infrastructures and capacities to support inventors of IP to protect, develop and exploit their inventions. An IP strategy may also be defined as a comprehensive national document system which outlines how all policies and implementations take place in a coordinated manner within a national framework.[24] China wanted a strategy outline with a series of policies to define its action in the future. But it is not an easy task.

According to the view at that time, China's national IP strategy should raise China's IP management level, utilize IP recourses from foreign and domestic markets, and improve home-developed innovation to support the main objectives of China's social and economic development. To implement the kind of national IP strategy, the Chinese government should cultivate innovative talents and enhance IP awareness.[25] China also realized the importance of participating in international IP affairs and making its own suggestions for improving the international IP institution.[26]

It was easier to reach consensus on the macro level than on the practical level. From the beginning, the experts and the ministers came with varied and even conflicting views on many policies. This drove the formulating tasks into deep water. For example, it was hard to define the

---

[24] WIPO has a misunderstanding about China's national IP strategy. It believes that the People's Republic of China had a clear national IP strategy in 2003. The national strategy WIPO referred to is only the IP section in China's *National Science and Technology Development Plan (2006–2020)*. But it is true that China has stressed the role of intellectual property in the context of harnessing national brands and increasing international competitiveness, as well as in the context of promoting scientific and research activities to obtain proprietary IPRs in key areas and facilitating a faster transition from research results to enhanced productivity was the main objective of the China's National IP Strategy. *See* WIPO, *National IP Strategies*, online at: http://www.wipo.int/ip-development/en/strategies/national_ip_strategies.html

[25] Zhang Qin, 'Reflections on China's National Intellectual Strategy', *Perspectives of Scientific and Technological Achievement*, 2005, No. 1, p. 4. Dr Zhang was a member of China's Leading Group of the National IP Strategy Formulation Working Group.

[26] For a comprehensive understanding of these, *see* Tian Lipu, 'The Implementation of Intellectual Property Strategy has effectively Supported the Construction of an Innovative Country', *China Intellectual Property Newspaper*, September 2013, online at: http://www.nipso.cn/onews.asp?id=18761

future policies and identify the standards of IP protection. It was also difficult to build a new and better system to implement the IP system, even though everyone knew that the disorganized IP management in China was troubling IP right holders.[27] There were also some fresh issues to be addressed such as traditional knowledge (TK) protection of Chinese Traditional Medicine (CTM).[28] Technical standards relating to patents were also a big concern for many multinational telecommunication companies.[29]

To address these disputes and the conflicts among many stakeholders, the Leading Group made great efforts to seek advice and suggestions. Multinational companies and Chinese domestic enterprises were invited to discussion meetings and ambassadors to China were encouraged to present their views to the Leading Group.[30] Well-known international IP experts such as Professor Michael Blakeney made trips to China to contribute to the making of China's IP strategy.[31]

The mission to formulate the IP strategy was not accomplished on time, but it was eventually finalized. The *IP Outline* was issued by the State Council of the People's Republic of China on 5 June 2008.

3. MAIN CONTENTS OF THE *IP OUTLINE*

The *IP Outline* shows in its preface the Chinese government's view on IP: in the world today, with the development of the knowledge-based economy and economic globalization, IP is becoming increasingly a strategic resource in national development and a core element in international competitiveness, as well as an important supporting force in building an innovative country and the key to holding the initiative in

---

[27]   Feng Xiaoqing & Shao Chong, 'On Improving China s Administration of Intellectual Property with Regulation of Market', *China Market*, 2012, No. 20, p. 39.

[28]   'Intellectual Property of Chinese Traditional Medicine Project Launched', *Science and Technology Daily*, 7 November 2005.

[29]   Tian Lipu, HouYunchun, Wang Jingchuan, Ni Guangnan, ChenDongqi & Wu Handong, 'Implementation of the National Intellectual Property Strategy', *Economic Daily*, 5 June 2009.

[30]   The Office of National Intellectual Property Strategy held meetings to hear the views from diplomatic bodies on IP strategy formulation. For further information, visit: http://www.sipo.gov.cn/ztzl/ywzt/zscqzl/zlzd/zlb/200804/t2008 0424_392465.html

[31]   Brief News, 'Intellectual Property International Forum Opening in Beijing', *Electronic Intellectual Property*, 2006, Vol. 3, p. 4.

development.[32] To some extent, this view reveals the fact that Chinese enterprises have not yet acquired sufficient IP capacities to compete with their international counterparts.

The preface also presents China's understanding of the role of the IP system. It is understood that the IP system should focus on the promotion of economic and social progress by adjusting the interests among different groups of people in the process of creating and utilizing knowledge and information. This standpoint defines the relationship between reward to the innovators and the progress of society. This indicates that China's IP strategy is established on the promotion of development, which is a very proper approach for developing countries such as China.[33]

The *IP Outline* specifies four main tasks – the creation, utilization, protection and management of IPRs. Japan's *Outline of the National IP Strategy* has three focuses: utilization, protection and human resources.[34] Both countries' understandings of the IP system emphasize capability-building within the IP institution and move beyond the conventional view that IP is simply about protection. To achieve these goals, China's *IP Outline* sets forth five strategic tasks: improving the IP system, promoting the creation and utilization of IP, strengthening the protection of IPRs, preventing abuses of IPRs, and fostering a culture of IPRs.

A priority of China's IP strategy is to strengthen the guiding role of IP in economic, cultural and public policies, and to improve domestic laws and regulations concerning IPRs. Obviously, this is an attempt to integrate IP with development policies. IP is not only a legal right that needs protection, but also an element that could be used to support the economy and China's development. The British government's *Report on Integrating Intellectual Property Rights and Development Policy* might have inspired the establishment of China's *IP Outline*.[35]

---

[32] Preface, *Outline of the National Intellectual Property Strategy*, issued by the State Council of the People's Republic of China on 5 June 2008.

[33] For instance, *see* Carlos Correa, 'Formulating Effective Pro-Development National Intellectual Property Policies', ICTSD-UNCTAD Dialogue, The Rockefeller Foundation's Bellagio Conference Center, 30 October–2 November 2002, available at: http://www.iprsonline.org/unctadictsd/bellagio/docs/C_Correa.pdf

[34] Strategic Council on Intellectual Property, Intellectual Property Policy Outline 2002, online at: http://www.kantei.go.jp/foreign/policy/titeki/kettei/0207 03taikou_e.html

[35] Ideally, the formulation of IP policy in a developing country should be based on a sound appreciation of how the IP system might be used to promote

At that time, Chinese enterprises were beset by IPR abuses. For example, some Chinese DVD manufacturers sued the patent pool of 3C and 6C for high patent royalty rates and package licences with non-essential patents. Due to the lack of relevant laws and regulations, the lawsuit was filed in the court of California, USA instead of in a court in China.[36] China needed the introduction of regulations and laws concerning antitrust and IP abuses.

To effectively promote its IP strategies, China needed to raise IP awareness among the general public. Thus the promotion of IP-related culture has become one of the key tasks in China's IP system. In the *IP Outline*, by emphasizing the significance of IP to China's future, the government calls on the general public to value IP and innovation. This includes organizing special events and functions for the general public's access to a better understanding of innovation, IP and respecting the rule of law.[37]

The *IP Outline* also includes some specific projects for patent, trademark, copyright, trade secrets, new varieties of plants and specific areas such as geographical indications, genetic resources, TK, folklore and integrated circuit layout designs. In general, these specific projects also focus on boosting innovation and improving IP protection. For example, the *IP Outline* urges the creation of more patents in some strategic and new technological fields such as biology, medicine, new materials, information technology, advanced manufacturing, new energy, oceanography, resources, environmental protection, modern agriculture, modern transportation, aeronautics and astronautics. These strategic and new technological fields meet the nation's strategic development needs as reflected in China's various policies and plans.[38] Using copyright as an

---

development objectives. UK Commission on Intellectual Property Rights, *Integrating Intellectual Property Rights and Development Policy*, London, September 2002, online at: http://www.iprcommission.org/home.html.

[36]   Zhang Zhicheng & Feng Xiaoquan, 'DVD Patent License Fee Event', *Invention & Paten*t, 2004, Vol. 10, p. 8.

[37]   *See* Tian Lipu, 'The Implementation of Intellectual Property Strategy Has Effectively Supported the Construction of an Innovative Country', online at: http://www.nipso.cn/onews.asp?id=18761.

[38]   China's IP strategy serves as a key part of China's construction of an innovative country. For instance, the new strategic technological fields that need to be supported by China's IP strategy can be well reflected from *The Guidelines on National Medium- and Long-term Program for Science and Technology Development (2006–2020)*, the Ministry of Science and Technology of the People's Republic of China, online at: http://www.most.gov.cn/kjgh/.

example, the government aims at assisting the development of copyright-related industries such as publication, radio, film, television, literature and arts, cultural entertainment, advertising design, arts and crafts, computer software and information networks.[39]

As mentioned above, the *IP Outline* is also set to balance different interests. One of the specific IP projects highlights China's view on balancing the interests of IP right holders and other stakeholders. For instance, the *IP Outline* states that copyright protection should parallel the promotion of information dissemination. The idea of balance appears several times in the *IP Outline*. In addition to copyright, trade secret and freedom of personnel flow and benefit-sharing of genetic resources and TK also reflect a balance theory.

To ensure the realization of its tasks and objectives, the *IP Outline* also puts forward strategic implementation measures. These include enhancing the capability of IP creation, encouraging the commercialization and utilization of IPRs, expediting the development of the IP judicial system, improving law enforcement, strengthening the management of IP, developing agent services, improving human resources, promoting IP culture and expanding international exchanges and cooperation.

4. IMPLEMENTATION OF CHINA'S IP STRATEGY

4.1 Organization

To organize strategic implementation is very difficult for any country, especially when such implementation has to engage many parties. In China, any major implementation inevitably involves the governments at central, provincial and city levels as well as different entities such as enterprises. The formulation of China's National IP strategy was such an undertaking.

Chinese policymakers have realized that implementation of the *IP Outline* would involve many government agencies, including the central government and local governments as well as many key enterprises from various industries. The State Council thus decided to establish an

---

[39] For instance, China is drafting a Movie Industry Promotion Law, in which copyright protection of original works is a focus. *See* Xiang Li, 'Copyright Protection: the Key to a Prosperous Movie Industry', National Intellectual Property Strategy Official Website, online at: http://www.nipso.cn/onews.asp?id=13399

Inter-Ministerial Joint Meeting for implementation work, with the Commissioner of SIPO and the Vice Secretary-General of the State Council to head the body, which consisted of more than 20 deputy ministry-level officials. These officials were responsible for the IP policy-making, drawing up the annual implementation plan and coordinating various important issues.[40] Within this structure, SIPO undertakes daily works as the Office of the Inter-Ministerial Joint Meeting. At the central governmental level, China's IP implementation system is to some extent similar to its Japanese counterpart. In Japan, the prime minister is in charge of Japan's implementation of its IP strategy, and other ministers act as members of the Leading Group of the IP strategy.[41]

Each year, the Inter-Ministerial Meeting Office drafts an annual implementation plan according to the *IP Outline*, as well as new studies and surveys over the past year.[42] The Inter-Ministerial Joint Meeting determines the actions to fulfil the *IP Outline* and identifies new and emerging issues. The relevant government entities are responsible for implementing specific actions and report directly to the State Council.

For China, merely having a central-government-level implementation mechanism is not sufficient. It is not easy to implement the IP strategy in China, which has huge differences in regional development. The government has to take into account various development levels and capabilities of different regions when implementing the IP strategy. As a result, within three years after the enactment of *the IP Outline*, most provincial governments had established their own leading groups for the implementation of China's national IP strategy with more detailed policy frameworks suitable for local needs. Some provinces have also put in place annual IP action plans and implementation projects.[43]

---

[40]   The State Council authorized the set-up of the Inter-Ministerial Joint Meeting of the State Council for IP Strategy implementation, online at: http://www.sipo.gov.cn/ztzl/zxhd/qzgyyzn/gjzl/200905/t20090522_461829.html.

[41]   Meng Haiyan, 'Report on the Implementation of Japanese and Korean IP Strategies', *SIPO Official Website* News, 25 May 2011, online at http://www.sipo.gov.cn/dtxx/zlgzdt/2011/201105/t20110526_605554.html

[42]   *The Implementation Plan of National Intellectual Property Strategies 2011*, online at http://www.gov.cn/gzdt/2011-04/26/content_1852660.htm. *The Implementation Plan of National Intellectual Property Strategies 2012*, online at http://www.gov.cn/gzdt/2012-05/04/content_2129681.html

[43]   'The National IP Strategy was Furthered to Establish a Foundational Planning Framework', *China Government Official News*, online at: http://www.nipso.cn/onews.asp?id=14202

Both the Inter-Ministerial Joint Meeting of the State Council and the leading groups at provincial level serve as the engine of the implementation of China's national IP strategy. This type of organization reflects the development stage of the market economy with Chinese characteristics. Because market participants in China still lack adequate IP awareness, the government has to be in place for leading the actual implementation of the *IP Outline*. This situation is very different from that in many developed countries where enterprises are capable of taking advantage of IP laws and incentives on the one side and the government simply needs to play the invisible hand.

4.2 Action

Effective IP protection is one of the main tasks in implementing the *IP Outline*. Many laws and regulations have been amended to strengthen IP protection in light of the *IP Outline*. For example, according to China's patent law, existing technology is redefined as technology that has been publicly disclosed in publications in China or abroad, or has been publicly used or made known to the public by other means in China or abroad, before the patent application date.[44] This means that even utility model patents,[45] or in other words petty patents, also need to adhere to the principle of universal novelty. According to the revised *Regulations on Custom Protection of Intellectual Property Rights*, customs can destroy imported infringing goods when the infringement features cannot be erased.[46]

At the same time, IP laws should also aim at keeping balance among different stakeholders. The revised patent law requires that a patent shall not be granted for inventions that are accomplished by relying on genetic resources obtained or used in violation of the provisions of laws and regulations.[47] China's new Anti-Monopoly Law was promulgated after the establishment of the *IP Outline*. It governs business operators' conduct to eliminate or restrict market competition by abusing their

---

[44] Article 22, *the Patent Law of the People's Republic of China*, revised in 2008.

[45] In China, there are three kinds of patents – invention patent, utility model patent and industrial design patent.

[46] *China Custom Protection IP Regulation of the People's Republic of China*, revised in 2010.

[47] Article 5, *the Patent Law of the People's Republic of China*, revised in 2008.

IPRs.[48] To put the law into practice, the State Administration for Industry and Commerce is now formulating the *Anti-Monopoly Guideline for Intellectual Property*. In 2012 *Measures for the Compulsory Licensing for Patent Implementation* was revised to allow SIPO to issue compulsory licences to local firms in cases of state emergencies, unusual circumstances or in the interests of the public. The new regulation may significantly improve the accessibility of medicine.[49] The central government also invests in the Cultural and Information Resources Sharing Project to improve access to knowledge and ensure affordability for the residents and poor people in remote areas.[50]

To strengthen IP protection, the Chinese government operates hotlines such as 12330 and 12315 to support patentees and other IPR holders in enforcing their rights. The government formulates an annual plan for IP protection and regularly takes actions to combat IPR infringements and counterfeit goods.[51] The *White Paper on IP Protection* is published annually.[52] Anyone who reports an illegal CD or DVD production line will be rewarded with cash by the authorities. In addition to the court system and customs border control, there is also an administrative enforcement system in China to help IPR holders to enforce their IPRs. Compared with lawsuits, the administrative system is more efficient, lower cost, and adaptable to Chinese conditions.[53]

IP awareness is very important for a society to create an environment that respects IPRs. Every year, the Chinese government spreads IP knowledge and information via websites, brochures, broadcasting, TV shows, cartoons and other activities. The government also conducts training programmes for officials and managerial personnel of IP in businesses. In university education in law, business and other subjects, IP is often an important course for students. In some southern provinces,

---

[48]   Article 55, the Anti-Monopoly Law of the People's Republic of China, 2008.

[49]   SIPO, *Measures for the Compulsory Licensing for Patent Implementation*, online at: http://www.sipo.gov.cn/zwgs/ling/201203/t20120319_654876.html

[50]   This can be exemplified by the activities organized by China's National Digital Cultural Network. For further details, please visit the official website of China's National Digital Cultural Network at: http://www.ndcnc.gov.cn/

[51]   Yang Jia & Ji Jie, 'The Hotline 12330 for IP Protection and Assistance Opened', *SIPO Official News*, online at http://www.sipo.gov.cn/yw/2009/200903/t20090318_446364.html.

[52]   *The White Paper on China's Intellectual Property Protection 2011*, online at: http://www.sipo.gov.cn/yw/2012/201204/t20120425_679211.html.

[53]   For a study on the administrative system, *see* Feng Xiaoqing (ed.), *Intellectual Property Law*, Wuhan: Wuhan University Press, 2009, pp. 17–18.

primary schools and secondary schools offer extra-curricular courses in IP knowledge. Many schools promote a culture of innovation by providing rewards to students.[54]

The ability to innovate and utilize IP in business communities is crucial to China's national IP strategy. There is a wide consensus in China that the rules of market economy limit the involvement of government roles in business operation. The government, on the other hand, serves to support business operation. SIPO has open databases available to the public to help enterprises to utilize patent information. It also has set up five IP information centres in key cities, including provincial capital cities such as Guangzhou, Wuhan and Nanjing. Together with the Ministry of Industry and Information Technology, SIPO also regularly releases patent information of specific industries.[55]

In order to facilitate patent applications by enterprises, SIPO has set up branch offices across China. There are also IP administrative offices at provincial and municipal levels to help enterprises to implement the IP system via training, mentoring, research and other tailored programmes. To guide Chinese enterprises to implement IP strategy, some IP offices at provincial level promote standardized IP management systems for improving the managerial behaviours of company managers. Many authorities also support enterprises to formulate company patent strategies through patent analysis. A survey shows that more than 75 per cent of the enterprises in Jiangsu Province, which is one of the most advanced provinces in China, now have in place company-level IP strategies.[56] The government also rewards enterprises that set a good example in IP management.[57]

4.3   An Innovative IP System

China's modern IP system is transplanted from developed countries. The legal environment at the beginning of the establishment of the People's

---

[54]   *The Implementation Plan of National Intellectual Property Strategies 2012*, online at http://www.gov.cn/gzdt/2012-05/04/content_2129681.htm.

[55]   State Intellectual Property Office, *Annual Report 2011*, p. 35. Online at: http://www.sipo.gov.cn/gk/ndbg/2011/201205/P020120507359268259958.pdf

[56]   Tang Heng & Zhu Yu, *The Implementation and Evaluation of Regional IP Strategies*, Beijing: Intellectual Property Publishing House, 2011, p. 65.

[57]   Inter-Ministerial Joint Meeting Office for the National Intellectual Property Strategy Implementation Work, Ministry of Human Resources and Social Security of the P.R. China, *Decision to Reward Advanced Workers and Units of National Intellectual Property Strategy Implementation Work*, Renshebufa No. 63, 2013.

Republic of China in 1949 did not fit the IP system well. In this context, an IP system had not been a priority until recently. To put the IP system into practice is an even greater challenge and can cause a mixture of positive and negative influences across China. How to promote the positive roles of IP in China's development and meanwhile prevent the negative effects are major concerns for the Chinese government. According to the popular view, to eliminate the negativities of TRIPS, developing countries should take advantage of the flexibilities of TRIPS in domestic law-making.[58] In reality, however, how to make the law work is a very real problem for developing countries.

China's IP laws have characteristics shared by many other developing countries. China's patent law includes three types of patents – invention, utility model and industrial design. The utility model patent protects petty inventions and is relatively easy and cheap to obtain. The objective of the system is to encourage innovation by the general public and small and medium-sized enterprises (SMEs), along with large enterprises. This suits China's conditions properly. In China, most users of the patent system are small enterprises and they cannot afford the high costs of the patent system.[59] For copyrights, the right holders in general need not register their rights, for they could formalize their copyrights. Of course, registration saves a lot of time when disputes arise in courts.[60]

To deal with the backlogs of patent and trademark examination, China has established three patent examination support centres and one trademark examination cooperation centre to lessen the burden on SIPO and

---

[58]   'To achieve that end, so far as possible developing countries should not be deprived of the flexibility to design their IP systems that developed countries enjoyed in earlier stages of their own development, and higher IP standards should not be pressed on them without a serious and objective assessment of their development impact.' UK Commission on Intellectual Property Rights, *Integrating Intellectual Property Rights and Development Policy*, London, September 2002. http://www.iprcommission.org/home.html

[59]   For example, the average fee for a patent application in the EU is about 35 000 euro. See Li Liming, 'Patent Application in the Europe is Costly', *China Council for the Promotion of International Trade official news*, online at http://www.ccpit.org/Contents/Channel_54/2006/0719/4007/content_4007.htm

[60]   WIPO NCAC, 'Study on the Impact of Enhanced Copyright Protection on the Development of the Textile Market Industry in Nantong, China', online at: http://www.wipo.int/export/sites/www/copyright/en/performance/pdf/impact_textile_market.pdf

China's Trademark Office.[61] This way SIPO could process a patent application within 24 months, which is more efficient compared with the completion periods in other national or regional patent offices in the world. In order to provide better support to the public and to patent examination, SIPO attaches great importance to the development of an automated system. Applicants could search patent information via electronic means.

For IP right holders, the greatest hurdle to enforcing their rights is the intolerable length of lawsuits and their associated costs. This institutional weakness in China's IP system seems inevitable due to the proceedings for IP rights verification, IP infringement and criminal procedures via three different courts. This could mean that the IP right holders have to suffer quite high legal costs when the infringers use legal procedure maliciously. For IPRs enforcement, China has now improved its IP judicial system, optimized the judicial resources and simplified procedures. Specifically, China's Supreme People's Court has an experimental project for the integration of administrative, civil and criminal systems into one IP court (three-in-one) to save time and money for IP right holders. Almost 100 Chinese courts have put in place the three-in-one system at local higher, intermediate and elementary court levels.[62]

5. ACHIEVEMENTS

In 2011 SIPO granted a total of 172 113 invention patents, up 27.4 per cent from 2010. Among them, 112 347 were granted to domestic inventors, accounting for 65.3 per cent of the total number.[63] According to a WIPO report, in 2011 ZTE Corporation was the biggest filer via the WIPO-administered Patent Cooperation Treaty (PCT) system, while Huawei Technologies, another giant telecommunications company of China, ranked third. 'Among the top filing countries, PCT applications from China (+33.4%), Japan (+21%), Canada (+8.3%), the Republic of Korea (+8%) and the US (+8%) saw the fastest growth in 2011.' China

---

[61] Approval for Establishing the Patent Examination Assistance Centers by the State Commission Office for Public Sector Reform, 2011, No. 102 Zhongyang bianban fuzi.

[62] The Supreme People's Court, *The White Paper on Intellectual Property Protection by Chinese Courts in 2010*. For further details of the role of China's IP judicial system, *see* Chapter 5.

[63] SIPO issued a report on granted invention patents in 2011, *China Report Intellectual Property*, 7 March 2012.

has become the fourth largest user of the PCT system.[64] To some extent, the numbers speak for themselves.

According to the Global Innovation Index 2012, which was jointly issued by the European Institute of Business Administration (INSEAD) and WIPO, China's ranking jumped from 43rd to 34th in 2010. China's performance on the key knowledge and technology outputs pillar is outpaced only by Switzerland, Sweden, Singapore and Finland. In the Global Innovation Efficiency Index, China leads the top 10 league of countries.[65]

Now, more and more Chinese enterprises have increased their awareness of the necessity of enriching the connotation of their trademarks, promoting brand value, and transforming trademarks into well-known marks. Chinese brands are enlisted into the World's 500 Most Influential Brands and four of them – CCTV, China Mobile, ICBC and State Grid – were published in the Top 100 by a World Brand Lab's report in 2011.[66] It is not a great achievement compared with companies in developed countries, but it is great leap for Chinese companies.

China has promulgated many policies to promote IP utilization, productivity and competitiveness. The utilization rate of patents reached 60.6 per cent in 2010,[67] which means a larger portion of granted patents has been commercialized. In recent years, IPRs pledge loans have represented a new approach to financing high-tech SMEs and cultural and creative industries. Over the past years, Chinese SMEs have obtained over 10 billion RMB of IPR pledge loans.

In some important technological fields, there are Chinese enterprises that have developed into active participants in establishing technical standards with their patents. Datang Telecom Technology & Industry Group, a Chinese company specializing in 4G mobile technology, has

---

[64]   'International Patent Filings Set New Record in 2011', *WIPO News*, Geneva, 5 March 2012, online at http://www.wipo.int/pressroom/en/articles/2012/article_0001.html

[65]   Soumitra Dutta, INSEAD (ed.), *The Global Innovation Index 2012 (GII): Stronger Innovation Linkages for Global Growth*, online at http://www.wipo.int/export/sites/www/freepublications/en/economics/gii/gii_2012.pdf

[66]   World Brand Lab: The World's 500 Most Influential Brands, 2011.

[67]   Survey Report by SIPO, 'Application Rate of Invention Patents Exceeding 60%', *SIPO News*, online at http://www.gov.cn/gzdt/2010-06/21/content_1632554.htm

been one of the core technology providers in TDSCDMA-LTE-Advanced – one of the international 3G mobile technology standards.[68]

The IP piracy rate in China has declined enormously (see Figure 2.2). According to a study, the IP piracy rate by cost fell from 41 per cent in 2010 to 38 per cent in 2011. The piracy rate of the operation system software was 24 per cent and the piracy rate of the office software was 39 per cent. According to the report of BSA (the Software Alliance), China's piracy rate dropped from 92 per cent in 2003 to 77 per cent in 2011 while the piracy rate in the Asian-Pacific region rose 7 per cent in general. Even by the stricter standards, IP right holders agree that IP protection in China has increasingly improved.[69]

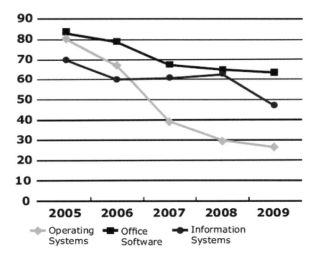

Source: Wang Guanqun, 'Software Piracy Rate Declining in China', *Xinhua News*, 11 May 2010, online at http://news.xinhuanet.com/english2010/china/2010-05/11/c_13286855.htm.

Figure 2.2   Decrease in software piracy cases in China

68   'Datang and Ericsson: Work Together to Internationalize the TD-SCDMA', *Xinhua News*, 21 April 2010, online at: http://news.xinhuanet.com/fortune/2010-04/21/c_1247647.htm
69   BSA, *2011 BSA Global Software Piracy Study*, online at http://globalstudy.bsa.org/2011/.

China has also enhanced international cooperation with the US, the EU, Japan, South Korea and Russia for IPR enforcement and the exchange of information. The *Guideline to Protect IP in China for EU SMEs* was formulated and released to the public with cooperation between China and the EU in 2010.[70] The *Business Confidence Survey 2011* conducted by the German Chamber of Commerce in China, which was based on opinions solicited from 188 German companies, indicated that only 19 per cent of German companies predicted that there would be more challenges for IP protection in the future. In an interview in 2012, the Commissioner of the United States Patent and Trademark Office (USPTO), David Kappos, stated that China is still facing the challenge of IP enforcement, but IP protection in China is improving or making progress.[71]

Culture plays a fundamental role in IP enforcement. In recent years, the Chinese government has paid great attention to IP education among the public. In a survey conducted by the Ministry of Commerce, more than 90 per cent of Chinese people living in cities are aware of IP although less than half of them do not reject using pirated or counterfeit goods. More and more Chinese people are coming to realize the significance of IP in China's modern and transforming economy.[72]

CONCLUSION: PROSPECTS OF CHINA'S NATIONAL IP STRATEGY[73]

This chapter has briefly described the contexts, establishment and operation of the national IP strategy of the People's Republic of China. Overall the strategy, guided by China's *IP Outline*, is designed to boost China's IP creation, utilization, protection and management in the light of the need to improve China's innovation capacity and its economic and social development. The implementation of China's national IP strategy

---

[70]   EU-China IPR2, *Guidance on China's Intellectual Property Protection 2010*, online at http://www.sme.gov.cn/web/second/ppt/CN/IPR2CNHAI.pdf

[71]   Zhang Yuan'an, 'Director of the United States Patent and Trademark Office: China Needs to Strengthen its IP Protection', *Caixin Online News*, online at http://international.caixin.com/2012-06-05/100397154.html

[72]   Han Xiu, 'The Ministry of Commerce: 90% of the Chinese People are Aware of IP in China', *China Radio*, 21 September 2012, online at: http://china.cnr.cn/gdgg/201209/t20120921_510964233.shtml

[73]   For further details, see Zhang Zhicheng, 'The International Situation in Intellectual Property Field and China's Countermeasures', *Science & Technology Review*, 2012, Vol. 33, pp. 15–17.

has already turned China into an IP power by numbers. Yet, more efforts should be made to maintain its sustainable development and it is necessary to improve the quality of invention patents and promote more famous Chinese brands. New thoughts and approaches should be introduced to improve China's IP system, especially the legal system. These could include the following few aspects:

First, public participation in IP law-making should be improved. Chinese legislative bodies should transform the stereotyped mindset of simply introducing laws to the society. The law-making process should not simply be viewed as a task of experts and governing bodies but should be expanded to include interested IP right holders and stakeholders so as to promote democratic and transparent law-making processes. This may further the localization and flexibilities of IP laws in China. It can also promote balance of interest in the legislative progress and thus meet the diverse demands for IPR protection at home. Through these channels, China's IP laws can better promote the development of a harmonious society and enhance the adaptability of IP laws in China's overall economic, scientific and technological development.

Second, the contents of IP legislation should reflect the overall demands of the changing Chinese market. IP management and operation are increasingly becoming skilful, integrated and strategic. The links between IP and capital are ever closer with capital's increased role in dominating and speculating IP assets. IP-related organizations, such as intellectual property alliances, IP activist groups, and right holders' groups, are flourishing. The vertical and top-down system has changed in China's IP system. It has turned into a networked and multi-dimensional system involving various interested groups, which leads to a notable phenomenon of imbalanced interest. Future law-making will have to address these issues, in the context of China's status quo as a global manufacturing power. This means regulating the IP fields in a timely manner, maintaining a proper market order, promoting appropriate marriages between capital and IP assets, and coordinating relations among interested groups such as inventors, innovation-oriented businesses and investors. A multi-dimensional IP system should be established in line with two key priorities – boosting the innovative development of China's real economy and meanwhile maintaining the public interest.

Third, the value orientation of the IP law-making process should continue to strengthen IP protection in China. At present, strengthened IPR protection is an international trend as well as a development objective for China. Although China is developing creative design and creating more brand-based businesses with some breakthroughs in certain areas, it remains principally at the low and medium end of the global manufacturing chain. Meanwhile, China's innovation capacities differ dramatically among different regions. Therefore, changes to China's IP system in the future should further protect petty inventions, designs and brand awareness. They should also improve reward systems to stimulate more innovation. In specific terms, a flexible, targeted, feasible and streamlined IP system should be established to improve the accessibility of China's IP system.

Fourth, the implementation and operation capacities in China's IP system need to be further improved. China's economic and social development, as well as the Chinese IP right holders' growing needs, require better implementation and operation capacities in respect of the IP administration system, law enforcement, the level of informatization, and the accessibility of IP and patent information by the general public, public awareness and the right holders' capability of utilizing the IP system. To improve China's IP system, we must seriously take into account the reality of China's development and highlight the required improvement of the fundamental capabilities of implementing IP strategies.

3. Implementation of China's rejuvenation through knowledge

Yang Lihua[*]

INTRODUCTION

Although China once had brilliant achievements in science and technology, it lags far behind Western countries in modern times. Since the People's Republic of China ('the P.R. China') was founded in 1949, the nation has attempted to overcome various challenges in its own development. In China today, the respect for and pursuit of knowledge and innovation are embodied in a set of laws, regulations and policies categorized into intellectual property or innovation, promotion of science and technology, education reform, talents cultivation, the protection of intellectual property rights and so on. All of these sail under the flag of 'relying on knowledge to rejuvenate China'.

This chapter provides a brief review of the P.R. China's rejuvenation-through-knowledge policies, laws and practices. Part 1 outlines the relevant thoughts of China's political leaders since the founding of new China. Part 2 discusses China's policy framework of relying on knowledge to rejuvenate the nation in science and technology, human resources, education and intellectual property. Part 3 briefly covers the legal system of rejuvenating China relying on knowledge. Part 4 discusses the implementation of laws and policies on relying on knowledge to rejuvenate China, and points out some achievements China has made, and the problems needed to be overcome. The conclusion points out that China's laws and policies on relying on knowledge to rejuvenate the nation change with time, the transformation of national economic systems and the change of the situations at home and abroad.

* The author wishes to thank Dr Liu Qijia and Dr Zhang Nan for their unselfish help in the modification of the English version. This paper is based on research data available in Mainland China.

1. FROM 'MARCH TOWARDS SCIENCE' TO 'BUILD AN INNOVATIVE COUNTRY'

Since the founding of the People's Republic of China in 1949, knowledge innovation factors such as science and technology, education and talents have been important components of national development strategies that have developed from the 'March towards science' during the Mao Zedong period to 'Science and technology is the first productive force' during Deng Xiaoping times, the strategy of 'Relying on science and education to rejuvenate the nation' in the Jiang Zemin era, and 'National innovation system construction' during the Hu Jintao period.

1.1 The Planned-economy Periods

The P.R. China's government had little to inherit from its predecessor, the Kuomintang government that fled to Taiwan in 1949. For example, only some 30 institutions of science and technology had been left in mainland China by the Kuomintang government.[1] In 1954 the first National People's Congress of the P. R. China proposed a grand goal: to realize the modernization of industry, agriculture, transportation and national defence. At the meeting, Premier Zhou Enlai pointed out that the key is to realize the modernization of science and technology.[2] The 'March towards science' is an important reflection of the thoughts of the first generation of the Communist Party of China (CPC)'s collective leaders.[3] This policy enabled new China to centralize all possible powers and mobilize various resources to carry out scientific research.[4] The slogan

---

[1] Bo Yibo, 'Review of Several Major Decisions and Events', Beijing: the Central Committee of the CPC School Press, 1991.

[2] Zhou Enlai, *Selected Work of Zhou Enlai*, Beijing: People's Publishing House, 1984, p. 412.

[3] The idea of science and technology is especially embodied in taking the planning of science and technology as the basic way of management of science and technology activities, and emphasizing the importance of planned development of science and technology. *See* Yu Lijun, 'From Marching towards Science to Building an Innovative Country: the Historical Evolution of the Thought of the Communist Party of China on Science and Technology', *Academic Journal*, 2011, No. 10, pp. 29–30.

[4] Deng Bin, 'On the Strategic Decision of the Party's First Generation of Central Collective Leaders on Marching towards Science', *Journal of Southwest Normal University* (humanities and social science), 2006, vol. 32, No. 4, pp. 123–26.

'March towards science' also suggests that under a difficult international environment in which the US-led Western countries did everything possible to blockade or even threaten war against new China, the CPC was able to progress in science and technology in a number of areas. However, due to the ten-year Cultural Revolution in Mao Zedong's era, intellectuals were attacked, and there were inherent development problems in China's science and technology.[5]

Karl Marx pointed out that productivity includes science and technology.[6] On this basis, Deng Xiaoping put forward his famous thesis that 'science and technology is the first productive force' at the beginning of post-Cultural Revolution China's economic reform.[7] The reason why science and technology is the first productive force is 'a dominant factor which plays a decisive role in all elements of productive force'.[8] At that time, after many years of unrest, China's economy and science and technology were backward. In this context, Deng Xiaoping decisively put forward the argument of 'science and technology is the first productive force', which was very forward looking in China's economic reform. Under the guidance of this thought, in 1985 the CPC Central Committee put forward a science and technology policy and development strategy, arguing that 'economic construction must rely on science and technology and scientific and technological work must be geared to the needs of economic construction'. Under the guidance of this policy, the Decision of the CPC Central Committee on the Reform of the Science and Technology System was passed in 1985,[9] which started a science and technology system reform, and emphasized how to strengthen the combination of technology and economy to make China's science and technology serve its economic construction better.

The view that 'Science and technology is the first productive force' is the essence of Deng Xiaoping's thought on science and technology, and

---

[5] Song Zheng, 'From Marching towards Science to Rejuvenating China by Relying on Science and Education: Comments on the Party's Policy of Science and Technology since the Founding of New China', *Journal of Hulun Buir College*, 2006, vol. 14, No. 5, pp. 78–80.

[6] *The Complete Works by Marx and Engels* (vol. 46), Beijing: The People's Publishing House, 1979, p. 211.

[7] Editorial Committee of the CPC Central Committee (ed.), *The Selected Works of Deng Xiaoping* (vol. 3), Beijing: The People's Publishing House, 1993, p. 274.

[8] Wang Yaodong, 'Deng Xiaoping's Thought that Science and Technology is the Primary Productive Force and its Development', *Social Sciences Journal of Colleges of Shanxi*, 2005, vol. 17, No. 4, pp. 5–7.

[9] Available at <http://www.techcn.com.cn/index.php?edition-view-138057-1>.

forms an important part of 'Deng Xiaoping Theory'. This thesis revealed the dialectical relationship between modern science and technology and economic development, clarified the role of science and technology in the development of social productive force, and enhanced the Marxist theory of science and technology to an unprecedented height.[10] It shows that the second-generation leaders of the CPC attached great importance to the development of science and technology, and pointed out a correct way that relies on scientific and technological progress and innovation to accelerate the development of productivity. At the time when China had just undergone a decade of unrest, Deng Xiaoping's proposal had a historic contribution for its positive impact on the development of Chinese science and technology, promoting the combination of Chinese technology and economy, playing the role of transforming science and technology into productivity, relying on scientific and technological progress to promote economic and social development. It thus laid a theoretical foundation for China's leaders later to put forward new strategies of relying on knowledge to rejuvenate the nation.

1.2   The Market-economy Periods

China entered into a socialist market economy in 1992. In this context, the strategy of relying on science and education to rejuvenate the nation was put forward by the P. R. China's third generation of collective leaders headed by Jiang Zemin.[11] In 1992, at the 14th National Congress of the CPC, Jiang Zemin pointed out that 'to revitalize economy, it must first revitalize science and technology', that 'science and technology must be geared to the main battlefield of economic construction', and

---

[10]   Song Zheng, 'From Marching towards Science to Rejuvenating China by Relying on Science and Education', pp. 78–80.

[11]   Some scholars think that the strategy of relying on science and education was formed by the efforts of three generations of collective leaders of the CPC. The first generation of collective leaders led by Mao Zedong cleared the way for the implementation of science and education development, the second generation of the collective leaders led by Deng Xiaoping constructed the theoretical basis of relying on science and education through practice, and the third generation collective leaders headed by Jiang Zemin formally took relying on science and education to rejuvenate the country as the guidelines and strategy of managing the country and turned it into actions. *See* Ji Zhihong, 'The Party's Exploration of the Strategy of Developing the Country by Relying on Science and Education after the Founding of New China', *Innovation*, 2009, No. 4, p. 72.

that 'education must be strategically placed in a priority position for development'.[12] In 1995, Jiang Zemin further put forward:

> Relying on science and education to rejuvenate the nation refers to full implementation of the thought that science and technology is the first productive force, to an education-oriented direction, to placing science, technology and education in an important position of economic and social development, to enhancing national science and technology strength and the ability to transform science and technology into real productivity, to enhancing the whole nation's scientific and cultural quality, and to transferring economic construction to relying on scientific and technological progress and improving labor quality.[13]

The 'Ninth Five-year Plan' and the '2010 Future Target Outline' passed at the 4th session of the 8th National People's Congress held in 1996 created a strategy of relying on science and education to rejuvenate the nation that was to be earnestly implemented in the next 15 years.[14] Later in 1997, at the 15th National Congress of the CPC, the CPC Central Committee further established the strategy of relying on science and education to rejuvenate the nation as a national development strategy across the century. The report of the 15th National Congress of the CPC reiterated the commitment to speed up the implementation of the strategy of developing the nation by relying on science and education and sustainable development strategy, which places scientific and technological progress in a key status of the social and economic development.[15] This is undoubtedly a specific implementation of Deng Xiaoping's ideas that 'science and technology is the first productive force'.

The proposal of the strategy of rejuvenating the country by relying on science and education in China was put forward against a unique

---

[12]   Xu Jing, 'From Marching towards Science to Relying on Science and Education to Rejuvenate the Country, *Science Management Research*, 2006, vol. 23, No. 5, pp. 71–87; Liu Guijun, 'From Science and Technology is the First Productive Force to the Construction of an Innovative Country', *Front Line*, 2010, No. 6, pp. 46–48.

[13]   Li Houqing, 'Jiang Zemin Thought on Relying on Science and Education to Rejuvenate the Country', *Xinjiang Social Science*, 2008, No. 4, p. 27.

[14]   Available at <http://www.npc.gov.cn/wxzl/gongbao/2001-01/02/content_50 03506.htm>.

[15]   Wang Kaishou, 'The Strategic Thought of the Third Generation of Collective Leaders of the Party on Relying on Science and Education to Rejuvenate the Country', *Journal of Huabei Coal Industry Normal College (philosophy and science)*, 2006, vol. 25, No. 4, p. 132.

background. Since the 1990s, science and technology have played an increasingly leading role in the global economy.[16] The global competitions in the so-called 'knowledge economy' have gradually turned out to be competitions of science, technology and talents. While post-1978 China's economy had maintained high-speed growth since the reform and opening-up policy was implemented from 1978 to the early 1990s, its economic growth mainly relied on a labour-intensive model. Technology industries were yet to become the common form. The level of development of science and technology was not high. Basic research was weak and original technology was not adequate. Overall, the contribution rate of science and technology to economic growth remained low.[17] In this context, China's economic growth and development needed an upgraded industrial structure. Thus, vigorously developing science, technology and education in China's economy and society had become the inevitable choice of China's economic and social development.[18]

Moving into the 21st century, the fourth generation of Chinese leaders led by Hu Jintao launched the strategy 'to construct an innovation-oriented country'. At that time, the rhythm of the world's science and technology revolution was greatly accelerating and the knowledge economy was generating a huge impact on the productivity of the world. This makes the innovation capacity of a nation the core of national competitive power.

Back to the early 2000s, China had already entered a historical stage in which it had to rely more on scientific and technological progress and innovation to promote economic and social development. After more than 30 years of rapid economic growth by adopting reform and the opening-up policy, China's development of science and technology has also made great progress, and even occupies a leading position in the world in some fields. China's general pattern of economic, scientific and technological development is still reliant on the introduction of foreign

---

[16] Statistics show that in developed countries in the early 20th century, science and technology contributed 5% to 20% in their national economic growth but today this rate has grown to over 50% and even to 90%. Wang Kaishou, 'The Strategic Thought of the Third Generation of Collective Leaders of the Party on Relying on Science and Education to Rejuvenate the Country', pp. 130–33.

[17] Song Zheng, 'From Marching towards Science to Rejuvenating China by Relying on Science and Education', p. 80.

[18] Feng Xiaoqing, *Intellectual Property Strategy for Enterprises*, Beijing: Intellectual Property Rights Press, 2008, p. 33.

capital and technology on a large scale or the so-called 'exchanging market for technology'. The self-sustainability rate of key technologies needed by China's industrial development is low. Key equipment with high-tech content relies on import. Most of China's industries are at the low end of the international division of labour and the global value chain.[19] This situation certainly is unsatisfactory. Therefore, the construction of an innovative country becomes an inevitable choice of 21st century China.

In this context, the CPC Central Committee with Hu Jintao as the General Secretary issued the call: 'adhere to the road of independent innovation with Chinese characteristics and strive for constructing an innovative country'.[20] In January 2006 Hu Jintao elaborated on the connotation of building an innovative country at China's 2006 National Conference on Science and Technology. He pointed out that:

> The core of building an innovative country is to enhance the independent innovation capacities as the basis of the development of science and technology, to create a road of independent innovation with Chinese characteristics, and to promote development of science and technology by leaps and bounds; it is to view the enhancement of independent innovation capacities as the key to adjusting industrial structures and transforming the pattern of economic development, to build a resource-conservative, and environment-friendly society, and to promote the good and rapid development of the national economy; it is to view enhancing our independent innovation capacities as a national strategy and carry it out through all aspects of the modernization construction, to arouse the spirit of innovation within the nation, to cultivate high-level innovation talents, to form systems and mechanisms conducive to independent innovation, vigorously promote theoretical innovation, institutional innovation and technology innovation, and to continuously consolidate and develop the great cause of Socialism with Chinese characteristics.[21]

Shortly after the 5th plenary session of the 16th National Congress of the CPC in 2006, the State Council promulgated 'The National Medium-term and Long-term Planning Outline of Scientific and Technological Development (2006–2020)' (hereinafter the NMLST), specifying independent

---

[19]   Chen Qi & Cheng Jianxin, 'Analysis of the Evolution and Characteristics of the Strategy of Developing the Country by Relying on Science and Education, to Building an Innovative Country', *Forum of Science and Technology in China*, 2007, No. 1, pp. 11–14; p. 113.

[20]   Available at <http://theory.people.com.cn/GB/41038/4545825.html>.

[21]   Available at <http://www.cast.org.cn/n435777/n435799/n561674/n562085/9487_2.html>.

innovation as the new strategic basis of China's science and technology development, and put forward the schedule of the construction of an innovative country, namely, by 2020 China will become one of the innovative countries. The report of the 17th Congress for the CPC once again stressed that to improve the capacities of independent innovation and build an innovative country are the core of national development strategy and the key to enhancing comprehensive national strength.[22] To build an innovation-oriented country is a key strategy that is based on China's national development strategy of the new century and aims at the world scientific and technological frontier. It also views Chinese enterprises as the main body of scientific and technological innovation in a market-oriented environment that combines production, learning and research.[23]

To summarize, after the founding of new China in 1949, the CPC leaders have put forward different slogans for science and technology, moving from 'March towards science' to 'science and technology is the first productive force', from 'rely on science and education to rejuvenate the nation' and 'to build an innovative country'. These slogans are not groundless, but represent the inheritance and development of Marx's theory that 'science and technology is productivity'.[24] That means the improvement of science and technology can lead to the rapid development of the economy and the improvement of science and technology must rely on talents and education. On account of this, scientific and technological progress and training and education come together in the policies and laws on relying on knowledge to rejuvenate the country and thus constitute a self-consistent and systematic project.

---

[22] Available at <http://news.xinhuanet.com/newscenter/2007-10/24/content_6938568.htm>.

[23] *The Opinion on Deepening the System Reform of Science and Technology and Speeding up the Construction of National Innovation System.*' Available at <http://www.gov.cn/jrzg/2012-09/23/content_2231413.htm>.

[24] Du Yang, 'On Jiang Zemin's Strategic Thought of Relying on Science and Education to Rejuvenate the Country', Northeast Forestry University, masters dissertation, p. 13.

2. THE POLICY FRAMEWORK OF RELYING ON KNOWLEDGE TO REJUVENATE CHINA

The policy framework of relying on knowledge to rejuvenate China is comprised of science and technology policy, talent policy, education policy, intellectual property policy and so on.

2.1 Science and Technology Policies

The improvement of the policy of science and technology is an important foundation of enhancing China's capacity for innovation and building an innovative country. These policies can be understood as 'the focused and coordinating measures adopted to promote the development of science and technology and to serve national goals by the means of science and technology'.[25] The Decision of the Central Committee of the CPC and the State Council on Accelerating the Progress of Science and Technology (hereinafter referred to as the DAPST) released on 6 May 1995 is an important policy document for China to promote the progress of science and technology.[26] Another important policy is the NMLST, promulgated in 2006.[27] Table 3.1 summarizes some important policies since the establishment of the People's Republic of China in 1949.

Table 3.1   Important scientific and technology polices of the P. R. China

Name	Year	Issued by	Contents
'The Perspective Plan for Science and Technology Development from 1956 to 1967' (hereinafter referred to as 'the Twelve-Year Plan for Science and Technology')	1956	The CPC Central Committee and State Council	Detailed provisions on scientific research systems, scientific research institution settings, scientific and technological personnel use and training, such as the general principles of the scientific research institutions, human and material resources, the principle of scientific research and personnel training and selection.

[25] Fan Chunliang, *The Policy of Science and Technology in the Era of Globalization*, Beijing: Beijing University of Technology Press, 2005, p. 32.
[26] Available at <http://news.xinhuanet.com/misc/2006-01/07/content_4021977.htm>.
[27] *See* Table 3.1.

Name	Year	Issued by	Contents
The 1963–1972 Plan for the Development of Science and Technology (hereinafter referred to as 'the Ten–Year Plan')	1963	The CPC Central Committee and State Council	Provisions on 12 aspects, such as professional research institution construction, training of research personnel, scientific investment management, appraisal and reward systems for scientific research achievements, technology promotion, involving the systems for personnel training, selection, assignment, transfer, reward, management, and research awards, etc.
The 1978–1985 National Science and Technology Development Plan (hereinafter referred to as 'the Eight–Year Plan')	1978	State Council	In addition to key research planning objectives, it singled out the goals of scientific research teams and institutional development. It proposed 14 aspects of security measures, including the development of higher education, accelerating scientific and technological personnel training; accelerating the popularization and application of scientific and technological achievements; establishment of national science awards system, etc.
The 1986–2000 Science and Technology Development Plan	1986	State Council	It emphasizes the combination of technology and economy, and pushing forward the reform of science and technology systems, unveiling science and technology plans such as the high-tech research and development plan (the 863 Plan), the Torch Program for promoting the industrialization of high-tech industry, the Spark Program to support rural areas, and National Natural Science Foundation to support basic research.

Name	Year	Issued by	Contents
The Ten-year Science and Technology Development Plan of the People's Republic of China and the Eighth 'Five-year' Plan (1991– 2000)	1991	State Council	Emphasized the reform of science and technology systems, reflected the changes in the reform from the planned economy to market economy system, proposed explicitly for the first time that the growth of investment in science and technology shall exceed that of GNP, and put forward clear objectives for R&D funds, and to take measures to promote scientific and technological progress.
The Science, Technology and Education Development Program of the 10th Five-year Plan for National Economic and Social Development	2001	The former State Planning Commission and the Ministry of Science and Technology	It proposed to establish a national innovation system, to improve the ability of independent innovation, to enhance the quality in science and technology, to continue to implement technological innovation projects, to encourage enterprises to become the subjects of technological progress and innovation, to establish national knowledge innovation system, and to promote knowledge innovation projects.
The Long-term Scientific and Technological Development Plan (2006–2020)	2006	State Council	This plan proposed the guidelines for scientific and technological work and is clearly put forward to build a national innovation system. The policies on promoting science and technology include: fiscal and taxation policies, government procurement, intellectual property strategy, monetary policy, science and technology investment system, and so on.

Name	Year	Issued by	Contents
National Eleventh Five-Year Science and Technology Development Plan	2006	The Ministry of Science and Technology	It proposed to establish a national innovation system with Chinese characteristics, including the technological innovation system with enterprises as subjects, the knowledge innovation system with the combination of scientific research and higher education, the innovation system of national defence science and technology, the regional innovation system, and the technology intermediary service system.
Twelfth Five-Year National Science and Technology Development Plan	2011	The Ministry of Science and Technology	It proposed to comprehensively promote the construction of a national innovation system, to speed up the implementation of the national science and technology major projects, foster and develop vigorously strategic emerging industries, strengthening the construction of science and technology innovation base and platform, vigorously foster innovative talents of science and technology, optimize the societal environment of innovation, etc.

Sources: The contents are available from the Ministry of Science and Technology website 'Science and technology plan', <http://www.most.gov.cn/kjgh>/. Also see 'Science and technology planning in the history', <http://www.most.gov.cn/kjgh/lskjgh/>.

Prior to 1995, especially before the reform and opening-up policy was carried out in 1978, the P. R. China's policy on the promotion of the progress of science and technology was mainly embodied in the devotion to developing the basic foundation of science and technology such as equipment, funding and human resources.[28] Under the planned economy system, the main policy on promoting scientific and technological progress was to concentrate the national scientific research strength on key breakthroughs that were to be achieved in a short time. During this

[28]   Chen Qi & Cheng Jianxin, 'Analysis of the Evolution and Characteristics of the Strategy of Developing the Country by Relying on Science and Education, to Building an Innovative Country', p. 14.

period, though China stressed the important role of science and technology within national development, it was not enhanced to a national development strategy level.

The Decision on Speeding up Scientific and Technological Progress was released in 1995 in the context in which China gradually entered into a socialist market economy. The opening of the Decision proposed to 'fully implement the thought that science and technology is the first productive force', and for the first time explicitly called for 'unswerving implementations of the strategy of relying on science and education'. That made the role of science and technology and education in modern China's national development become vital.

The promulgation of the NMLST in 2006 marked another profound change in China's policy on the promotion of science and technology. It clearly proposed to establish a 'national innovation system'.[29] 'To construct national innovation system' was established as the basic strategy of national development by the NMLST. The subsequent 'National Eleventh Five-year Science and Technology Development Plan' promulgated in 2006 and 'National Twelfth Five-Year Science and Technology Development Plan' promulgated in 2011 further deepened this outline.

2.2 Human Resource Development Policies

Human resources are essential to economic development. 'A country depends on talents to revitalize, and political affairs rely on talents to manage.'[30] Competition in the era of the knowledge economy is ultimately competition between talents. Therefore, the cultivation of talents, the enhancement of science and technology innovation ability, and the formulation of talent policy appear to be critical.[31] Human resources are even being viewed as 'the first resources'.[32] Here talent policy plays a vital incentivizing role. Talent policy refers to 'a series of policies and regulations concerning bringing the ability and role of talents into play, and regulations, measures and action made or taken by the government to

---

[29] Available at <http://www.gov.cn/jrzg/2006-02/09/content_183787.htm>.

[30] Li Duanxiang, 'On the Thought of Jiang Zemin on Reinvigorating China through Human Resource Development', *Administrative Management in China*, 2004, No.11, p. 39.

[31] Deng Songlu & Cui Yi, 'Human Capital and Relying on Science and Education to Rejuvenate the Country', *Science, Technology and Dialectics*, 2000, No. 2, p. 64.

[32] Jin Wenzhi, 'Why Human Resources are the First Resource', *Chinese Talent*, 2002, No. 8. pp. 25–29.

play the role of talents with regard to the activities such as cultivation, development and utilization of talents'.[33] Talent promotion policy is the core of talent policy, and is the pointer of talent cultivation and maximizes the energy of human resources. The policy on talent promotion is an important part of China's strategy of rejuvenating the country by relying on knowledge.

As to specific policies, a series of talent projects have been brought out. These include the National Hundred, Thousand and Ten Thousand Talent Project (1995) jointly implemented by seven ministries or commissions including the Ministry of Personnel, the Ministry of Science and Technology, and the Ministry of Education,[34] and the Yangtze River Scholars Program carried out by the Ministry of Education in 1998.[35] The strategy of reinvigorating China through human resource development is the basic orientation of China's policy on talent promotion, and is the sub-strategy to carry out the strategy of developing the country by relying on science and education, and the national strategy of constructing an innovative country. Implementing the strategy of reinvigorating China through human resource development is the correct choice to respond to economic globalization, and is the inevitable choice of promoting the strategy of rejuvenating China by relying on science and education and building an innovative country.

On the basis of theoretical research and practical experience in the talent policy, the General Office of the Central Committee of the CPC and the State Council jointly issued the 2002–2005 National Talent Team Construction Plan (hereinafter referred to as the Talent Team Plan) on 7 May 2002.[36] The second part of the Talent Team Plan, 'the guidelines and objectives of the talent team construction', clearly proposed to 'implement the strategy of reinvigorating China through human resource development'. Specific chapters were dedicated to talent team constructions for the government and enterprises, patents and technology, talent development and introduction for China's western regions, attraction and

---

[33]   Song Yuqiang & Zhuang Xinying, 'Talent Policy Research Review', *The Small and Medium-sized Enterprise Management and Science and Technology*, 2012, No. 4, pp. 238–39.

[34]   The project's main goal is to develop hundreds of world-leading scientists, thousands of nationwide leaders in different fields, and tens of thousands of young key experts. Available at <http://baike.baidu.com/view/793718.htm>.

[35]   The project is jointly initiated by the Ministry of Education and the Li Ka Shing Foundation. Available at <http://baike.baidu.com/view/56929.htm>.

[36]   Available at <http://www.edu.cn/20020613/3058823.shtml>.

use of overseas talents, strengthening of education and training, establishment and improvement of the talent incentive mechanisms, and guiding the rational flow of talents. The Plan has laid a solid foundation for the further improvement of China's policy on talent promotion, and the further deepening of the strategy of reinvigorating China through human resource development.

In 2003 the CPC Central Committee and the State Council held the national conference on talent work for the first time since the founding of new China,[37] and issued the Decision on Further Strengthening the Talent Work (hereinafter referred to as the Decision) on 26 December 2003.[38] In 2006 the strategy of reinvigorating China through human resource development was listed as an independent chapter in the '11th Five-year Plan Outline of National Economic and Social Development of the People's Republic of China'.[39] This was the first time that the P. R. China explicitly put forward the implementation of the strategy of reinvigorating China through human resource development. On 6 June 2010 the National Medium- and Long-term Talent Development Plan (2010–2020) (hereinafter referred to as the Talent Plan) was released. This Plan put forward the basic guidelines for the medium- and long-term talent development and China's overall strategic objectives of talent development. These objectives include that by 2020 China is to be one of the leading talent countries of the world, and that the total amount of human resources will reach 180 000 000, etc.[40]

The fulfilment of the policy on reinvigorating China through human resource development and talent promotion in China has prompted a large number of creative talents to stand out.[41] In this wave, a clear trend is that human resources have increasingly become a vital theme of China's construction of its national innovation system.

---

[37]   Available at <http://news.sina.com.cn/o/2003-12-22/13061404086s.shtm>.
[38]   Available at <http://www.llrsrc.gov.cn/llrsrc/info/view_47.html>.
[39]   Available at <http://www.gov.cn/ztzl/gmjj/>.
[40]   Available at <http://www.chinanews.com/gn/news/2010/06-06/2326040. shtml>.
[41]   There are of course some problems in the implementation of the talent programmes, such as short vision and formalism. For details, see Zhang Hongwei, 'Irrational Tendency and Its Control of Talent Project', *Talent Development*, 2006, No. 4, p. 17.

2.3   China's Education Policies

Education is a central value of Chinese civilization. Today, education is viewed as the cradle of talent growth. Therefore it becomes an important factor and part of rejuvenating the country through knowledge. 'Without the solid support of education, the development of science and technology would not be sustained, stable and healthy.'[42] China's education policy has been undergoing various changes in past decades as responses to various challenges such as the domestic education level, low education penetration, unbalanced development, needs of science and technology development etc.

On 13 February 1993 the State Council promulgated *China's Education Reform and Development Compendium*. It proposed to form the basic framework of socialist education with Chinese characteristics in the 21st century. It sets specific targets for nine-year compulsory education, high school education, and the development of higher education, with a focus on various aspects of strength of the central and local governments to create about 100 key universities and a group of key disciplines and specialties.[43] Guided by the above policy, great changes have taken place in China's education system. The 21st-Century Education Revitalization Plan formulated in 1998,[44] aimed at establishing a new system of education, and was the construction blueprint for the cross-century education reform and development, which was put forward for implementing the Education Law and Chinese Education Reform and Development Compendium. Subsequently in June 1999, the Central Committee of the CPC and the State Council held a national conference on education and issued 'The Decision on Deepening Education Reform, Comprehensively Promote Quality Education'.[45]

On 5 May 2010, former Chinese Premier Wen Jiabao chaired a State Council executive meeting, which reviewed and passed the National

---

[42]   Li Guang, 'Relying on Science and Education to Develop the Country: Correlation and Overall Function of Science and Education', *The Advance of Science and Technology and Countermeasures*, 1997, No. 1, p. 16.

[43]   Available at <http://www.gov.cn/jrzg/2010-07/29/content_1667143.htm>.

[44]   Formulated by the Ministry of Education on 24 December 1998, and approved and forwarded by the State Council on 13 January 1999. Available at <http://news.sina.com.cn/richtalk/news/china/9902/022523.html>.

[45]   Issued by the general office of the Central Committee of the CPC on 13 June 1999. Available at <http://www.jyb.cn/info/jyzck/200602/t20060219_10716. html>.

Medium-and-long-term Education Reform and Development Plan Outline (2010–2020) (hereinafter referred to as the Education Planning Outline).[46] This is another major policy adjustment on China's education reform and development. The Education Planning Outline includes four parts: overall strategy, development tasks, institutional reform, and implementation measures. It sets the overall future target and direction of China's educational reform and development. For example, it proposed to realize the modernization of education by 2020 and also put forward specific targets of education development and human resources development.[47]

As can be seen from the above brief discussion, China's education reform and education policy has been constantly adjusted under different situations, but has been following this trend: first, the important position of education in rejuvenating the country through knowledge and the promotion strength of the policy has been increasing. This can be seen from the increase in education funding, reform of the education system, and the implementation of the large-scale educational project such as the 211 Project and the 985 Project. Second, the extent of standardization, systemization, education modernization and internationalization becomes wider and wider. The increase of standardization is reflected in the improvement of the education laws and regulations. A systematic education network has been formed. This network ranges from primary and secondary to higher education in both vocational and academic models. Increasingly, less developed regions in central and western China have experienced significant growth in education networks. The embodiment of the modernization and internationalization first lies in the change of educational philosophies, the transformation of the mentality of education from exam-oriented education to quality education, from school education to lifelong education, and the increase of international education cooperation and exchange, etc. In the 21st century, China's comprehensive national strength and international competitiveness will be increasingly dependent on the level of education development, science and technology and knowledge innovation. Education will remain a key driving force for China's development.

---

[46] Available at <http://www.gov.cn/jrzg/2010-07/29/content_1667143.htm>.
[47] *Ibid.*

2.4 Intellectual Property Policies

The intellectual property system is an important system to promote innovation and enhance the national core competitiveness. On 5 June 2008 the State Council promulgated the National Intellectual Property Strategy Outline (hereinafter referred to as 'NIPSO').[48] It is a milestone in the development of China's intellectual property system. The contexts and contents of the NIPSO have already been discussed in Chapter 2 of this book. The reiteration here is just to show that the NIPSO is an integral part of the strategy of rejuvenating the country through knowledge. China's intellectual property policy of rejuvenating the country through knowledge is closely related to the above-mentioned policies on science and technology promotion, personnel promotion and education promotion but it has its own unique function.

Intellectual property strategy reflects 'a process of the legalization of public policy and the trend of turning legal system into public policy'.[49] It can be said that the implementation of the NIPSO is a major strategic plan for China to realize its rejuvenation through knowledge. From 2009 to 2013, China published five annual schemes to promote the national intellectual property strategy.[50] All provinces and cities over the country have issued regional intellectual property strategies in combination with regional development situations.[51] Based on their functions, ministries of the State Council have successively issued their own solutions or opinions on the implementation of the NIPSO.[52] As can be expected, as China speeds up the pace of building an innovative country and develops its intellectual property system rapidly, China's intellectual property policies, which serve innovation, protect innovation achievements and promote the application of innovation achievements, will gradually become more mature under the environment of rejuvenating China through knowledge.

---

[48] Available at <http://www.gov.cn/zwgk/2008-06/10/content_1012269.htm>.
[49] Zhang Zhicheng, *Studies of Intellectual Property Strategy*, Beijing: Science Press, 2009, p. 2.
[50] See the national intellectual property strategy network: http://www.nipso.cn/index.asp.
[51] For instance, in May 2009 the Beijing municipal government issued *Opinions on the Implementation of Capital Intellectual Property Strategy*, and in March 2010 the *Intellectual Property Strategy Compendium of Hainan Province* was passed.
[52] Such as the *Work Plan of the Ministry of Science and Technology on Carrying out the Strategy of Intellectual Property*, promulgated in June 2012.

3. THE LEGAL SYSTEM OF REJUVENATING CHINA THROUGH KNOWLEDGE

Rejuvenating the country through knowledge is regulated by a set of laws. These include laws on the promotion of science and technology, education reform, fiscal system and tax, government procurement, science and technology reward, and intellectual property, etc. In addition, there are regulations, local laws and policies and implementation measures that form a whole system.

3.1 The Laws on Promoting Science and Technology

The Law on the Progress of Science and Technology enacted in 1993 and revised in 2007 is China's most comprehensive legislation concerning the promotion of science and technology.[53] With eight chapters and 75 articles, it includes scientific research, technology development and the application of science and technology, technological progress in enterprises, scientific and technological research and development institutions, science and technology personnel, safeguarding and legal responsibility.[54] It legalizes China's policy on the promotion of science and technology, such as the implementation of the strategies of developing the country by relying on science, education, innovation, building a national innovation system, promotion of the freedom of science and technology research and development, encouragement of scientific exploration and technological innovation, and respect for labour, knowledge, talents and creation. Financial investment, tax, government procurement, and establishment of a reward system for science and technology are the focuses of the law.

In addition to the above law, China's laws on science and technology promotion include the Law on the Promotion of the Conversion of Scientific and Technological Achievements,[55] the Law on the Popularization of

---

[53] It was passed on 2 July 1993 and revised on 29 December 2007. The revised law came into effect on 1 July 2008. Available at <http://www.gov.cn/flfg/2007-12/29/content_847331.htm>.

[54] *Ibid.*

[55] It came into force on 1 October 1996. Its purpose is to promote the transformation of scientific and technological achievements into real productive forces, to govern the transformation of scientific and technological achievements, and to speed up scientific and technological progress. Available at <http://www.npc.gov.cn/wxzl/wxzl/2008-12/15/content_1462105.htm>.

Science and Technology,[56] the Ordinance of the State on Science and Technology Reward[57] and other laws and administrative regulations. Furthermore, various ministries and commissions under the State Council promulgated a number of administrative rules or regulations for the sake of implementation of the medium- and long-term programme for science and technology development, involving financial investment and management, tax incentives, financial support, government procurement, construction of technology innovation base and platform, etc.[58]

3.2   The Laws on Education and Talents

The Education Law was implemented on 1 September 1995.[59] In addition, according to different types of education and objectives, China has introduced the Compulsory Education Law,[60] the Higher Education Law,[61] the Vocational Education Law,[62] the Teacher Law[63] and the Private Education Promotion Law[64] as well as a number of administrative rules and regulations, such as the Compulsory Education Law Implementing Rules, the Notice of the State Council on Several Issues of Implementing the Teacher Law of the People's Republic of China,

---

[56]   It came into force on 29 June 2002. Its purpose is to improve citizens' scientific literacy through the popularization of science and technology. Available at <http://www.npc.gov.cn/wxzl/wxzl/2002-07/10/content_297301.htm>.

[57]   It was issued by the State Council on 20 November 2003. Its purpose is to motivate scientific research and technological inventions by creating the national science awards. Available at <http://www.most.gov.cn/fggw/xzfg/200601/t2006 0106_53402.htm>.

[58]   See the Ministry of Science and Technology website: <http://www.most. gov.cn/ztzl/gjzctx/>.

[59]   Available at <http://www.gov.cn/banshi/2005-05/25/content_918.htm>.

[60]   It came into force in 1986 and was revised in 2006. It guarantees that children and youths will receive nine years of compulsory education free of charge. Available at <http://edu.people.com.cn/GB/4547065.html>.

[61]   It came into force on 1 January 1999. Available at <http://www.gov.cn/ banshi/2005-05/25/content_927.htm>.

[62]   It came into force on 1 September 1996. Available at <http://www.npc. gov.cn/wxzl/gongbao/2000-12/05/content_5004660.htm>.

[63]   It came into force on 1 January 1994. Its purpose is to protect teachers' rights and improve teaching quality. Available at <http://www.gov.cn/banshi/ 2005-05/25/content_937.htm>.

[64]   It came into force on 1 September 2003. It is the legal norm on school education activities run by non-fiscal funds. Available at <http://www.gov.cn/test/ 2005-07/28/content_17946.htm>.

Regulations of the Teachers' Qualification, the Regulations on Implementing Private Education Promotion Law, the Ordinance of Teaching Achievement Award, the Literacy Work Regulations and so on.[65]

With China's implementation of the strategy of developing the country by relying on science and education, the needs of the development of educational undertakings call for education law-making in China:

> Since the reform and opening up policy was implemented 30 years ago, China has formulated a number of educational laws and special laws, administrative regulations, local regulations and government rules, and has preliminarily established the framework of educational law system, which is an important symbol of comprehensively going into the orbit of administering education according to law.[66]

China's education legal system with the Education Law, as its core, aims at providing access to education for different groups of people. It undoubtedly plays an irreplaceably important role in China's educational development.[67]

3.3   Intellectual Property Laws

From the early 1980s to the early 1990s, the P. R. China had established various intellectual property laws.[68] So far, China's intellectual property legal system has been in line with international standards.[69] Back to the beginning of the founding of new China, the national leaders attached

---

[65]   These documents are administrative rules and regulations issued by the State Council and are the implementation measures of the relevant laws. These documents can be obtained from the Ministry of Education's official website: <http://www.moe.gov.cn>.

[66]   Lao Kaisheng, 'The Construction of Legal System of Education during 30 years of Reform and Opening up', *Research on Education*, 2008, No. 11, pp. 3–10.

[67]   Of course, there are problems that need to be solved. For example, there are still many blank areas within China's education laws; the existing laws do not have long-term and comprehensive planning; and the education laws do not have a necessary level of authority and often conflict with other policies and regulations. *Ibid.*, pp. 76–78.

[68]   The Trademark Law of the People's Republic of China was implemented on 1 March 1983. The Patent Law of the People's Republic of China was implemented on 1 April 1985.The Copyright Law of the People's Republic of China was implemented on 1 June 1991.

[69]   So far, China has participated in the major international conventions on the protection of intellectual property rights.

importance to intellectual property legislation. For example, in 1950, the then Administration Council approved the Provisional Regulations on Guarantee of the Inventory Rights and Patents.[70] However, because of the implementation of the planned economy and the Cultural Revolution (1966–1976),[71] China's economic development and legal construction was greatly damaged, and the intellectual property protection system had been unable to develop. In 1978, after ten years of domestic chaos, the government started to establish modern intellectual property laws.

With the revolution of science and technology and the change of economic patterns, the intellectual property system in the world has been changing rapidly. China is no exception. As a result, China had to reform various aspects of its intellectual property laws. For example, the Copyright Law experienced two amendments in 2001 and 2010. The Trademark Law experienced modification twice in 1993 and 2001. The Patent Law was revised three times in 1992, 2000 and 2008. At present, these laws are respectively in their third or fourth amendments.[72]

From the perspective of promoting innovation and improving the ability of national innovation, China's legal system of intellectual property constitutes an important part of the national innovation system. Intellectual property law itself has a very close relationship with technology innovation: the law protects and encourages technological innovation. In addition, the legal system of intellectual property is not only the means of protecting innovation achievements, but also an important index of evaluating whether a technology innovation is successful.[73] At present, intellectual property laws are becoming more and more important in supporting China's overall strategies in building an innovative country.

---

[70]   Available at <http://www.cnki.com.cn/Article/CJFDTotal-SXBA1950090 02.htm>.

[71]   Available at <http://baike.baidu.com/view/1921.htm>.

[72]   With regard to the background and contents of several legal changes, *see* Feng Xiaoqing, *Intellectual Property Law*, Beijing: China University of Political Science and Law Press, 2010.

[73]   Feng Xiaoqing, 'Research on the Technical Innovation and Intellectual Property Strategy and Its Legal Protection System', *Intellectual Property*, 2012, No. 2, pp. 3–10.

4. IMPLEMENTATION OF CHINA'S LAWS AND POLICIES

Since the new China was founded, with the help of powerful policy promotion and legal protection China has made remarkable achievements in science, technology, and education and talents that have contributed significantly to China's economic and social development. There have been some scientific and technological breakthroughs during the period of the P. R. China's period of planned economy, such as in the fields of nuclear power, geological science, synthetic insulin and rice breeding technology.[74] By the 1990s, China's science and technology fields had developed into a relatively comprehensive stage, which covers the basic research supported by such projects as the 863 Plan, the Torch Plan, the Spark Program, the construction plan for a national engineering research centre, the state key industrial experiment plan and a series of major action plans for science and technology. These implementations have witnessed a number of important growths such as the establishment of key equipment in the state key laboratories.[75]

In recent years, China has experienced further rapid changes. Following the pace of leading scientific development in the world, China is entering the stage of innovation and development. China has been successful in leading computing science, has participated in the international human genome project and has successfully carried out super rice breeding. In important high-tech fields such as IT, biology and new materials, China's scientific research personnel have mastered a number of core technologies with independent intellectual property rights, which have significantly enhanced China's capacity for innovation.[76] These examples of success are closely connected with the implementation of the laws and policies of China's rejuvenation through knowledge.

There has also been significant progress in increased performance in R&D funding, output of science and technology, talent projects, and the construction of innovation parks or high-tech development zones, which demonstrate the implementation objectives of the laws and policies of China's rejuvenation through knowledge.

---

[74] For China's scientific and technological achievements at that time, *see* Gui Changlin, *China's Scientific and Technological Achievements Overview*, Hefei: University of Technology Press, 2011.

[75] Liu Guijun, 'From Science and Technology is the First Productive Force to the Construction of an Innovative Country', pp. 46–8.

[76] *Ibid.*

The changes of input and output of science and technology from 1990 to 2001 are good examples. The national research and development investment increased more than six times. The annual industrial output of national high-technology industry grew by an average of 20 per cent. The proportion of national high-tech industry in the national economy increased from 1 per cent to 15 per cent.[77] National financial allocation to science and technology increased from 16.07 billion RMB in 1991[78] to 490.26 billion RMB in 2011.[79] The number of papers published in China in 1991 indexed by SCI, EI and ISTP three systems was only 13,542.[80] In 2011 the number had grown to 300 000.[81] In addition, by the end of 2011, the number of China's various innovation parks and high-tech development zones represented by Beijing Zhongguancun Science and Technology Park and Shenzhen High-Tech Industry Development Zone had reached 88 in total. About 39,343 high-tech enterprises had been established in these zones and parks. In 2012, at the National People's Congress and Chinese People's Political Consultative Conference, the government work report provided the following data: the five-year central government budget for investment in science and technology totalled 872.9 billion RMB, and the average annual growth was more than 18 per cent. The whole society research and experimental development spending had increased from 1.4 per cent in 2007 to 1.97 per cent in 2012. R&D spending in enterprises accounted for more than 74 per cent.[82]

In terms of education development, after the Cultural Revolution there were only 598 higher education providers across the country with 850 000 students.[83] In 2011 the number of higher education providers in China was 2,409 and the number of undergraduate and college students

[77] Song Zheng, 'From Marching towards Science to Rejuvenating China by Relying on Science and Education', pp. 78–80.
[78] Data collected from the website of China Science and Technology Statistics. Available at <http://www.sts.org.cn/sjkl/kjtjdt/data1998/dtbk32.html>.
[79] *China Science & Technology Statistics Data Book*, Ministry of Science and Technology, the P. R. China.
[80] Data collected from the website of China Science and Technology Statistics. Available at <http://www.sts.org.cn/sjkl/kjtjdt/data1998/dtbk44.html>.
[81] *China Science & Technology Statistics Data Book*, Ministry of Science and Technology, the P. R. China.
[82] 'Great Achievements Have Been Made in the Strategy of Reinvigorating China through Human Resource Development – Important Data in Government Work Report about Human Resource Development', *The Talent of the People's Republic of China*, 2013, No. 7, p. 1.
[83] Available at <http://www.stats.gov.cn/tjgb/ndtjgb/qgndtjgb/t20020331_153 72.htm>.

was 23.0851 million.[84] The construction of the 211 Project led to great achievements.[85] So far, universities having China's 211 Project status amount to 112.[86] The investment funds in the 211 Project had reached 36.826 billion RMB in 2005.[87] In the last ten years, the 211 Project universities have produced a large number of leading scientific research outcomes and account for about a third of China's total winners of important science and technology prizes.[88]

Several talent projects implemented by China have also made significant progress. By 2012 the 'Thousands-of-People Plan' had introduced many top-quality talents into various leading areas.[89] By 2010 the national-level candidates of the National Hundred, Thousand and Ten Thousand Talent Project had amounted to more than 4,100.[90] By 2012, according to the Yangtze River Scholars Program, 1,801 individuals had been appointed as Yangtze River Scholars by Chinese universities, including 1,190 distinguished professors and 611 chair professors. Eighty-five Yangtze River Scholars were successively elected as academicians of the Chinese Academy of Sciences or academicians of the Chinese Academy of Engineering.[91] In 2012 the government work report pointed out that the implementation of China's human resource and innovation strategies and policies have created over 8.6 million and 8.8 million professional and high-skill talents respectively, and had attracted 540 000 overseas Chinese returnees.[92]

---

[84]   Available at <http://www.moe.gov.cn/publicfiles/business/htmlfiles/moe/moe_633/201208/xxgk_141305.htm>.

[85]   The 211 Project is a Chinese government initiative aiming to develop about 100 leading universities in the 21st century. For further details, visit the website of China's Ministry of Education: <http://www.moe.edu.cn/publicfiles/business/htmlfiles/moe/moe_846/200804/33122.html>.

[86]   Available at <http://www.moe.gov.cn/publicfiles/business/htmlfiles/moe/moe_94/201002/82762.html>.

[87]   Available at <http://www.moe.gov.cn/publicfiles/business/htmlfiles/moe/moe_1983/200804/9077.html>.

[88]   Available at <http://www.moe.gov.cn/publicfiles/business/htmlfiles/moe/moe_1978/200803/9602.html>.

[89]   Available at <http://www.chinanews.com/gn/2012/07-25/4058759.shtml>.

[90]   Available at <http://www.mohrss.gov.cn/SYrlzyhshbzb/zwgk/szrs/ndtjsj/tjgb/201206/t20120605_69908.htm>.

[91]   Wang Wenle, 'Interpretation of New Cheung Kong Scholars Program', *Shenzhou Economist*, 2012, No. 7, pp. 12–13.

[92]   Available at <http://www.ccnt.gov.cn/xxfbnew2011/xwzx/lmsj/201203/t20120316_233571.html>.

In addition, China's improved enforcement of intellectual property is starting to work. As Chapter 5 will indicate, China's judicial protection of intellectual property pays more and more attention to stimulating innovation and safeguarding the legal order of fair competition and intellectual property rights protection. In 2012, for example, in the civil trial of intellectual property cases, the Chinese court strengthened patent protection by centring on enhancing the innovation-driven development momentum; strengthened the protection of trademark rights by centring on cultivating brand competitive advantage; strengthened the copyright protection by centring on improving the overall strength and competitiveness of culture; and strengthened the protection of competition by centring on stimulating the development vitality of all kinds of market subjects.[93]

The amount of intellectual property litigation has been constantly rising in China. Through fair protection of the lawful rights and interests of Chinese or foreign intellectual property owners and other parties concerned, the Chinese court effectively promotes the effective enforcement of intellectual property in China.[94] Compared with other countries and regions in the world, China's protection of intellectual property includes not only judicial protection, but also administrative measures.[95] For example, from October 2010 to June 2011 the Chinese government launched a nine-month nationwide special operation against the infringement of intellectual property rights and the production of fake and inferior goods, which led to remarkable achievements.

CONCLUSION

This chapter's analysis is no more than the tip of an iceberg of the relevant topics that have been extensively discussed in China. However, it provides a window to see the development of China's laws and policies

---

[93] The Supreme People's Court, *The State of Judicial Protection of Intellectual Property Rights in China in 2012*. Available at < http://www.chinacourt.org/article/detail/2013/04/id/949841.shtml>.

[94] For instance, in 2012, the Chinese court received 87,419 intellectual property civil cases of first instance, and concluded 83,850. The increase rate was 45.99%. *Ibid.*

[95] Broadly speaking, 'special operations' taken by the Chinese government at all levels on intellectual property rights infringement also belong to the category of intellectual property administrative enforcement. *See* Feng Xiaoqing (ed.), *Intellectual Property Law*, Wuhan: Wuhan University Press, 2009, pp. 17–18.

on its rejuvenation through knowledge. China firmly believes that knowledge can build a state, that knowledge can rejuvenate a state, and that knowledge can make a state powerful.

The author now summarizes the following conclusions: First, China's laws and policies on its rejuvenation through knowledge are changing with the passage of time, the transformation of economic systems, and the difference in the situation at home and abroad; they have experienced the complex transformation from the planned system to the socialist market economic system, from the simple stimulation of innovation inputs to the overall stimulation of a national innovation system. Second, China's laws and policies on its rejuvenation through knowledge reflect improved understandings of the state concerning knowledge and innovation; in the national development strategy the role of knowledge and innovation is increasingly becoming important. Third, in different periods, China's laws and policies on its rejuvenation through knowledge have been guided by corresponding strategies in rejuvenating the country through knowledge, have experienced the evolution process of 'march towards science', 'science and technology is the first productive force' and 'rely on science and education to rejuvenate the country'.

Currently China is facing a historic opportunity to upgrade its economic development model and industrial structure. To improve the nation's innovation ability and realize the grand goal of ranking as an innovative country in 2020, it is necessary to further form a good atmosphere and innovation culture for innovation, to encourage innovation in the whole society, and at the same time to carry out in-depth reform in such aspects as economy, the science and technology system, and the education system. It is also necessary to form a market-oriented technology innovation system with Chinese enterprises at the centre of innovation, to combine learning, research and innovation further, and to gradually construct the national innovation system.

In addition, further reforms of China's intellectual property policies and laws are needed for encouraging and protecting innovation, promoting the effective application of innovation, and providing a fair competition environment for innovation activities and institutional guarantees. As can be expected, although China will encounter many difficulties and obstacles in implementing the strategies of building an innovative country, China's policies and laws on rejuvenating the country through knowledge and its implementation will become better with the enhancement of China's innovation capacity and the construction of an innovative country.

4. Challenges to China's self-driven innovation and intellectual property practice

Feng Xiaoqing[*]

INTRODUCTION

In modern times, innovation is not only an essential requirement for an enterprise to survive and develop, but also a symbol of national competitiveness. The goal of China's *zizhu chuangxin* (self-driven innovation) is to improve China's ability in innovation. The key is to realize the combination of the breakthrough of core technologies with institutional innovation; its basic meaning is to emphasize the autonomy of innovation, or to consider that self-driven innovation is the advanced stage of technological innovation or scientific and technological innovation.

Translating China's current innovation policies (*zizhu chuangxin*) into 'independent innovation' is highly misleading, because none of them reflect the fact that China's innovation policies do not encourage unnecessary repetition of technologies that have already been produced, or relying on domestic enterprises to complete everything in every technology sector.[1] Actually, self-driven innovation emphasizes that Chinese enterprises should depend on their own strength to control innovation achievements and intellectual property rights (IPRs). For this purpose, technology import is also very important for China to realize its

---

   * The author would like to thank Dr. Liu Qijia and Dr. Tao Qian for their unselfish help in the modification of the English version and Professor Ken Shao for his invaluable support in revising this chapter. This work is predominately based on ample research data available in the Chinese language.
   [1] Ken Shao, 'Zizhu chuangxin and China's Self-driven Innovation: Calling for a Holistic Perspective', *Cardozo Law Review de novo*, 2013, p. 171; p. 186.

self-driven innovation strategy.[2] Therefore, self-driven innovation in China largely refers to innovation with independent intellectual property rights, not self-made inventions.[3] The main goal of self-driven innovation is to improve the ability of self-driven innovation.

In 2006 China enacted the National Intellectual Property Strategy Outline.[4] The promotion of the IP strategy is designed to support China's construction of its national innovation system.[5] In recent years, China has achieved substantially in promoting innovation policies and implementing intellectual property strategies.[6] However, there are still some institutional, legal and infrastructural defects. The main target for realizing self-driven innovation is to overcome the defects of the outdated system so as to provide a reliable system for supporting the innovation activities of Chinese enterprises.[7] Only when these weaknesses were overcome could Chinese enterprises succeed in promoting self-driven innovation and intellectual property.

This chapter will explore the achievements and weaknesses in implementation of self-driven innovation and intellectual property in China from the perspective of institutional and legal challenges, challenges in managing science and technology parks, challenges in implementing national, regional, industrial and enterprise intellectual property strategies, as well as challenges faced by innovation and intellectual property management in Chinese enterprises. This chapter concludes that although China faces many challenges, its determination to construct an innovative country is unwavering.

1. INNOVATION ACHIEVEMENTS

China's innovation policies and its national intellectual property strategy programme have increased Chinese enterprises' innovation. In 2009

---

[2]   Yang Xiaoling, 'On Technology Import and Independent Innovation, and on China's Independent Innovation Strategy to Promote Technological Progress', *Tianjin Social Science*, 1999, No. 6, pp. 68–72.

[3]   Jia Xueying, 'Independent Innovation: New Engine of Economic Development', *China Financial News*, November 22, 2010.

[4]   *See* Chapter 2 of this book.

[5]   *See* Chapter 1 and Chapter 2 for more details.

[6]   There are many Chinese studies available in this regard. Some chapters of this book provide certain analyses.

[7]   Dong Binghe, *Study on the System for Legal Protection of Technological Innovation – a Focus on the Intellectual Property System*, Beijing: Intellectual Property Press, 2006, p. 71.

China's total investment in research and development ranked number 5 in the world and accounted for 1.62 per cent of China's GDP for the year.[8] According to the Global Innovation Index 2012, China ranked 34th in overall innovation but its efficiency index of innovation ranked the first in the world. China has achieved great successes in knowledge and technologies export, infrastructure and the maturity of market and enterprises, in which China's output of critical knowledge and technology only fell behind that of Switzerland, Sweden, Singapore and Finland.[9] According to *the National Competitiveness Bluebook: Report of National Competitiveness of China* published in October 2010, China's ranking of competitiveness rose from 37th in 1990 to 17th in 2009 and its innovation competitiveness rose to 22nd.[10] Based on the report of National Innovation Index 2010 issued by the Chinese Institute of Science and Technology Strategic Development, the innovation index of China ranked 21st among 40 major countries in that year, and some of the critical indexes ranked among the best.[11] For example, the total number of research staff comes first and the total amount of expense for research and development ranked number 4. This important data demonstrates that great improvements have been achieved in both investment and achievement of innovation in China. In particular, the ranking of innovation index of Chinese enterprises rose dramatically from 25th in 2000 to 12th in 2010.[12] The achievements are reached owing to an improved innovation environment for Chinese enterprises.

Knowledge creation and development in Chinese enterprises also benefit from technology import. Researches show that technology import

---

[8]   This information comes from the speech of Tian Lipu, Director of State Intellectual Property Office (SIPO), at a ministerial session of WIPO (September, 2010) in Geneva. For more details, please visit <http://www.sipo. gov.cn/yw/ 2010/201009/t20100927_539415.html>. It must be noted that input is an important factor and indicator that affects the performance of knowledge creation in enterprises. *See* Han Xinyan & Wu Tianzu, 'Factors and Measures which Affect Technology Innovation and the Overall Level of Performance', *Science of Science and Management of Sci. & Tech.*, 2003, No. 3, pp. 19–23.

[9]   Ren Xiaoling, 'The Issue of 2012 Global Innovation Index Report', available at <http://www.sipo.gov.cn/dtxx/gw/2012/201207/t20120717_725791. html>. It should be noted that, before the publication of the book, the 2013 Global Innovation Index has been issued. However, there exist few changes as to the situation in China. For details, please refer to <http://www.gov.cn/gzdt/2013-07/05/content_2440998.htm>.

[10]   Available at <http://www.ylagri.gov.cn/info/1177/30585.htm>.

[11]   Available at <http://news.cntv.cn/20110302/116428.shtml>.

[12]   *Ibid.*

has positive influences in innovation.[13] In addition, reforms in China's innovation system have enabled some enterprises to implement innovation strategies in China's industrial structure upgrading.[14] Cooperative innovation has also become increasingly common among Chinese enterprises in various forms. This includes industrial clusters, regional innovation systems and collaborations among production, learning and research.[15] In general, self-driven innovation consists of original innovation, integrated innovation and independent innovation after digesting and assimilation. Chinese enterprises attach importance to the three innovative models. A survey conducted by the State-owned Assets Supervision and Administration Commission (hereinafter referred to as SASAC) shows that the above self-driven innovation models constitute 37.3 per cent, 20.9 per cent and 41.8 per cent respectively among Chinese enterprises.[16] Some innovation demonstration zones and experimental enterprises act as pathways to feasible models of innovation and their innovation experiences are then introduced to other enterprises and sectors.[17] Hence, Chinese enterprises have come to a positive and dynamic innovation stage after the stage of net technical import and imitation.

---

[13]   Chen Rong & He Caiyin, 'An Empirical Analysis of the Relationship between Independent Innovation and Import of Technology', *Contemporary Economy*, 2013, No. 3, pp. 124–25.

[14]   Shao Xianwen, 'Technology Integration: A Mode of Independent Innovation in Enterprises', *Collection of Articles of National Youth Academic Seminar of the 9th Harbin Science and Technology Progress and Development in Contemporary World*, 2003, pp. 156–60.

[15]   Du Chuanzhong & Cao Yanqiao, 'Success of Collaborative Innovation and Independent Creation in Chinese Enterprises', *Present Day Finance & Economy*, 2009, No. 7, pp. 61–66.

[16]   Li Qua, 'Intellectual Property: Weakness of Chinese Enterprises and Proposed Route for Improvement', *WTO Trends and Research*, 2008, No. 10, p. 25.

[17]   According to statistics, by June 2011 a total of 550 national innovation demonstration enterprises had been approved. The input of these companies in research and development and their innovation capacities are significantly higher than average. *See* Feng Xiaoqing, 'Research on the Integration of Legal Operational Mechanism of Technology Innovation and Intellectual Property Strategy in Enterprises', *Research Report of National Social Science Fund*, June 2013, p. 120.

2. INSTITUTIONAL AND LEGAL CHALLENGES

Institutional reform remains a key reform agenda for China today. After the establishment of the People's Republic of China, the country formed a management system for science and technology under the planned economy. This system covers the initiation of research projects, distribution and use of funding, appraisal of achievements and awards for the popularization and application of achievements.[18] The value of the creator's achievements is decided through external bodies, and the government or other relevant authorities are the driving force to carry out such an approach. Thus rewards are not linked to the market application of the achievement and its benefits, and the mechanism for deciding rewards may be subjective.[19] Under the planned economy model, technical personnel's enthusiasm and creativity were limited.[20] On the other hand, enterprises under the planned economy did not view intellectual property as important, which led to a lack of intellectual property ownership and the loss of intangible assets. Today, this government-led system still exists but assessment criteria for scientific and technological achievements now include the possibility of commercialization.[21]

Intellectual property is a system that protects IP rights as private rights, with the internal incentive mechanism that mobilizes people's creativity.

---

[18]   Tan Wenhua, *On Science and Technology Policy and Science and Technology Management*, Beijing: People's Publishing House, 2012.

[19]   Feng Xiaoqing, *Intellectual Property Management for Enterprises*, Beijing: Press of China University of Political Science and Law, 2012, pp. 11–13; Wu Kai, 'The Structure Problems of the Reward System of Science and Technology in China and Optimization Measures', *Scientific and Technological Progress and Countermeasures*, 2011, No. 18, pp. 95–99.

[20]   Wang Keqiang, 'Deepening the Reform of Science and Technology System Should Solve Three Problems', *Chinese Science News*, 18 August 2012; Zhang Weibin & Li Lang, 'Analysis of the Present Situation of China's Scientific and Technological Achievements Management and the Countermeasures', *Science and Management*, 2010, No. 1, pp. 41–44.

[21]   China implements the national, provincial scientific and technological achievements reward system. In accordance with the provisions of the State Science and Technology Reward Ordinance, in order to reward citizens and organizations that have made outstanding contributions in science and technology progress activities, stimulate the enthusiasm and creativity of scientific and technical workers, accelerate the development of science and technology, and improve the comprehensive national strength, the State shall reward the contributing science and technology which has generated huge economic or social benefit via the commercialization of the technology (Article 1 and Article 8).

At present, in order to strengthen the organic combination of the management of enterprise achievements with intellectual property management, the Chinese government regulates and guides enterprises to carry out innovation by way of policies and laws. Intellectual property management is integrated into the development of technology and the marketization of new technologies and products. The management system reform of science and technology involves many aspects such as organization, resource allocation, ownership of scientific and technological achievements, distribution of benefits, commercialization and industrialization, motivation, the environment of science and technology innovation, etc. The goal is to eliminate the problems caused under the planned economy and to strengthen the important position of Chinese enterprises in technological innovation.[22]

Chinese economic system reform in recent years has undoubtedly laid a good foundation for its economic and social development. The direction and idea of institutional reform in science and technology is to combine the goals of technology innovation with the intellectual property protection environment. However, owing to the inertia of the old institution, we still have obstacles against such reform in terms of self-driven innovation and enforcement of intellectual property rights, and we have to make efforts on many aspects, such as standards of innovation evaluation and cohesion of the management mechanism, etc.[23]

The basic goal of providing legal protection to technological innovation is to create a good institutional environment for the enterprise to conduct technology innovation, give full play to the enthusiasm of enterprises and other related parties for innovation, and safeguard the legitimate rights and interests of the parties that contribute to the

---

[22]   The key is to 'establish the science and technology innovation system with the enterprise as the main body'. Achievement evaluation should mainly consider application value. *See* Zhang Xiaogong & Zhang Jinchang, 'The Management System Reform of Science and Technology', *Technical Economics and Management Research*, 2011, No. 8, pp. 50–53.

[23]   For further details, *see* Yang Cengxian, 'The Defects of Administrative Science and Technology System and the Urgency of the Reform', *Social Science Forum*, 2008, No. 4, pp. 52–63; Li Li, Tang Shuxiang & Wu Xianfeng, 'The Problem of Scientific and Technological Achievements Evaluation System in China and the Countermeasures', *Science and Technology Information*, 2012, No. 26, pp. 97–98; Huang Tao, 'To Study the Countermeasures of Deepening the Reform of Science and Technology System from the Prominent Problems in Scientific Research Management', *Technology and Innovation Management*, 2013, vol. 34, No. 1, pp. 27–31.

innovation, and thus provide 'motivation for technology innovation'.[24] However, China's legislation today follows the philosophy of 'being coarse rather than precise'. For many aspects we do not have detailed regulations or do not have well-functioning coordination among different public and private stakeholders. Thus further improvements are necessary.

2.1   Challenges of the Intellectual Property Laws

As can be seen from China's current intellectual property legislation, some important matters are only covered in the form of administrative regulations, and the degree of protection is not high enough. Therefore it is necessary to enhance the level of legislation.

In terms of China's *Patent Law*, its third revision in 2008 was to highlight the important role of the patent system in enhancing innovation ability, and to promote the transformation of scientific and technological achievements and technology innovation in China.[25] However, there are still some improvements needed: firstly, the definition of 'employment invention' is too simple and the reward to employment inventors is modest and no measures are available to many enterprises that do not strictly follow the reward system.[26] Secondly, the patent approval procedure cannot cope with the situation that patent filings are surging rapidly, and cannot serve the patent information construction and internationalization.[27] Thirdly, the provisions of the current Patent Law on the limitation of rights are too abstract and are not easily applied in judicial

---

[24]   Dong, *Study on the System for Legal Protection of Technological Innovation*, p. 45.

[25]   Peng Dongyu, 'The Patent Law for the Third Time Revision: Realize the Change of Legislative Purpose', *China's National People's Congress*, 2009, Vol. 1, pp. 37–38; Feng Xiaoqing, 'The Interaction between Enhancing the Capacity for Independent Innovation and Patent Protection: A Perspective on the Third Amendment to the Patent Law of the P. R. China', *Journal of Technology Law and Policy*, 2009, Vol. 1, pp. 1–129; Feng Xiaoqing & Liu Youhua, *The Patent Law*, Beijing: Law Press, 2010, pp. 25–33.

[26]   Feng Xiaoqing & Liu Di, 'On the Service Invention System in the Mainland of China', *Patent Consultation*, 2013, Vol. 14, pp. 1–27.

[27]   China's patent examination requires administrative approval and is subject to the management system and approval procedures, etc. *See* Xiao Xingwei, 'Patent Examination and Approval System and the Cultivation of Clean Government in China', *Intellectual Property*, 2012, No. 2, pp. 3–12.

practice.[28] Fourthly, the provisions of the existing Patent Law are obviously insufficient to promote the popularization and application of innovation and to promote the commercialization of the invention. There are no relevant provisions on commercialization issues such as the pledge of patents, patent investment and securitization of patents. Currently these issues are only carried out through administrative regulations.[29] Fifthly, there are problems with regard to weak enforcement measures on patent infringement and the lack of clauses on abuse of patent rights.[30]

There exists a big gap between China's current Copyright Law and the requirements of promoting the copyright industry. Although the law has experienced two revisions, it still demonstrates some characteristics of the planned economy. In addition, its response to the rapid development of digital technology and internet technology is not sufficient.[31] The challenges faced by China's Copyright Law include the following. Firstly, the provisions on the ownership of works cannot meet the needs of practice.[32] Secondly, it has not stipulated the special right of database with originality, resulting in conflicts between the database industry and the public interest.[33] Thirdly, the adjustment of the law, including the introduction of public lending right, artist's resale right, etc., needs to be considered in response to the needs of social development.[34] Fourthly, in

---

[28] For example, the current Patent Law has no complete provisions on priority rights and use concerning scientific research and experiments. *See* Xiang Ling, 'Patent Restriction System in China: the Path of Innovation – Based on the Analysis of the Comparison Method', *Intellectual Property*, 2013, No. 11, pp. 83–88.

[29] Feng Xiaoqing, 'The Operating Strategy of the Enterprise Intellectual Property Capital in China', *Journal of Shanghai University of Finance and Economics*, 2012, Vol. 14, No. 6, pp. 45–52.

[30] However, the provisions of China's current Patent Law on compulsory licensing involve the abuse of the compulsory licence system. In addition, there are general provisions to regulate the abuse of intellectual property rights in Article 55 of China's Anti-monopoly Law.

[31] Feng Xiaoqing, *The Theory and Practice of Intellectual Property Law*, Beijing: Intellectual Property Press, 2002, pp. 296–325.

[32] Such as for film works and works in a similar way of film production, the current Copyright Law provides that except authorship right, the copyright shall be enjoyed by the producer, which definition varies.

[33] Wen Quan & Huang Jilan, 'On the Database Copyright Protection', *Library*, 2011, No. 2, pp. 1–2.

[34] In the third amendment (draft) to the Copyright Law of China, the artist's resale right is incorporated, which reflects the efforts to cope with the development of China's art market. Available at <http://economy.caijing.com.cn/2012-04-04/111800710.html>.

practice, producers of audiovisual products and broadcasting organizations do not enjoy the right of performance, which causes irreparable damage to their interests.[35] Fifthly, the provisions of the Copyright Law on the limitations and exceptions of the copyright are limited to fair use and statutory licence, but there are no provisions on private copying, exhaustion of rights, moral rights, etc. Also, there are no systematic provisions concerning uploading, digital transmission, the dissemination and utilization of digital works in remote education, and the public information service of libraries.[36] Sixthly, the current law needs to improve its copyright infringement list so as to give the courts better guidance.[37] These problems hinder the development of cultural industry and may fail to meet the needs of self-driven innovation.[38]

In addition, abuse of intellectual property rights exists in China, especially by multinational companies, which constitutes unfair competition against Chinese enterprises.[39] Meanwhile, in overseas markets, some multinational companies frequently take advantage of American clause 337 to suppress Chinese enterprises' access to the US market.[40]

---

[35]   In the third amendment (draft) to the Copyright Law of China, the right of performance of producers of audio and video and radio organizations has been incorporated.

[36]   For example, the provisions of Article 3 of the Interpretations of the Supreme People's Court on the Trial Involving the Law Applicable to the Copyright Disputes over the Computer Network were not embodied in the Ordinance for the Protection of Information Network Transmission Right. *See* Lin Peiwen, 'The Expansion and Restriction of Copyright under the Network Environment', *The Academic Forum,* 2012, No. 5, pp. 63–67.

[37]   Feng Xiaoqing, *Copyright Law*, Beijing: Law Press, 2010, pp. 230–260.

[38]   Aiming at solving the problems of China's existing Copyright Law, on 18 December 2012 the National Copyright Administration launched the third amendment (draft). With regard to the studies of the revision, *see* Liu Chuntian, 'The Third Revision of the Copyright Law is the Requirement of the Great Change of Situation', *Intellectual Property*, 2012, No. 5, pp. 7–12; Wu Handong, 'The Third Revision of the Copyright Law: Background, Style and Emphasis', *Law and Business Research*, 2012, No. 4, pp. 3–7; Li Mingde, 'The Third Revision of the Copyright Law in China and Suggestions', *Intellectual Property*, 2012, No. 5, pp. 19–25.

[39]   As to the definition of abuse, Chinese scholars have basically reached an agreement. *See* Song Baihui & Wang Yuan, 'The Expansion of Intellectual Property Rights, the New Definition of Intellectual Property Rights Abuse', *Scientific Management Research*, 2011, No. 6, pp. 64–67.

[40]   Zhu Pengfei, 'The Legitimacy of the American Section 337 and China's Countermeasures, in the Perspective of WTO General Exception Clauses', *Nanjing Social Science*, 2013, No. 1, pp. 81–86.

However, China's Antitrust Law, Unfair Competition Law and intellectual property laws and the administrative regulations on the abuse of intellectual property rights are not very workable, for instance on restrictive licensing, tying sale, restriction on competition and the abuse of technical standards. From the perspective of promoting innovation among Chinese enterprises, we must improve the intellectual property system to prevent right abuse and monopoly from damaging China's innovation resources, innovation environment and the foundation of innovation so as to fairly and reasonably protect the legitimate rights and interests of all parties.

2.2 Challenges of the Finance and Taxation System

China's existing finance and taxation system has the following characteristics and shortcomings. Firstly, most of the tax policies are scattered in various rules and regulations formulated separately or issued jointly by the Ministry of Finance or the State Administration of Taxation. The legislative level is low, and these policies lack stability.[41] Secondly, policies of tax preferences focus on high-tech enterprises and the initial stage of transformation of scientific and technological achievements, but tax incentives for the development stages are neglected.[42] Thirdly, the preferential tax policy is regional, with a focus on high-tech development zones and economic development zones, and the enterprises outside of them cannot enjoy such benefits.[43] Fourthly, the current policy is not conducive to encouraging the development of innovation under the model of a production-learning-research combination.[44] The role of these tax measures is limited in helping Chinese enterprises to carry out self-driven innovation and administrative discretion worsens tax inequality.

In addition, China's tax policies still favour foreign enterprises in China. Studies show that the average tax rate for China's foreign enterprises is 11 per cent, while that of domestic enterprises is 22 per cent, and that of large state-owned enterprises is 30 per cent. As a result, the production of Volkswagen Company in the Chinese market accounts for just 14 per cent of its global production, but its profits in the Chinese

---

[41] Li Shuhua, 'The Tax Policies on Promoting Technology Innovation of China's Science and Technology Enterprise', *Tianjin Economy*, 2009, No. 10, pp. 49–51.
[42] Zhou Ying, 'Analysis of the Preferential Tax System of Hi-tech Enterprises in China', *High-tech Enterprise in China*, 2013, No. 2, pp. 146–48.
[43] *Ibid.*
[44] Wang Shufang, *On the Research and Development of Enterprises*, Beijing: Press of Beijing Normal University, 2010, pp. 468–76.

market accounts for 80 per cent of its total profits; the United States GM production in China only accounts for 3 per cent of its global production, but its profits obtained from the Chinese market accounted for 25 per cent of its global profits.[45] Of course, we cannot deny that the preferential tax policy has attracted foreign investment to set up factories in China but now China's market environment and competition structure are not as the same as that at the beginning of reform and opening-up. Especially under the WTO, full attention should be paid to how to reform the tax preferential policies on foreign enterprises.[46]

2.3   Challenges of the Investment Legal System

The financing system is of greater significance to innovation in China's small-and-medium-sized enterprises (SMEs) because insufficient funding is the widespread development bottleneck for them. Empirical research holds that the increase of the government's subsidies, enterprise equity capital and bank loans helps improve the capacity for self-driven innovation in China's high-tech enterprises.[47] Venture capital is conducive to promoting innovation because innovation activities need money while venture capital can share the risk of innovation. Currently, the lack of technology innovation funds and poor channels of investment and financing greatly suffocate innovation in Chinese SMEs. China's venture capital investment has not been developed well enough. The current investment structure tends to invest in quick-return projects.

Because the mechanism for evaluating intangible assets is not sound in China, investment institutions lack trust in innovation, which results in the phenomenon that 'good projects cannot find investors, and venture capital companies cannot find good projects'.[48] Empirical research shows that China's venture capital investment has not played a significant role

[45]   Yang Weiwen, Zhu Keli & Yao Yao, 'The Present Situation of Development of Independent Intellectual Property of Chinese Enterprises and Countermeasures', *Finance and Banking*, 2008, No. 5, pp. 54–59.

[46]   Li Xiao, 'On the Reform of Preferential Tax Legal System of Foreign-invested Enterprises in China', *Modern Economic Information*, 2011, No. 6, p. 12.

[47]   Song Xianzhong & Liu Zhen, 'On Financing Efficiency of Technology Innovation of High-tech Enterprise', *Journal of Accounting*, 2008, No. 8, pp. 10–12.

[48]   Wang, *On the Research and Development of Enterprises*, pp. 486–90.

in technology innovation, and venture capital investment has not stimulated technological innovation as expected. Instead, most domestic patents are generated by R&D investments.[49] Some regions of China have already developed some venture capital investment but it takes time to promote these patterns.[50]

2.4 Challenges of Government Procurement

Government procurement is not only an effective tool for promoting innovation, but also a measure unbound by the WTO.[51] However, China's government procurement policies do not demonstrate full support for self-driven technological products. The main problems are as follows:

Firstly, the support of the government procurement mainly stays at the policy level. It is not mentioned at all in the Government Procurement Law, which lacks specifications on the procurement of self-driven innovative products. Article 25 of the Law on the Progress of Science and Technology is beneficial, but it remains as a principle and does not have implementation measures.

Secondly, compared with developed countries, China's government procurement is not sound, and the proportion of the products procured by the government in GDP is too small. Research data shows that the proportion of government procurement in the GDP of a country is about 12–20 per cent on average. China's GDP in 2011 was 45.8 trillion RMB. If estimated in the proportion of 20 per cent, the Chinese public procurement market would be about 9 trillion RMB, but China's government procurement was only 1.13 trillion RMB.[52] Even if all government procurement is used to support innovation, the effect of the Chinese government procurement on innovation is very limited.

---

[49] Deng Junrong & Long Rongrong, 'An Empirical Study on the Role of Venture Capital in Technological Innovation in China', *the Technical Economics and Management Research*, 2013, No. 6, pp. 49–52.
[50] Tian Ming, 'The Impact of the Growth Enterprise Market on the Development of China's Venture Capital', *Business Culture*, 2010, No. 3, p. 92; Li Hui, 'On the Impact of the Growth Enterprise Market on Risk Investment', *Economic Forum*, 2008, No. 10, pp. 112–13.
[51] Li Xuejing, 'Theoretical Analysis of the Government Procurement to Promote China's Technological Innovation', *Journal of Zhenjiang College*, 2004, No. 3, pp. 80–83.
[52] Lou Zhibin & Mao Huohua, 'New Thinking about the Role of Government Procurement to Promote Scientific and Technological Innovation', *East China Science and Technology*, 2013, No. 4, pp. 16–18.

Thirdly, to a great extent, the Chinese public still has doubts over government procurement of self-driven innovation products. For instance, a self-driven innovation product achieved by leading Chinese enterprises such as Anshan Steel has made two core technological breakthroughs. This project has made outstanding contributions to the nationalization of China's metallurgical equipment, and received the first prize of scientific and technological progress at the National Science and Technology Award Congress in 2007. But so far, only one Chinese enterprise dares to use it, while other companies still prefer imported products at high prices.[53] Since 'foreign' brands have superiority in the minds of some government officials, domestic products are ignored even though they have intellectual property. This tendency has adverse impacts on government procurement, because it may set a negative guide for ordinary people. Further improvements are needed to develop government procurement for domestic products with intellectual property rights.[54]

3. CHALLENGES OF SCIENCE AND TECHNOLOGY PARK MANAGEMENT

The construction of science and technology parks, especially high-tech industrial parks, is an important pattern for China to promote enterprise self-driven innovation, to vigorously develop high and new technologies, and to stimulate economic and social development. So far China has already approved and run a batch of high-tech industrial parks across the country, and has made great achievements in the promotion of self-driven innovation and the protection of intellectual property. Some industrial parks have been listed as demonstration units of intellectual property rights.[55] Statistics show that since the national intellectual property demonstration units came into being in 2002, 44 demonstration units had

---

[53]   Zhou Li, 'On Chinese Enterprises' Independent Innovation of Intellectual Property', *Market Forum*, 2008, No. 4, pp. 86–87.

[54]   For the related research, *see* Ma Li & Wu Jinguang, *Government Procurement and Independent Innovation of Enterprises*, Beijing: Economic Management Press, 2012; Wang Hui, 'The Countermeasure of Government Procurement to Promote Scientific and Technological Innovation', *Journal of Liaoning Administration College*, 2012, Vol. 14, No. 8, pp. 23–25.

[55]   He Ming, Xia Enjun & Liu Yiwen, 'Research on Technology Innovation Model of High-tech Enterprises in Zhongguancun Science Park', *Scientific and Technological Progress and Countermeasures*, 2010, Vol. 27, No. 3, pp. 9–11; Zhao Chaoyi, *The Standardization of the Capital: Empirical Studies of Zhongguancun Science Park*, Beijing: Science Press, 2011.

sprung up by 2011. For instance, many companies in Nanchang high-tech Industrial Development Zone rely on self-driven innovation for mastering core patented technologies. Since 2008 the number of patent applications and approvals in Hangzhou High-Tech Industry Development Zone have doubled and increased five-fold respectively.[56] The development of these parks has contributed to local economic transformation and upgrading, and also has ushered in the trend of self-driven innovation among other Chinese enterprises.

However, not all science and technology parks in China have a high level of management. Take the Private Science and Technology Park in Zhengzhou as an example; the problems are as follows. Firstly, the area is small, and the infrastructure needs to be improved. Secondly, human resources in the park are unstable. The professional and technical personnel and management personnel tend to work for state-owned enterprises which provide better incentives. Thirdly, financing for the enterprises in the parks is limited. Fourthly, the technology innovation after-effect of the Park enterprises is insufficient. Private enterprises are short of strategic planning and long-term perspective on management, and are unable to invest in long-term funds and thus are unable to cope with dynamic changes in the technology markets.[57] In the Agricultural Science and Technology Park of Sichuan Province, there exists such problems as irrational construction, uneven distribution, poor demonstration capacities, and weak research abilities and so on.[58] Due to these problems, self-driven innovation in those parks is hindered.[59]

---

[56]   Zhao Jianguo, 'The Important Mission of the Pilot Demonstration Parks for Restructuring', *China Intellectual Property Newspaper*, 28 June 2011.

[57]   Wang Zhongkui, 'The Problems Existing in the Development of Private Science and Technology Park of Zhengzhou City and Countermeasures', *Journal of Henan Institute of Science and Technology*, 2013, No. 1, pp. 17–19.

[58]   Teng Lianze, Zhang Hongji & Luo Yongdeng, 'Problems and Counter-measures for the Development of Agricultural Science and Technology in Sichuan Province', *Modern Agricultural Science and Technology*, 2013, No. 1, pp. 299–300.

[59]   How to strengthen the construction of high-tech parks to promote innovation in China naturally becomes an important part of building an innova-tive country in China. *See* Li Jun, Xiong Fei & Cheng Jun, 'Accelerating the Construction of the Zhongguancun Science Park –Take Fengtai Science Park for Example', *Science and Technology Management Research*, 2010, No. 7, pp. 68–70; Wang Shuilian & Li Baoshan, 'The Systematic Thinking about Innovation Platform Mechanism of Science and Technology Park', *Science and Technology Management*, 2009, No. 1, pp. 61–65.

4. CHALLENGES OF THE IMPLEMENTATION OF INTELLECTUAL PROPERTY STRATEGIES

In recent years, China has established various intellectual property strategies at central and local levels under the guidance of the National Intellectual Property Strategy Outline.[60] The following will discuss the problems and difficulties of the implementation of China's intellectual property strategies.

4.1   Challenges for the National Intellectual Property Strategy

Since the National Intellectual Property Strategy Outline came into existence in 2008, it has resulted in huge public responses and played an important role in the construction of an innovative country.[61] In the fields of economy, science and technology, and foreign trade, the management of intellectual property and the establishment of an intellectual property system are not perfect, and many core technologies depend on foreign countries.[62] The national intellectual property strategy's focus is deviated and the implementation measures are inadequate.

Firstly, consciousness of intellectual property strategy is poor.[63] China's manufacturing exports are limited to tangible goods without a deep exploitation of the cultural industry.[64]

Secondly, in the fields of economy, science and technology, and foreign trade, the management of intellectual property and the establishment of an intellectual property system are not perfect. Many laws and

---

[60]   *See* Chapter 2 of this book.

[61]   Liu Ren, 'Good Beginning: Full Implementation of the National Intellectual Property Strategy', *China Intellectual Property Newspaper*, 5 June 2009; Zhao Jianguo, '3-year Implementation of the Outline of the National Intellectual Property Strategy: Prominent Achievements', *China Intellectual Property Newspaper*, 10 June 2011.

[62]   Mei Shuwen & Lin Kaichuan, 'The Implementation of the Strategy of the National Intellectual Property Strategy and Performance Evaluation', *International Academic Dynamic*, 2010, No. 1, pp. 7–10.

[63]   Gu Huaxiang, 'On Several Issues of Implementing the National Intellectual Property Strategy', *Journal of Hunan Finance and Economics University*, 2012, Vol. 28, pp. 4–5.

[64]   Dong Jia, 'Study on the Intellectual Property Strategy of BRIC', doctoral dissertation, Jilin University, 2011, p. 122.

policies are quite rough and abstract and require clearer and more detailed plans for specific industries.[65]

Thirdly, the national intellectual property strategy in foreign trade is missing. Research shows that at present the number of Chinese export companies owning brands accounts for only about 20 per cent of the total of those engaging in foreign trade. According to a report released by Nielsen and the *Campaign Asia-Pacific* magazine, no Chinese enterprise has been ranked in 'the 2012 annual top 100 most valuable brands in the Asian market'.[66] Nowadays when intellectual property is becoming increasingly important, we must rely on brand and technology to participate in international competition. Weak intellectual property will undoubtedly have adverse effects on the role of Chinese enterprises in the international market. With the transformation and upgrading of the Chinese economy, the model of foreign trade relying on high input and high consumption has come to an end. To vigorously implement the national intellectual property strategy in foreign trade is the only way to realize the shift from 'driven by element' to 'driven by innovation'.[67]

Finally, the government plays a key role in implementing China's national intellectual property strategy, but the orientation and practical experience of the government are insufficient. China has reached an important phase of further reform. A focus is on an improved relationship between the government power and the market – the 'invisible hands'. At present, administrative intervention of intellectual property remains, especially in the fields of the grant and evaluation of intellectual property rights. In many cases, the implementation of the national intellectual property strategy can easily lead to government showcases that care more about the government's performance assessment rather than the commercialization of intellectual property.[68]

---

[65] Available at <http://www.most.gov.cn/fggw/zfwj/zfwj2010/201008/t201 00817_78927.htm>.

[66] Xu Yuan, 'Study on China's Current Implementation of the National Intellectual Property Strategy in the Field of Foreign Trade', *International Trade*, 2013, No. 4, pp. 27–30.

[67] *Ibid.*

[68] The problems existing in the implementation of the national intellectual property strategy and challenges can also be understood from the following three points: from an international perspective, China is under pressure to further improve the protection standard of intellectual property rights; domestically, the overall development level of intellectual property is not high, and effective support to the innovation economy is still weak. In recent years, new phenomena

4.2 Regional Challenges

In the light of the national intellectual property strategy, regional intellectual property strategies have been formulated across China. A regional intellectual property strategy is formulated and implemented within a specific region. Its main task is to formulate the regional intellectual property strategy and the relevant implementation plan, to promote the development of regional economy, science and technology, and culture by utilizing the intellectual property system, to improve regional competitiveness, and to provide policy and institutional support for the effective promotion of the national intellectual property system in the region.[69]

Regional intellectual property strategies are the connecting point between the national intellectual property strategy and intellectual property strategies of Chinese enterprises.[70] Strategic and policy guidance for the enterprises within the region should be provided and reasonable planning should be undertaken in order to develop an intellectual property strategy. However, the implementing effect is not ideal.

Firstly, the contents of the regional intellectual property strategy are usually imitating versions of the national intellectual property strategy. The local government, according to the national intellectual property strategy, formulates local intellectual property strategies.[71] However, take Hubei Province for example: except in reference to the corresponding policy of Wuhan City, the Western Hubei Ecological-Culture Tourism Circle, and the Yangtze River Economic Belt of Hubei Province, its basic contents are all from China's national intellectual property strategy.[72] Such a strategy lacks regional characteristics and carefully targeted deployment, and to an extent is simply the counterpart of the macro policies.

---

and new problems have emerged endlessly with respect to intellectual property. *See* Zhang Zhicheng, 'Thinking on the Formulation and Implementation of the National Intellectual Property Strategy', *Science and Technology for Development*, 2012, No. 7, pp. 11–15.

[69] Feng Xiaoqing, *Intellectual Property Strategy for Enterprises*, Beijing: Intellectual Property Press, 2008, p. 25.

[70] Jin Minghao, 'The Construction of Coordination Mechanisms for Implementation of the Regional Intellectual Property Strategy System and Its Implementation Path', *Journal of Nanjing University of Science and Technology (social science edition)*, 2013, No. 2, pp. 50–59.

[71] *Ibid.*

[72] Information from *Hubei Daily*, 25 August 2010.

Secondly, the key problem of the regional intellectual property strategies is regional coordination, but the existing intellectual property strategy cannot take full advantage of the role of the policy to allocate resources. 'In the process of implementation of the regional intellectual property strategy, there exist mutual interest relationship and matching relationship between various resource elements and organizational elements, and they interact and influence the collaborative process and the final result of the implementation of the regional strategy.'[73] In formulating regional strategies, it needs to fully distribute various kinds of resources, including innovators, innovation resources and innovation capacities within a region and among different regions so as to make up regional inadequacies and reduce high costs and risks caused by independent operation of individual parties. This is very much absent in most regional strategies.[74]

4.3 Challenges Facing Industries

An industrial intellectual property strategy is directly related to industrial competitive advantages.[75] It is formulated and carried out by a specific industry, and its main content and task are to study how to formulate and implement the intellectual property strategy in the industry for improving the industry's ability for creation, protection, management and utilization of intellectual property, improve the industry's overall technological innovation capability and core competitiveness, and effectively cope with intellectual property challenges and risks. China's industry intellectual property strategy is crucial to the relevant industries. However, the academic discussion on China's industry intellectual property strategies is weak, and the particularities of each industry put forward difficulties in implementing these strategies, which makes the implementation of these strategies face enormous challenges.

---

[73]   Supra note 70.
[74]   For China's regional intellectual property strategy research, *see* Luo Aijing & Gong Xueqin, 'Studies of Regional Intellectual Property Strategy', *Forum on Science and Technology in China*, 2010, No. 2, pp. 88–91; the Legal Division of the State Intellectual Property office, *Collection of Studies of the Regional Intellectual Property Strategy*, Beijing: Intellectual Property Press, 2012.
[75]   Zhan Ying & Wen Bo, 'The Industry Intellectual Property Strategy and Access to Competitive Advantage – the Rise of the Indian Software Industry', *The Science of Science and Management of S. & T.*, 2011, Vol. 32, No. 4, pp. 98–104.

For some industries, the number of patents is low, and their innovation ability is insufficient. For instance, in the textile machinery industry, there exist challenges that the number of patent applications for domestic textile is low, and thus innovation capability of the domestic textile enterprises is obviously insufficient. Meanwhile, patent complaints from foreign loom manufacturers are increasing.[76] In practice, due to industrial diversities, it is difficult for the main contents of the industry intellectual property strategies to follow a unified model.[77] This is the individuality of the industry intellectual property strategy. The challenges and risks for the implementation of the industry intellectual property strategy are as follows:

Firstly, different industries in China have different levels of awareness of the necessity for an intellectual property strategy. China's first national industry intellectual property strategy pilot – the railway industry intellectual property strategy – was initiated on 30 June 2008. However, the Ministry of Railways, the Ministry of Science and Technology and the State Intellectual Property Office (SIPO) are still working together on formulating the intellectual property strategy compendium for China's railway industry. This means that the railway industry has not yet formed complete strategy outlines. According to the latest statistics, as of 30 June 2011, the number of patent applications in the field of information technology in China had climbed to 1.364 million with an increase of 20 per cent. Among them, the growth of high-tech invention patents is notable. The total number of applications was more than 910 000, and increased by 20 per cent, for the first time exceeding the number of applications by foreign companies.[78] This shows that China's IT industry has achieved remarkable results under the guidance of the intellectual property strategy. The development phase of technology among different industries is different, and the degree of importance that different industries attach to intellectual property is different. Hence, the implementation of the intellectual property strategy is also quite different.

Secondly, the coordination mechanism leaves much to be desired. Generally speaking, there is competition as well as common interests within an industry. Within the same industry, the actual situations of

---

[76]   Wang Hao, 'On the Intellectual Property Strategy of Textile Machinery Industry', *Intellectual Property*, 2004, No. 5, pp. 19–22.

[77]   Zhan Ying, 'Basic Problems of the Industry Intellectual Property Strategy', *Huxiang Forum*, 2009, No. 6, pp. 12–16.

[78]   'Adhere to the Implementation of the Industry Intellectual Property Strategy, Promote Transformation and Upgrading of the Industry', *Electronic Intellectual Property*, 2011, No. 12, p. 17.

different enterprises are different, and the industry strategy formulated by the leading enterprises is not a 'universal' model, which results in the enterprises within the industry tending to act on their own will. Industry coordination bodies do not have management power. They can only guide enterprises through suggestions. This mechanism cannot be effective. For example, a management body that can provide timely feedback and deal with intellectual property issues in China's railway industry is missing.[79]

Finally, the implementation of the intellectual property policy by industry is weak. As for the protection and management of existing achievements, industries have not played a role as organizers. Competitions of intellectual property within an industry are often very fierce. The disputes relating to intellectual property should have been coordinated by the industry. However, except in a few cases like the Smoking Set Association of Wenzhou, there are few industry associations which can protect legal rights on behalf of enterprises. This situation has weakened the positive role of industry associations, and it gives little incentive to follow an industry strategy.[80]

Therefore China needs to improve the functions of industry associations in promoting the formulation and implementation of industrial intellectual property strategies, to strengthen the coordination and implementation of intellectual property strategies within an industry, to pay more attention to the allocation and integration of resources, to establish a platform between regional intellectual property strategies and enterprise intellectual property strategies, and to enhance the competitiveness of industries.

4.4 Challenges Facing Enterprises

The enterprise intellectual property strategy is an important part of the intellectual property strategy system of a country or a region, and is the foundation and safeguard of the final actualization of the national, regional and industrial intellectual property strategies.[81] Many enterprises

---

[79] Zhou Zhiwei & Xiao Hai, 'On the Intellectual Property Strategy of China's Railway Industry, *Journal of Chongqing Jiaotong University* (social science edition), 2012, No. 2, pp. 27–30.

[80] Yang Yong, 'The Role of Guilds in the Building of Industry Intellectual Property Strategy System', *Industrial & Science Tribune*, 2008, Vol. 7, No. 9, pp. 166–67.

[81] Feng Xiaoqing, 'The Implementation of the Enterprise Intellectual Property Strategy in China: A Perspective of National Intellectual Property Strategy', *Journal of Hunan University (social science edition)*, 2010, No. 1, pp. 116–23.

in China do not have intellectual property strategies, and existing strategies are insufficient. Specifically, the challenges faced by Chinese enterprises during the implementation of intellectual property strategies are as follows:

The enterprise's weak awareness of intellectual property rights has influenced the actual effect of the strategy system. To formulate and implement an intellectual property strategy is an important guarantee for enterprises to improve their competitive advantages. Chinese enterprises have obvious shortages in the utilization of intellectual property rights. The SASAC, in a survey of 2,716 enterprises, found that only 347 enterprises, less than 13 per cent, have intellectual property strategies or planning, and even fewer have made specific programmes to apply their strategies. Even among those having the programmes to commercialize their intellectual property achievements, most of them did not closely combine the patent strategy and the brand strategy with their development strategy.[82] In 2011 the Torch Center of the Ministry of Science and Technology conducted a survey among 1,991 enterprises which were located in 57 high-tech development zones in China and another survey of 1,038 non-high-tech enterprises. Those high-tech enterprises which formulated five-year intellectual property strategy planning accounted for only 12.7 per cent, while those who formulated one-year intellectual property strategy planning accounted for 18.9 per cent.[83] This situation shows that intellectual property plays a limited role in Chinese enterprises.

The cohesion between the enterprise intellectual property strategy and the macro intellectual property strategy is poor. The enterprise intellectual property strategy is the key to the implementation of the national, regional and industry intellectual property strategies. Only when the enterprises combine their own advantages and make full use of strategic thinking to improve China's overall intellectual property strategies can the implementation of the latter become active. This is because Chinese enterprises have paid insufficient attention to intellectual property strategies and do not realize this important cohesion. Also, their, strategy planning is rough and infeasible.

---

[82]   Supra note 69, p. 8.
[83]   Tang Heng, Fu Liying & Feng Chujian, 'Analysis of High-tech Enterprise Intellectual Property Management and Performance', *China Science and Technology Forum*, 2011, No. 5, pp. 80–85.

Nearly one year after China's National Intellectual Property Strategy Outline was released, the SASAC notified 53 large central-government-owned enterprises and other qualified central-government-owned enterprises to develop and implement their enterprise intellectual property strategies by the end of 2009, for the purpose of creating a number of big companies or groups that have strong intellectual property rights and famous brands and improved international competitiveness.[84] However, even the enterprises which have formulated an intellectual property strategy did not fully grasp the meanings of the intellectual property strategy. An enterprise intellectual property strategy is a systematic strategy. Only by making full use of the various policy systems which can ensure its implementation can it create maximized benefits.[85] Simple repetition of the policy is useless. If so, the enterprise intellectual property strategy planning will disconnect from its actual implementation. Therefore, it is absolutely important to strengthen the strategic coordination of enterprise intellectual property strategies in China.[86]

Chinese enterprises have some difficulties in implementing all levels of intellectual property strategy. They fail to notice that intellectual property can increase their market competitiveness. They think that to formulate an intellectual property strategy is just to satisfy the inspections of the authorities, and to give a good impression to the authorities of their excellent intellectual property management.[87] The implementation of national, regional and industrial intellectual property strategies thus becomes a formalistic approach. In China, of course, enterprises have few intellectual property rights and thus are unable to form aggregation effects. This means that the economic benefit of strategic use of intellectual property rights is not obvious, and in turn, there is a reluctance to make a long-term investment in intellectual property strategy. Although it is a bit premature to expect to see the actual effect of the intellectual property strategy at China's current stage, the actual effect is what China ultimately needs to pursue. Only when we fully explore various paths to the implementation and sum up experiences in a

---

[84] Wen Yuan, 'The Central Enterprises Comprehensively Implement the Enterprise Intellectual Property Strategy', *Guangming Daily*, 1 May 2009.

[85] Chen Wei, 'Studies of the Safeguard System for Implementation of the Enterprise Intellectual Property Strategy', *Economic Aspect*, 2007, No. 12, pp. 129–31.

[86] Yu Liyan, Wu Zhenggang & Cheng Xiaoduo, 'Research on Synergy Based on the Operation Process of the Enterprise Intellectual Property Strategy', *Management Modernization*, 2012, No. 5, pp. 84–86.

[87] Supra note 69, p. 385.

timely manner can we actually set examples of implementing the intellectual property strategies.

The implementation of the enterprise intellectual property strategy faces severe international competition. Along with economic globalization and the internationalization of domestic markets, Chinese enterprises also face fierce competition from foreign multinationals, even at home. At present, multinational companies have set up a rigorous intellectual property blockade in China, which presents a serious challenge for Chinese enterprises to realize innovation and industrial development. For example, Chinese enterprises have encountered technology barriers and intellectual property challenges in the United States.[88] From 2002 to 2010, Section 337 investigations against Chinese enterprises in the United States grew by an average of 18 per cent a year and this has caused huge market pressures and economic losses to Chinese enterprises.[89] Many Chinese enterprises lack core technologies and depend highly on foreign technologies. They are greatly restricted by foreign policies regarding the export of advanced technologies and the control of key technologies, which is also an important bottleneck for implementing intellectual property strategies.[90] Core technologies and intellectual property rights are linked together. Since Chinese enterprises lack core technologies, and foreign enterprises implement strict control over their core technologies and even abuse intellectual property rights,[91] Chinese enterprises have difficulty in carrying out their strategies for self-driven innovation.

---

[88]   'Countermeasures for Chinese Companies to Cope with Patent Barriers', *Cooperative Economy and Science and Technology*, February 2008, pp. 18–19.

[89]   Xiang Zheng & Gu Xiaoyan, 'On the Development Trend of the American 337 Investigation on China's Enterprises and the Countermeasures of China's Strategic Emerging Industries', *Science and Technology Management Research*, 2012, No. 24, pp. 144–49.

[90]   Li Dun, 'The Status, Causes and Countermeasures of External Dependency Technology in China under the Strategy of Independent Innovation', *International Trade*, 2009, No. 9, pp. 26–30.

[91]   Gao Lanying, 'On the Regulation of the Anti-monopoly Law on the Abuse of Intellectual Property Rights by Multinational Corporations in China', *Hunan Social Science*, 2011, No. 2, pp. 79–82; Hong Jing, 'On the Abuse of Intellectual Property Rights by Multinational Companies in China and Countermeasures', *International Business Research*, 2007, No. 5, pp. 25–29.

5. CHALLENGES FOR INNOVATION AND IP MANAGEMENT IN CHINESE ENTERPRISES

The construction of innovation systems and intellectual property management systems in Chinese enterprises is far from perfect and many problems still exist. For Chinese enterprises have experienced Deng Xiaoping's economic reform in the late 1970s, the development and attraction of capital since the 1980s and the reform in the property rights system in the 1990s.[92] So there are very few Chinese enterprises that pay serious attention to innovation and intellectual property.

5.1 Some Problems

Some Chinese enterprises view an intellectual property management system as creating additional costs. Due to a lack of strategic planning of intellectual property, the level of utilization, industrialization and commercialization of intellectual property for those enterprises remains low, even after obtaining intellectual property.[93] Secondly, Chinese enterprises do not have many management specialists for intellectual property. Many companies are suffering from a lack of specialists for management of intellectual property, especially those who can integrate intellectual property management and the business of enterprises.[94]

Thirdly, professional departments for management of intellectual property in enterprises are missing. For instance, according to a survey conducted in Sichuan Province in 2006, among 212 surveyed high-tech enterprises, 26.88 per cent had not established intellectual property management departments, 66.04 per cent simply assigned intellectual property related works to another department, and only 7.08 per cent had established specialized intellectual property management departments.[95]

---

[92] Ma Lixing, *Research on the Reform of Property Right System of Chinese State-owned Enterprise*, Shanghai: Shanghai Academy of Social Sciences Press, 2012; Lu Zheng & Huang Sujian, *Research of the Reform in the 30 Years for Chinese State-owned Enterprise*, Beijing: Economy Management Press, 2008.

[93] Ye Yueping, 'Analysis of the Problems and Solutions in Intellectual Property Management', *Business Economy*, 2009, No. 1, pp. 92–94.

[94] Tao Xinliang (ed.), *China Intellectual Property Training Colleges and Universities*, Beijing: Intellectual Property Publishing House, 2011.

[95] Wang Tao & Gu Xin, 'Management Situation, Problems and Counter-measures for our High-tech Enterprises', *Science and Technology Management Research*, 2006, No. 4, pp. 8–11.

This suggests that the majority of Chinese enterprises have not set up any intellectual property management functions.

Fourthly, the management system of intellectual property in enterprises is incomplete. A survey conducted by SIPO about enterprise intellectual property management in Qingdao City shows that of the 121 model companies, 20 have set up patent management systems, 22 have completed part of it, 31 are on the way to completion, and 48 enterprises have done nothing.[96] This suggests that the construction of management systems of intellectual property in enterprises is not yet achieved.

The problems reflected by insufficient intellectual property management systems in Chinese enterprises can explain the overall insufficient capacity of innovation in the Chinese economy. This results from, on the one hand, the lack of consciousness of innovation, inadequate investment and the shortage of innovation systems, and on the other hand, failure to access core technologies when China introduces foreign capital as well as fierce domestic competitive pressures.[97]

Many enterprises attach more importance to technology import than on the digestion and absorption and innovation of the imported technology. China is highly dependent on foreign technology. According to a survey of 2,716 enterprises by SASAC, dependence on foreign technology in Chinese enterprise is 50 per cent.[98] Some enterprises rely too heavily on importing technology but ignore the digestion, absorption and innovation of the imported technology. Besides, when allocating innovation resources and funds, enterprises have failed to distribute the fund reasonably among introduction, digestion, absorption and re-innovation and the proportion of funds for re-innovation is strikingly low.[99]

For example, according to a survey of industrial enterprises in China implemented in 1991–2006, the proportion of technology import in

---

[96]   Li Li, Xing Guang, Zhang Zhanzhen *et al.*, 'Status Survey and Feature Analysis of Patent Management in Enterprises – Take 284 Key Enterprises in Qingdao as an Example', *Economic Theory and Business Management*, 2009, No. 4, pp. 75–80.

[97]   Wang Ruijie & Xu Hanming, 'The Cultivation of Independent Creative Capability in Open Economy in China', *Journal of Liaoning Normal University* (Social Science Edition), 2005, No. 5, pp. 29–32.

[98]   Bi Xunlei, 'Analysis of Innovative Performance in Chinese Enterprise: A Perspective Based on the Relationship between Innovation Capability and Innovative Motivation', *Science & Technology and Policy*, 2011, No. 28, pp. 94–98.

[99]   For further studies, *see* Ni Shuowen, 'Learn from the U.S. Patent System and Facilitate Independent Innovation', *Journal of Hubei Administration Institute,* 2007, No.5, pp. 74–76.

China to that of digestion and absorption is 1:0.079, while this proportion was 1:3 in developed countries.[100] According to a 2009 survey for Small and Medium-sized Enterprises in Laiwu City, although an iron and steel enterprise spent a large sum of money in technology development, most of the fund was spent on technical updates, which accounted for 54.36 per cent of the total funds; its spending on import of technology accounted for 35.71 per cent, digestion and absorption 6.02 per cent, and the purchase of domestic technology 3.91 per cent.[101]

Quality experts in innovation are in short supply among Chinese enterprises. Most of them work for universities and research institutes. In other words, China's innovative human resources mainly work in universities and research institutes and the proportion in enterprises is too low. Original innovations are mostly found in colleges and universities, research institutes and a small number of large enterprises. At present, the mechanism of production-learning-research does not work properly. Talents in research institutes and universities cannot serve innovation activities in Chinese enterprises so enterprises are running short of innovative talents. Therefore, enterprises cannot attract enough talents for innovation, which naturally affects the innovation activities of Chinese enterprises.[102]

Another problem is that the system of self-driven innovation is not yet sound. Self-driven innovation needs the support of a healthy culture, including material culture, norm culture and conceptual culture.[103] Only by effective connections among cultural systems can the environment and motivation for innovation be created and developed. The lack of incentive mechanisms for innovation is another issue. Surveys show that Chinese enterprises do not have sound incentive mechanisms. According to a 2009 survey for Small and Medium-sized Enterprises in Laiwu City,

---

[100] Chen Ao, 'Exploration of Association Mechanism in Technology Transfer, Product Innovation, and Patent Output – on the Basis of Data in Large and Medium-sized Industrial Enterprises between 1991–2006', *Research and Development Management*, 2009, No.3, pp. 57–62.

[101] Zhuang Xiao, 'Problems and Solutions for Intellectual Property Management for SMEs of Laiwu', *Economy and Technology in Cooperation*, 2010, No.9, pp. 24–25.

[102] A survey shows that 59.4 per cent of operators believe 'shortage of innovative talents' is the key factor that hinders innovation. CEO Survey System in China, 'Innovation in Enterprises: Current Status, Problems and Policies: Special Survey Report of the Development of Chinese Entrepreneurs', *World of Management*, 2001, No. 4, pp. 71–80.

[103] Wang Mianqing, 'Cultural Supply in Independent Technological Creation', *Science and Technology and Law*, 2009, No. 3, pp. 13–16.

Shandong Province, an iron and steel enterprise established an incentive system that allowed an employee who had made significant technological breakthroughs to receive 5000 RMB as a reward. However, an employee's request for the bonus after accomplishing the technology breakthrough was rejected for the reason that the breakthrough was not distinctive enough. Besides, even those who finally got the bonus were also unhappy with the small amount.[104]

In fact, only a very limited proportion of Chinese enterprises have set up research and development institutions. Statistics show that only 25 500 enterprises above a certain size had established their own R&D institutions in China in 2011, accounting for only 7.8 per cent of the total enterprises above a certain size. Among the 25 500 R&D institutions, 12 000 were located in large and medium-sized industrial enterprises, accounting for 19.8 per cent of all large and medium-sized industrial enterprises.[105] Faced with the above-mentioned internal and external constraining factors, the innovative vitality in Chinese enterprises cannot be completely released.

5.2   Some Solutions

To handle the challenges faced by Chinese enterprises in management of intellectual property, it is necessary to employ the following measures:

First, strengthen the sense of management of intellectual property and innovation. Usually it is necessary to strengthen the training and education of leaders and staff of the business in intellectual property. This training and education involves popularization of knowledge about intellectual property, the system and management of intellectual property related to the enterprise, strategies about intellectual property and their implementation.

Secondly, facilitate the organic integration of management of both technology achievements and intellectual property. To realize such integration, it is necessary to make full use of intellectual property strategy in research and development and the implementation of innovation, and mix intellectual property management in with management of technology

---

[104]   Zhuang, 'Problems and Solutions for Intellectual Property Management for SMEs of Laiwu', pp. 24–25.

[105]   Yu Sibian & Zhao Yongxin, 'Substantial Increase of the Proportion of Enterprises to Establish R & D institutions', *People's Daily*, 1 March 2013.

achievements.[106] Companies need to establish innovation-oriented innovation management systems and include intellectual property in the whole process of management of the enterprises' technology achievements.

Thirdly, establish and improve the management and innovation systems to promote the formation of independent intellectual property in enterprises. The management system of intellectual property in enterprises should be established from the perspective of systematic planning. The relevant experience of Chinese and foreign enterprises has demonstrated that the management system of corporate intellectual property is an important guarantee to improve the mechanism of intellectual property in enterprises.[107]

Fourthly, establish and improve the management system of intellectual property in Chinese enterprises. The management system of intellectual property in enterprises needs to be reflected from various aspects of intellectual property creation, utilization, management and protection. Improvement of these systems helps to provide a solid systematic guarantee for management of intellectual property.

Fifthly, improve the human resources for the management of intellectual property in Chinese enterprises. Human resources of intellectual property management in enterprises are the basic safeguards for management of intellectual property. They include personnel for intellectual property strategies, the daily management of intellectual property, legal issues, and management of international intellectual property rights. To improve the level of management of intellectual property in enterprises, it is necessary to introduce and cultivate interdisciplinary talents for intellectual property management.

Sixthly, establish an incentive system. An effective incentive system is a systematic mechanism that encourages employees to be engaged in knowledge creation. To establish such an incentive system, it is essential to regulate the relationship between companies and employees, especially between the rights and obligations of companies and their technology personnel. This incentive system involves a technology creation system and the distribution of benefits. Besides, an assessment system demonstrating the value of knowledge creation should be created.

As for innovation, an innovative platform is the basic foundation for enterprises to carry out technology innovation. It is also an entity for enterprises to promote China's innovative system in its national industrial

---

[106] See Part One of this Chapter for further details.

[107] Feng Xiaoqing, *Strategies of Intellectual Property for Enterprises* (3rd edn.), Beijing: Intellectual Property Publishing House, 2008, pp. 478–90.

development. Most of China's enterprises do not have effective innovative platforms. It is essential for enterprises to build technology, experiment and engineering centres so as to integrate innovative resources and strengthen the effective combination of industries, universities and research institutes, form large and medium-sized enterprise technology alliances, and build platforms for critical and generic technologies and a number of bases for research and development. Generally speaking, enterprises need to construct innovative platforms with their own funds and human resources. For major projects, it is necessary to establish national and local innovation centres and key laboratories so as to provide safeguards in budget and policy.

In addition, the construction of a service system for knowledge innovation in enterprises in China must be focused on the following two aspects:[108]

First, construct a public service platform for knowledge creation. The construction of a service platform for knowledge creation can improve the service functions of enterprise technology innovation. The construction of a public technology service platform calls for support from government departments. The central and local authorities can also construct public information service platforms, such as information service platforms for intellectual property[109] and network service platforms for scientific and technological information.[110]

Secondly, establish and improve agency services for science and technology. Currently China has different types of agencies for IP transactions, technology transfer, asset appraisals, business consultation and management, and so on. To strengthen the management of such agencies, it is necessary to develop and improve the policies that promote the development of these agencies and enhance their roles in enterprise knowledge creation and the protection of intellectual property.[111]

Innovative human resources are the fundamental guarantee of knowledge creation in enterprises and China is highly committed to cultivating

---

[108]   Feng Xiaoqing, 'Research in Construction of Service System for Intellectual Property Strategy Based on Technological Innovation and Intellectual Property', *Science & Technology Progress and Policy*, 2013, No. 1, pp. 1–3.

[109]   Feng Xiaoqing, 'Research on the Construction of Information Network Platform of Intellectual Property in China', *Journal of Hunan University* (Social Sciences Edition), 2013, No.3, pp. 137–142.

[110]   *The Twelfth Five-Year Plan of the State Intellectual Property Career*, issued in 2012. Available at <http://www.gov.cn/jrzg/2011-10/14/content_1970 050.htm>.

[111]   Supra note 108, pp. 2–3.

innovative talents. It is necessary for China to establish and improve the incentive mechanisms for innovative talents and improve the evaluation systems for selection and assessment of innovative talents. In addition, given that a lot of technical personnel are not engaged in the front line of enterprises but in colleges, universities and research institutes, we need to set up systems that encourage and attract these talents to flow to the enterprises.[112]

In addition, disconnection exists among universities, research institutes and enterprises. Many superior and cutting-edge facilities belong to research entities and are not open to enterprises for sharing. Therefore, we need to integrate knowledge creation resources and share resources. Chinese enterprises can also cooperate with foreign enterprises or scientific research institutions to implement international technology cooperation plans and introduce core parts and technologies and intellectual property. They can then be digested and absorbed for further innovation.

Last, the production-learning-research alliance needs to be improved. Enterprises, universities and research institutes should exercise their respective advantages and complement each other so as to better integrate innovation resources, especially in conducting major projects. In constructing the production-learning-research alliance, it is also important to encourage the technology innovation achievements of universities and scientific research institutes as well as their innovation talents to flow to enterprises.

CONCLUSION

In the process of implementing intellectual innovation, Chinese enterprises are facing many challenges. There are differences between modern intellectual property systems and the model of science and technology management under China's previous planned economy. Their coexistence has hindered patent commercialization. The lack of market incentives is not only unfavourable for the commercialization of patented technology, but also unfavourable for attracting funds for Chinese enterprises to conduct research and development. China's intellectual property laws, tax law, investment law and the Government Procurement Law follow the legislative principle of 'being coarse rather than precise', and thus a clear

---

[112]   Feng Xiaoqing, 'Research on the Improvement of Technology Innovative System and the Public Policy', *Journal of Jishou University* (Social Science Edition), 2013, No. 2, pp. 53–57.

system providing incentives to innovation is absent. Although China's science and technology parks have played a significant role in the stimulation of innovation, due to unbalanced economic and technological development progress, the quality of parks varies and further adjustment is necessary to meet the needs of self-driven innovation. Chinese enterprises also lack experience in self-driven innovation. This includes insufficient enterprise intellectual property strategy experience, lack of supporting systems for implementation of intellectual property strategies, insufficient enterprise self-driven innovation abilities, poor industrialization and marketization of enterprise innovation achievements, and the severe international situation faced in the implementation of enterprise intellectual property strategies. This puts Chinese enterprise into a vicious cycle: insufficient motivation on innovation causes insufficient supporting funding and experience, which conversely causes insufficient capacity for innovation.

However, although China faces many challenges, its determination to establish an innovative country is unwavering. In the process of internationalization, only the vigorous promotion of self-driven innovation and utilization of intellectual property will lead Chinese enterprises to stand steadily in the world. The fundamental key is to overcome the deficiencies in the systems, laws, facilities and business operations.

5. Efforts and tendencies in China's judicial practice of intellectual property

Kong Xiangjun and Du Weike

INTRODUCTION

The courts in the People's Republic of China bear the duty to protect intellectual property rights. Tribunals specializing in intellectual property cases in China have been established for some years, at both central and local levels (hereinafter IP tribunals). Their purpose is to respond to the highly specialized nature of IP laws in general and to China's own conditions in particular. In July 1993 the High People's Court of Beijing set up the first tribunal for hearing intellectual property cases in China, followed by the establishment of the Intellectual Property Tribunal of the Supreme People's Court in 1996. At present, tribunals specializing in hearing intellectual property cases exist in every High People's Court, as well as in almost every Intermediate People's Court and the Grassroots People's Court in regions where economy, society and technology are relatively developed.

One 5 June 2008, the State Council issued the National Intellectual Property Strategy Outline, which requires 'strengthening the judicial protection system'. IP tribunals are required to 'play a leading role in protecting intellectual property' in China.[1] The people's courts at all levels in China have been playing such a role in judicial protection. By means of the establishment of judicial interpretations and judicial policies by the Supreme People's Court, and through cases judged by the people's courts at all levels, IP tribunals have effectively clarified the standards of the application of law for China's intellectual property laws, and the legal rules relating to intellectual property disputes. Collectively, these efforts

---

[1]   Available at <http://www.gov.cn/zwgk/2008-06/10/content_1012269.htm>.

have promoted the development of rule of law in the intellectual property sectors in China.[2]

This chapter aims at discussing some of the new tendencies of China's efforts in judicial practice in intellectual property laws and its roles in fostering China's knowledge-based economy. Part 1 focuses on our considerable efforts in judicial interpretations of and the application of IP laws, which play fundamental roles in China's legal system in general and of course in the relatively new areas of intellectual property. Part 2 discusses the judicial polices on judging IP cases issued by the Supreme People's Court. These policies cover a wide range of issues that guide Chinese local courts in China's dynamic internal and global environments. Part 3 elaborates on typical IP cases decided by the Supreme People's Court. These typical cases reflect our steady efforts and significant progress in achieving high-quality judicial practice of IP laws in China. In particular, we strive to create balance among the knowledge creators and the varying interests of the public in different regions of China.

This chapter clearly outlines China's tendencies in intellectual property law practice, namely promoting China's innovation-based economy. This term does not simply mean that the courts should provide maximized and unreasonable protection to IP right owners. Rather, balance needs to be consistently sought among different stakeholders in each given IP case. Our judicial practice in patent lawsuits, for instance, aims at both effectively protecting patent rights and preventing their abuses. The innovation economy is not only about commercial interests. It is also about continuous and sustainable innovations into the future and their benefit to be shared by the public.

1.   IMPROVE THE WORK ON JUDICIAL INTERPRETATION AND UNIFY THE STANDARDS OF THE APPLICATION OF IP LAW

According to the Resolution of the National People's Congress (NPC) Standing Committee on Strengthening the Legal Interpretation Work (hereinafter the Resolution), and the provisions of Law of China on the Organization of the People's Courts (hereinafter the Court Organization

---

[2]   Kong Xiangjun, *Basic Issues of the Application of Intellectual Property Law: Judicial Philosophy, Judicial Policy and the Method of Adjudication,* Beijing: Law Press, 2013, p. 1.

Law), when dealing with the specific application of law by the courts, the Supreme People's Court can base itself on the relevant laws and the legislative purposes to issue judicial interpretation.[3] It is important to note that judicial interpretation plays a crucial role in contemporary China's legal system. It serves a similar function to the judge-made law in common law jurisdictions. This system ensures that the application of law can keep up to date and suit the dynamic needs of social changes. This is particularly relevant to China, which has been undergoing very rapid transitions in the last 30 years.

The Supreme People's Court's judicial interpretations explain specific definitions of the law and their consistent application often in the form of provisions, which are legally binding on the people's courts at all levels. In recent years, the Supreme People's Court has issued various judicial interpretations based on summarized trial experiences so as to achieve consistency in justice and ensure the implementation of law in China's courts. This represents our considerable efforts responding to a vast number of legal disputes taking place in contemporary China's unique transitional period.

The following part will now elaborate on key judicial interpretations concerning intellectual property laws and disputes.[4] Considering the relatively new profile of IP laws in post-World Trade Organization (WTO) China, these judicial interpretations represent great efforts of the judiciary in promoting improved intellectual property law practices.

1.1 Judicial Interpretation on Patent

In 2001 the Supreme People's Court issued Several Provisions on Issues Concerning the Application of Law to the Trial of Cases of Patent Disputes. This was an effort responding to the needs after China's accession to the WTO and the amendment of China's Patent Law in

---

[3]   Article 2 of the Resolution provides that the detailed application of laws and decrees in trials is interpreted by the Supreme People's Court. Article 32 of the Court Organization Law provides that, during the trial, the Supreme People's Court is responsible for the interpretation of the specific application of laws and decrees.

[4]   As to the basic theory and philosophical thinking for the understanding and application of the judicial interpretations in China, *see* Kong Xiangjun, *Judicial Philosophy and Legal Method*, Beijing: Law Press, 2005; Kong Xiangjun, *A Perspective of Legal Method: The Selection and Application of Legal Norms*, Beijing: The People's Court Press, 2006.

2001.[5] Patent disputes heard by the courts in the last 20 years have been systematically summarized in this judicial interpretation, which covers such areas as the types of acceptable patent cases, jurisdictions, suspended proceedings, claims to explain, the doctrine of equivalents, and calculation of damages for compensation.[6]

On 27 December 2008 China's Patent Law was amended for the third time, making it more suitable for China's status quo. The relevant new changes required the Supreme Court to issue a new interpretation in December 2009 – Interpretation on Several Issues concerning the Application of Law in the Trial of Cases in Patent Infringement Disputes (hereinafter the Interpretation on Patent Cases). It summarizes new and key issues in the relevant trials, and standardizes various applications of law in detail for patent infringement. This interpretation dramatically improves the environment for patent litigation in China. It further regulates the principles and specific rules for the explanation of patent claims; improves the judgment standards of the doctrine of equivalents; adds the provisions of the principle of estoppel and contribution; sets up necessary restrictions for the application of the doctrine of equivalents; clarifies the principles of determining design patent infringement; clarifies the assessment standards for prior art counterplea, existing design counterplea and the prior right counterplea; and adds provision of non-infringing litigation, etc.[7] Undoubtedly, these aspects are crucial to any modern patent law as well as to China's rising innovation economy.

1.2   Judicial Interpretation on Copyright

In response to China's accession to the WTO and the amendment of China's Copyright Law in 2001, the Supreme People's Court issued Interpretation on Several Issues Concerning the Application of Law in the Trial of Copyright Cases in Civil Disputes in October 2002. This judicial interpretation regulates some basic legal matters concerning copyright,

---

[5]   With regard to the issue of the WTO and TRIPS and related intellectual property, *see* Kong Xiangjun, *TRIPS Agreement and the Domestic Application*, Beijing: Law Press, 2002; Kong Xiangjun, Wu Jianying & Liu Zeyu, *The Rules of WTO and Intellectual Property Law: Theory, Rule and Cases*, Beijing: Qsinghua University Press, 2006.

[6]   Kong Xiangjun (ed.), *The Comprehension and Application of the Judicial Interpretation of Intellectual Property by the Supreme People's Court*, Beijing: China Legal System Press, 2012, pp. 26–27.

[7]   For the Interpretation on Patent Cases, *see* <http://www.court.gov.cn/qwfb/sfjs/201001/t20100129_759.htm>.

including: the scope and admission of civil cases over copyright; jurisdictions; evidence assessment in copyright civil cases; copyright protection for certain works; and calculation of damages for compensation.[8]

The rapid development of the internet, information technology and information network dissemination has brought unknown challenges to the traditional patterns of copyright law. The world's largest internet user, China is not immune. On 19 December 2000 the Supreme People's Court issued Interpretation of Several Issues Concerning the Application of Law in Trial of Cases of Copyright Disputes over Computer Network. It regulates the jurisdictions of copyright disputes in cyberspace, ownership of copyright for digitalized and internet-disseminated works, determination of copyright infringement, liability of internet service providers (ISPs), and damages for compensation. To suit rapid social changes, it was amended in 2003, and again in 2006.[9]

IP laws in China are certainly not isolated but are part of China's broad legal reforms that respond to overall economic and social changes. For instance, the establishment of China's Tort Liability Law[10] has made some contents of the above-mentioned judicial interpretations out of date. In this context, the Supreme People's Court issued Provisions on Several Issues Concerning the Application of Law in the Trial against the Civil Disputes of Information Network Dissemination on 26 December 2012.[11] The purpose of this interpretation is to unify the trial standards of the civil disputes on the right to disseminate information networks, to provide legal protection to both the right to disseminate information and the public interest. The purpose is to create a healthy environment for the prosperity of China's internet industry. Thus, the interpretation specifically addresses cutting-edge issues such as the criteria of infringing acts of the right to disseminate information networks, the ISPs' legal liability for aiding and abetting infringement, and the liability of online storage providers.

---

[8]   Supra note 6, pp. 178–201.

[9]   The amendment is mainly for the adoption of the formulation of the Regulation of Protecting the Right to Disseminate Information Network, which was passed during the 135th executive meeting of the State Council, on 10 May 2006, and came into effect on 1 July 2006.

[10]   The Tort Liability Law of China was passed during the 12th session of the Standing Committee of the 11th National People's Congress of China, and has become effective since 1 July 2010. Article 36 thereof is related to illegal acts in cyberspace and its legal liabilities.

[11]   Wang Yanfang, 'Interpretations and Applications of the Provisions of the Applicable Law in the Trial against the Civil Disputes of Information Network Dissemination', *The People's Justice*, 2013, No. 9, p. 14.

1.3   Judicial Interpretation on Trademarks

The Trademark Law in modern China is over 30 years old. Trademarks have flourished in the course of China's 30-year economic reforms with a total number of over 20 million trademarks, ranked number 1 in the world.[12] This creates an enormous amount of work for both the Trademark Office and the courts.

The Supreme People's Court has continuously summarized trial experiences and standardized the application of trademark law on time. Since 2001 the Supreme People's Court has formulated six interpretations on trademarks.[13]

Following the Trademark Law amendment in 2001, the Supreme People's Court in January 2002 issued the Interpretation on the Issues Concerning the Jurisdiction and the Scope of Application of Law for Hearing Trademark Cases and the Interpretation of Applicable Law on Ceasing Infringement upon the Exclusive Right to a Registered Trademark before Trial and the Preservation of Evidence. These two interpretations mainly focus on issues such as the application of law and pre-trial provisional measures. Nine months later, in October, the Interpretation on Several Issues Concerning the Application of Law in the Trial of Cases of Civil Disputes Arising from Trademarks was issued to clarify a number of important legal issues, such as the acts that 'caused other damage to the owner of a registered trademark', which is stipulated by Article 52 of the Trademark Law, the protection standards of well-known trademarks, a few other legal concepts important in the verdict of trademark infringement, such as 'related public', 'similar trademarks' and 'similar goods'. They also clarify the provisions of the principle of judgment and comparison of trademark infringement, as well as registered trademark licensing, calculation of damages for compensation, and the limitation of action.[14]

In China's transforming economy, legal disputes can be complicated. In order to solve the conflict of rights in intellectual property adjudication practice, protect the legitimate rights and interests of the parties, prevent unfair competition, and improve market order, the Supreme People's Court issued the Provisions on Several Issues Concerning the

---

[12]   Zhang Silu, 'China's Trademark Applications Counts over 20 Million in 2012', *CRJ Online*, <http://gb.cri.cn/42071/2013/04/26/5951s4097241.htm>.

[13]   For further understanding of the application of the Trademark Law in China, please refer to: Kong Xiangjun, *Basic Issues of the Application of Trademark Law*, Beijing: Press of China Legal System, 2012.

[14]   Supra note 6, pp. 95–114.

Trial of Civil Disputes Relating to Registered Trademark, Enterprise Name and Conflicts of Prior Right on 18 February 2008. This judicial interpretation intended to solve urgent issues such as acceptance of civil disputes on conflicts between trademark and prior rights; conflicts between enterprise names; cause of action in conflicts of rights in civil cases; and so on.[15]

Well-known trademarks have traditionally been important to both trademark owners and consumers. The formidable size of the Chinese economy today creates both the demand of well-known trademarks and difficulties in defining them. In order to further improve the judicial protection for well-known trademarks, the Supreme People's Court quickly responded to existing problems in relevant areas and issued the Interpretation on Several Issues Concerning the Application of Law in the Trial of Civil Dispute Relating to the Protection of Well-known Trademarks in 2009.[16] This interpretation further clarified the legal definition of well-known trademarks, the applicable conditions of assessing well-known trademarks, and the criteria of cross-category protection of well-known trademarks.[17]

1.4 Judicial Interpretation on Other Intellectual Property Rights

With regard to new plant variety disputes, the Supreme People's Court issued the Interpretation on Several Issues Encountered in the Trial of Cases of New Plant Varieties Disputes on 5 February 2001, which set up

---

[15] Supra note 6, pp. 117–28. Also *see* Jiang Zhipei, Kong Xiangjun & Xia Junli, 'The Understanding and Application Regarding the Trial of Civil Disputes Relating to Registered Trademarks, Enterprise Names and Conflicts of Prior Right' (Part I), *Administration of Industry and Commerce*, 2008, No. 8, pp. 32–35; Jiang Zhipei, Kong Xiangjun & Xia Junli, 'The Understanding and Application Regarding the Trial of Civil Disputes Relating to Registered Trademarks, Enterprise Names and Conflicts of Prior Right' (Part II), *Administration of Industry and Commerce*, 2008, No. 9, pp. 50–53; Kong Xiangjun, 'Standard of Logic and Policy Regarding the Judicial Dealing with Rights of Conflicts in Commercial Marks', *Qsinghua Legal Science*, 2007, No. 2, pp. 126–47; Kong Xiangjun, 'On the Clarification of the Civil Justice and Administrative Procedure in the Settlement of Rights of Conflicts in Intellectual Property', *Henan Social Science*, 2005, No. 6, pp. 9–14.

[16] As to this research in detail, *see* Kong Xiangjun, 'The Understanding and Application Regarding the Interpretation on Several Issues concerning the Application of Law in the Trial of Civil Dispute Relating to the Protection of Well-known Trademarks', *People's Justice*, 2011, No. 17, pp. 46–52.

[17] Supra note 6, pp. 137–46.

rules on case acceptance, jurisdiction and termination of the proceedings. It further issued the Regulation of Issues on Applicable Law in the Trials of Cases of Infringement Dispute for New Plant Variety Right on 12 January 2007, which focuses on legal issues such as the cognizance of the interested parties and infringement; technical appraisals; determination of damages for compensation of the infringement; handling the infringing items; and, importantly, exemption from compensation liability of farmers.[18] The Supreme People's Court's efforts in these judicial interpretations once again show its timely response to cutting-edge issues concerning intellectual property.

Technology contracts are crucial to the realization of the commercial value of intellectual property.[19] For China's booming high-tech economy, this is of particular relevance. The Supreme People's Court issued, on 24 December 2004, the Interpretation of Issues of Applicable Law in the Trial of Technical Contract Dispute. This was to define the concepts of and rights to technology achievements, execution and termination of technology contacts, and validity, invalidation or revocation of the contracts.[20]

Recognizing the important role of competition law to IP areas, the Supreme People's Court issued the Interpretation of Issues of Applicable Law in the Trial of Civil Cases concerning Unfair Competition on 12 January 2007.[21] It covers the cognizance of counterfeiting, trade secret infringement, and civil liabilities of unfair competition. The lack of antitrust in an IP legal framework creates fundamental flaws. With antitrust becoming an important sector of the people's courts since the implementation of the Anti-trust Law on 1 August 2008,[22] the Supreme People's Court issued Regulations on Issues of Applicable Law in the Trial of Civil Disputes Caused by Monopoly on 3 May 2012, which

---

[18]   Supra note 6, pp. 235–41.

[19]   Kong Xiangjun, 'Using New Thought to Protect Creation – New Thinking of the Current Intellectual Property Trial', *People's Justice*, 2013, No. 9, p. 38.

[20]   Supra note 6, pp. 289–308.

[21]   With regard to the theoretical research and application of the issue of anti-competition law in China, *see* Kong Xiangjun, *The Application of Anti-Competition Law and Its Upgrading*, Beijing: Law Press, 2000; Kong Xiangjun, *Trademark and Unfair Competition Law: Theory and Cases*, Beijing: Law Press, 2009; Jiang Zhipei, Kong Xiangjun & Wang Yongchang, 'The Understanding and Application Regarding the Interpretation of Issues of Applicable Law in the Trial of Civil Cases concerning Unfair Competition', *Legal Application*, 2007, No. 3, pp. 21–26.

[22]   According to the distribution of work in the People's Court, the Intellectual Property Tribunal hears civil cases of dispute over anti-monopoly.

signified the establishment of a linked system between IP and antitrust requirements.[23]

2. ESTABLISH AND IMPROVE JUDICIAL POLICIES AND STANDARDIZE THE APPLICATION OF LAW

Intellectual property is an area in which public policies play a clear role. The discretionary power of IP judges thus creates spaces for forming judicial policies.[24] When protecting intellectual property, the judiciary can be both a policy-maker and a receiver of judicial policies.

The basic policy of China's intellectual property is determined by law.[25] The judiciary formulates policies only within the realm of the law. These policies are usually formulated to ensure the proper and uniform exercise of discretionary power. Through judicial policies, the Supreme People's Court guides Chinese courts in the application of IP laws.[26] Considering China's development stage as both the world's largest manufacturing economy and an emerging modern knowledge-based economy, the competitive and rigorous international environment, as well as the spirit of IP protection, the Supreme People's Court sets the basic IP policies to be 'strengthened', 'categorized', and 'appropriately restricted'.[27] First, 'strengthened protection' is the largest challenge and the most important policy orientation suitable for China's current development stage. But strengthened protection cannot be simplified and needs to be categorized and appropriately restricted.

Whilst strengthening the protection, we need to provide different implementation measures for different intellectual property with different characteristics. Such 'categorization' of course must operate within the realm of the law. 'Appropriate restriction' means that we should consider China's social and economic conditions and its overall development stage

---

[23]   As to the main contents, *see* supra note 6, pp. 263–64.

[24]   Supra note 2, p. 23.

[25]   Kong Xiangjun, 'Law, Policy and Politics in Adjudication: Take Intellectual Property Trail as an Example', *Intellectual Property Law: Case and Academic Studies (General Volume)* (Intellectual Property Monographic Series: Case and Academic Studies), Feng Xiaoqiing (ed.), Beijing: Encyclopaedia of China Publishing House, 2010, pp. 77–86.

[26]   Supra note 2, p. 24.

[27]   Speech of Xi Xiaoming, Vice-president of the Supreme People's Court, delivered at the Third National-level Conference of Intellectual Property Trail, 21 March 2013.

when strengthening the protection. Strengthening the protection thus does not mean unreasonable protection.[28]

Guided by the above-mentioned basic policies, the Supreme People's Court has made efforts to create detailed policies. To date, the Supreme People's Court has issued 16 judicial policy guidelines, covering the trial of intellectual property for the broad conditions of China, the promotion of the development and prosperity of socialist culture, and safeguarding the construction of China's national innovation system. This represents the forming process of China's judicial policy framework for intellectual property.[29]

2.1 The Main Judicial Policy on Patents

According to the changes of domestic and international conditions, the Supreme People's Court has requested local courts to increase the efforts in patent protection, and correctly implement the 'appropriate restricted' policy. Through establishing proper standards with regard to claim constructions, doctrine of equivalents and other discretionary rules to suit the levels of innovation, the needs of specific industries, and the characteristics of the relevant technologies. Such a flexible approach can benefit China's economic and social development and innovation in its own context.[30]

With regard to the scope of patent protection and the explanations of claims, the Supreme People's Court has pointed out the necessity of adhering to a balanced approach that sufficiently respects patent law's universal role of being open for public inspection (OPI), and reasonably delineates the legal boundaries between patent rights and the public interest. By this we want to protect the right holders' legitimate interests and prevent the intrusion of private rights into the public domain. Otherwise, technology innovation can be harmed.[31] The scope of patent protection cannot be simply limited to the literary meanings of patent

---

[28] Speech of Xi Xiaoming, Vice-president of the Supreme People's Court, delivered at a training course of the Directors of the Intellectual Property Tribunals, 8 February 2010.

[29] *Ibid.*

[30] *Ibid.*

[31] Opinions of the Supreme People's Court on Giving Full Play to Trial Functions to Provide Judicial Safeguard for Deepening the Reform of System of Science and Technology and Speed up the Construction of National Innovation System (hereinafter the Opinions on the Reform and Innovation), 2012. Available at <http://www.court.gov.cn/xwzx/fyxw/zgrmfyxw/201207/t20120724_177810.htm>.

claims. Nor can it be based on arbitrary interpretation of the relevant technologies. These are two extreme ends. Instead, the interpretation of claims should provide fair protection to the patent owners and meanwhile ensure reasonable stabilities of the law among the public.[32]

With regard to hearing the cases of confirmation of patents, the Supreme People's Court emphasizes the aims of adjusting the judicial assessment standards of patents, encouraging invention and creativity, improving the quality of patent assessment through standardized and professional procedures, and improving the rules on evidence and efficiency.[33]

2.2 The Main Judicial Policy on Copyright

Copyright is very important to cultural areas, and thus for judicial protection of copyright the Supreme People's Court has developed the following policies:[34]

Balance of interest is a fundamental policy consideration in judging IP cases in China under the basic policy of 'appropriately restricted'. And it is also a universal copyright principle in the world.

The freedoms of creation, research and expression are related and under the influence of copyright protection, and should be guided by the principle of balance of interest. For China, balance is not only needed for the relationships among culture creators, commercial users and the public, but also among incentives, the broad development of cultural industry and the protection of fundamental cultural rights of the people. Regional development varies greatly across China and all parties should benefit from copyright and knowledge dissemination.[35]

The extent to which copyright exists largely depends on the definition of originality, which is an underlining and universal concept of modern copyright law. Judicial protection of copyright should safeguard the unity of the standards of determining originality, which must first meet the

---

[32]   Opinions of the Supreme People's Court on Issues concerning the Intellectual Property Trial Service to General Situation under the Current Economic Situation, 2009. Available at <http://www.court.gov.cn/qwfb/sfwj/yj/201002/t20 100224_1916.htm>.

[33]   *Ibid.*

[34]   Supra note 28.

[35]   As for the general research on the issue of balance of interests in copyright protection, *see* Kong Xiangjun, 'On the New Mechanism of Balancing of Interests in the Protection of Copyright in Cyberspace, *People's Justice*, 2011, No. 17, pp. 53–62.

minimum threshold. On the other hand, a higher level of originality requirement may be needed for certain cultural industries or specific subject matters of copyright. To implement the principle of balance of interest, the courts are required to adequately assess the conditions of a piece of work, the space for future creativity, industrial policies and the public interest. Only by doing so can a court determine the reasonable protection level for a given work.

The courts are required to properly deal with the relationship between copyright protection and the promotion of the development of the information industry and the dissemination of information networks. Infringement of copyright in cyberspace is common, often hidden and beyond the limit of physical boundaries and is thus quite difficult to discover and stop. China has the world's largest population of internet users. The internet has certainly become one of the most important methods of access to information for sharing ideas, opinions and entertainment. For copyright protection in cyberspace, the courts are required to consider the difficulty for copyright owners to protect their rights, and at the same time, the necessity of promoting the development of internet technology, the commercial models of the Chinese internet service industry, and the public interest. At present, an important principle and yet a challenge for China's copyright practice is how to seek balance among the copyright owners, ISPs and the public.

Last but not least, China is a country with an enormous amount of cultural heritage, which deserves judicial attention. In recent years, developed countries have obtained exclusive rights through the intellectual property system by using their technological advantages to collect, develop, modify and commercialize Chinese folklore, traditional knowledge and genetic resources. They have made huge profits from it. However, those who have created, maintained and inherited this Chinese intangible culture heritage do not have a fair and reasonable return. Rather, they suffer from expensive fee payments. China has huge intangible cultural heritage reservations. If intangible cultural heritage can be protected by the existing legal system of intellectual property, it should be protected. This requires an innovative way of thinking that is not confined or prevented by conventional definitions of subject matters, limited time term and scope and other intellectual property jargon. In practice, the principle of disclosure of origin should be insisted upon. The rights to information, consent and benefit sharing should be encouraged. The purpose is to ensure the interests of the key stakeholders can be reasonably coordinated and balanced during the process of discovery, inheritance, protection, development and utilization.

2.3 The Main Judicial Policy on Trademarks

Distinctiveness and protecting the consumer from confusion are the essential features of any trademark law. China has the world's largest amount of trademark registration. Preventing confusion thus becomes a core objective of our judicial policy on trademarks. China is a country with a tradition of respecting and valuing well-known brands. Thus we focus on preventing malicious acts of squatting of well-known commercial brands and 'free-riding' behaviours, and providing a supportive legal environment for the development of famous brands. Based on existing experience in trial and China's specific conditions, the Supreme People's Court has developed a series of judicial policies relating to trademarks that strengthen trademark protection, clearly define the boundaries of the market, leave space for trademark creation, and create a friendly environment for economic development.[36]

Defining the boundaries among trademarks is a serious business in practice. The protection scope of a trademark is essentially determined by the mark's distinctiveness and its reputation among its consumers. In theory, a trademark with a higher degree of distinctiveness and/or better recognition deserves a wider scope of protection. Discretionary power is also needed to decide on trademark principles prescribed by law. These include trademark similarities, similarities in goods, prior use marks with market influence and trademark registration through fraud or dishonest acts. The main target is to prevent squatting of other well-known commercial logos and 'free-riding' behaviours. That being said, it is also necessary to allow in specific cases coexistence of trademarks that contain similar elements so that the business owners can develop themselves with tolerance of each other. Such tolerance should only be limited to exceptional circumstances, such as coexistence resulting from complex historical reasons or other external factors.[37]

2.4 Other Major Judicial Policies on Intellectual Property

As to judicial protection of trade secrets, the Supreme People's Court recognizes the difficulties in terms of burden of proof and confidentiality in trade secret disputes, and thus allocates the burden of proof properly between the parties. It also assures the standards of proof of confidentiality and unfair means are adequately handled, so as to reduce the plaintiffs' common difficulty in resorting to lawsuits.

---

[36] Supra note 1, p. 79.
[37] Supra note 28.

The courts also recognize the market reality of an increasing level of flow of human resources in China. Laws should protect both trade secrets and promote free flow of human resources, including promoting the flow of elites or talents between scientific research institutes/universities and enterprises, which represent a common and encouraged model by the Chinese government's pro-innovation policies.[38] The courts are also required to balance the relations between protection of trade secrets and non-competition clauses properly.

With respect to liability for infringement, the Supreme People's Court emphasizes the needs to increase the compensation for damages and the degree of punishment and deterrence effect; to reduce the cost of lawsuits; and to increase the cost of infringement. The courts are required to actively guide the parties to claim compensation by way of calculating their actual damages or the infringer's profits obtained from the infringement, and avoid simplified use of statutory compensation. When there is difficulty in proving a specific amount of damages or profits, but there is evidence indicating that the amount is significantly higher than the maximum limit of the statutory compensation, the court shall evaluate all the evidence, and determine the proper amount of compensation at a level higher than the statutory limit. Excepting wherever prescribed by law, the courts shall reasonably include in the calculation the legal costs.[39]

In terms of the equal protection of intellectual property, the Supreme People's Court is firmly against any form of local protectionism. The courts are required to equally protect the local-foreign, domestic-foreign parties' legitimate rights and interests, promote consistency for the opening up of domestic markets, improve the investment environment and enhance investors' confidence, and improve the international reputation of China and Chinese enterprises. The courts should properly handle important trade-related intellectual property disputes, and actively serve both the domestic and international markets. The purpose is to comply with international trade and economic treaties with no prejudice to China's national interests, economic safety, and innovation.[40]

3. THE GUIDING ROLE OF TYPICAL CASES

So far we have briefly covered judicial interpretations and judicial policies issued by the Supreme People's Court for IP laws. These

---

[38] *See* Chapter 1 for further discussion.
[39] *See* supra note 32.
[40] *Ibid.*

demonstrate the huge efforts the Chinese courts have made to serve the nation's complex social and economic transition into a more developed, competitive and innovation-based economy. Now we will proceed to discuss how specific and difficult IP cases are guided under China's judicial hierarchy.

One of the essential features of China's court system is the central role of typical cases in guiding trials. Since 2008 the Supreme People's Court has regularly published annual reports, as well as ten most important and fifty typical cases involving judicial protection of intellectual property in China.[41] These huge efforts are results of systematic analyses of many cases concerning intellectual property decided by Chinese courts.

3.1 Typical Patent Cases

3.1.1 Interpretation of written claims

Interpretation of claims is a fundamental legal issue concerning patent infringement, the grant of patents and confirmation of the grant of patents. The degree and scope of interpretation will determine the extent of patent protection, and in turn, the relationship between patent owners and the public.[42] With respect to the interpretation of claims, Article 59 of China's Patent Law states: 'the scope of protection of the invention patent or utility model patent is determined by the content of its claims. The specification and drawings may be used to interpret the content of the claims.' However, Article 59 only acts as a principle. To implement it, the Supreme People's Court has established a judicial interpretation and has ruled a series of typical cases that provide detailed guidance to the relevant cases.

With respect to the distinction between interpretation of claims and modification of claims, in the *Longsheng Cable Factory* case, the Supreme People's Court stated that when the ordinary technicians in the field can clearly identify the related concept of the claim, and in the specification there is no specific description of the claim, the understanding of the content by the ordinary technicians in the field shall prevail. To

---

[41] The report of the Work on Strengthening the Trial of Intellectual Property and Promoting the Construction of an Innovative Country, in the 30th meeting of the 11th Session of the National People's Congress Standing Committee, by Wang Shengjun, the then President of the Supreme People's Court. Available at http://www.court.gov.cn/zscq/dcyj/201205/t20120509_176748.html.

[42] Kong Xiangjun, Wang Yongchang & Li Jian, 'The Understanding and Application of the Interpretation of Issues in the Trial of Patent Disputes of Infringement', *Electronic Intellectual Property*, 2010, No. 3, p. 27.

put it another way, patent infringement proceedings shall not be used as opportunities to seek modification of the claim in question.[43] This measure is needed for preventing patent abuse and accords with many developed countries' practices.

In some claims there are technical characteristics of the background or conditions of the invention in the claim. These 'environmental character-istics' can affect the scope of patent protection. The Supreme People's Court pointed out, in the *Shimano Inc.* case, that the environment characteristics written in the claim are necessary technical features, and determine the scope of protection of the claim. The degree to which such determination is achieved is a case-by-case analysis. In general, it should be understood that the requested protection object can be, and does not necessarily have to be, used in such environment, with the exception that, after reviewing the patent claim, the specification, and the patent assess-ment files, the ordinary technicians in the field can clearly and reason-ably state that the protected object must be used in such environment.[44]

3.1.2   The doctrine of equivalents and estoppel

The 'doctrine of equivalent' is an important principle for protecting patent rights.[45] It overcomes the limitations of the literary expression of a patent claim. This doctrine, however, is carefully exercised and is only used to interpret confusing literal expressions.[46] In judicial practice, the Supreme People's Court strictly and cautiously applies the doctrine of equivalent, in that an abuse of this doctrine may create an unreasonable level of patent monopoly and thus hinder the freedom of innovation and the public interest.[47] For this purpose, the 'principle of estoppel' is applied to regulate the doctrine of equivalent.[48]

---

[43]   In this case, the petitioners are Wuxi Longsheng Cable Factory & Shanghai Tin Shing Cable Material Co. Ltd., and the respondent is Xi'an Qinbang Telecommunication Material Co. Ltd., while the defendant in the first instance is Furukawa Electrician (Xi'an) Optical Communication Co. Ltd. The Supreme People's Court (2012) Mintizi, no. 3.

[44]   In this case, the petitioner is Shimano Inc. and the respondent is Ningbo Sunrun Industry & Trade Co. Ltd. The Supreme People's Court (2012) Mintizi, no. 1.

[45]   Chinese Patent Law does not formulate provisions on the doctrine of equivalent, but Article 17 of *the Interpretation on Patent Cases* does.

[46]   *See* supra note 1, p. 133.

[47]   *See* supra note 42, p. 27.

[48]   China's Patent Law does not formulate provisions on the principle of estoppel, but Article 6 of the *Interpretation on Patent Cases* does.

With respect to the cognizance standards of equivalent infringement, the Supreme People's Court has pointed out, in the *Jingye Co.* case, the following rules: when judging whether the accused infringing product's technical features are equivalent to the technical features of the patent, the court needs to consider not only whether the technical features of the alleged product can be anticipated by the ordinary technicians of the field without any creative and imaginative work, but also whether the technical features of the accused infringing product apply similar technical means, seek similar functions or achieve similar results, in comparison with the patent technical features. Only when the two aspects of conditions above are both met can the court hold that these two have equivalent technical features.[49]

The principle of estoppel, as the above has mentioned, acts as a restriction to the doctrine of equivalent. In the *Shen Qiheng* case[50] and the *Wushi Co.* case,[51] the Supreme People's Court held that if the patent applicant or patentee has given up the technical schemes through the modification of the claims, specifications or statement of opinion during the process of the grant or invalidation, these technical schemes will not be included in the scope of patent protection in patent proceedings. When determining whether equivalent infringement exists, even if the accused infringer did not ask for the use of the principle of estoppel, the court may apply this principle based on ascertained facts for the purpose of limiting the scope of equivalent. This interesting and practically workable feature is to ensure that the principle of equivalent is not abused.

3.1.3 Inventiveness

Inventiveness is one of the three requirements for proving patent validity. In patent practice in China, inventiveness is a hotspot and a very difficult issue in confirmation of granted patents.[52] In recent years, the Supreme

---

[49] In this case, the petitioner is Shanxi Jingye Glass Steel Co. Ltd., and the respondent is Yongchang Sekisui Composites Co. Ltd. The Supreme People's Court (2010) Minshenzi, no. 181.

[50] In this case, the petitioner is Shen Qiheng, and the respondent is Shanghai Shengmao Transport Facilities Engineering Co. Ltd. The Supreme People's Court (2009) Minshenzi, no. 239.

[51] In this case, the petitioner is Hubei Wushi Pharmaceutical Co., Ltd., and the respondent is Aonuo (China) Pharmaceutical Co., Ltd., and the defendant is Wang Junshen. The Supreme People's Court (2009) Mintizi, no. 20.

[52] Refers to when the parties do not accept the decision of the Patent Re-examination Board of the State Intellectual Property Office (hereinafter the PRB) during the patent re-examination and invalidation procedure, he or she by law can bring a lawsuit to the People's Court.

People's Court has held various proceedings related to granting patents, in which inventiveness is widely involved.

Evidence other than the patent application may be used to prove the existence of inventiveness. In the *Welman Co.* case, the Supreme People's Court held that the technical contents disclosed in the patent specification when applying for the patent was the basis on which the patent administration department of the State Council had examined the application. It is also the foundation for the public to study, disseminate and utilize the patented technology. Therefore, technical schemes and technical effects that have not been disclosed in the patent specification by the applicant, in general, cannot be treated as the basis for evaluating whether the patent qualifies for statutory confirmation of patent rights. Otherwise, it will be inconsistent with the 'first-to-file' principle of the Patent Law, and thus deviate from the essential nature of 'disclosure in exchange for patent protection' principle.[53]

In the *Takeda Pharmaceutical* case, the Supreme People's Court reconfirmed that those technical schemes and technical effects that have not been disclosed in the patent specification, in general, cannot be used as the basis for evaluating whether the patent complies with the statutory confirmation of patent rights. Experimental data that was submitted after the date of application is not part of the contents written and disclosed by the original application documents, for the public has no access to such data. If it was not disclosed by the application, and thus it would be unfair to the public if the patent right was granted. In addition, the court added that when the applicant or patentee attempts to prove the inventiveness of his technical schemes compared with the existing technology by way of submitting comparative experimental data, the presumption for accepting such data must be that the data aims only to support the technical effect written clearly in the original application documents.[54]

3.1.4 The claim shall be based on the specifications
The degree to which intellectual property is protected must suit the level of innovation in a country. In the area of patent law, the claim shall be

---

[53] In this case, the petitioner is Beijing Double-Crane Pharmaceutical Co. Ltd. and the respondent is Xiangbei Wei'erman Pharmaceutical Co. Ltd. In the second instance trial, the appellee is the PRB. The Supreme People's Court (2011) xingtizi, no. 8.

[54] In this case, the petitioner is Takeda Pharmaceutical Co. Ltd. and the respondents are the PRB and Sichuan Haisike Pharmaceutical Ltd. & Chongqing Pharmaceutical Institute Ltd. The Supreme People's Court (2012) zhixingzi, no. 41.

fully supported by the specification, which is a practice that meets the relevant international standards. In the *Eli Lilly & Co.* case, the Supreme People's Court considered that the protection of the technical scheme in the claim shall be the scheme that can be generalized or summarized by the technicians in the field from the disclosed content of the technical specification. Furthermore, the technical scheme shall not exceed the scope disclosed by the specification. If the technicians in the related field have reasonable doubt that the generalization cannot resolve the technical issue of inventiveness and reach the same result of the claim, the claim shall be considered as receiving no support from its specification.[55]

Defects and mistakes are often unavoidable when drafting patent applications. Given the legislative purpose and the practice of China's Patent Law, the Supreme People's Court has stated that the legal effect of the patent right cannot be simply denied due to reasons such as poor drafting skills.[56] For instance, in the *Hong Liang* case, the Supreme People's Court held that the drafting errors in the claim do not necessarily mean the specification cannot support the claim; if the errors exist clearly in the claim, and the technicians in the field can obtain exclusively correct understanding of the scheme according to the specification and drawing, the court shall accept the modified technical scheme as the basis of protection, and then move to examine whether the claim is supported by the specification.[57]

3.1.5 Patent infringement concerning obviously unclear protection scope

Judicial protection of intellectual property rights depends on the validity and legitimacy of an issued patent. Under certain circumstances, a patent is unable to be protected due to fundamental lack of validity.[58] In the *Bo Wanqing* case, the Supreme People's Court held that defining the scope of patent protection is a prerequisite of deciding whether the alleged

---

[55]   In this case, the petitioner is Eli Lilly & Co. and the respondent is the PRB. The Supreme People's Court (2009) zhixingzi, no. 3.

[56]   The Opinions on the Reform and Innovation requires a full consideration of the objective limitations of patent drafting; within the scope of patent disclosure, the court shall try its best to grant patents to inventions so that the patent application can receive the patent right matching his contribution to the relevant technology; the purpose is to maximize the support of science and technology to economic and social development.

[57]   In this case, the petitioner is Hong Liang and the respondent is PRB, Song Zhanggen. The Supreme People's Court (2011) xingtizi, no. 13.

[58]   Kong Xiangjun, 'Protection of Innovation with Innovative Way', *People's Justice*, 2013, No. 9, p. 35.

infringement technology scheme constitutes infringement. If the court fails to determine the specific content of the technical terms in the claim and the scope of the patent right as per the patent specification and the common general knowledge in the relevant field, then a meaningful comparison between the alleged technical scheme and the patent cannot be reached. Hence, the alleged technology shall not be regarded as an infringement to the patent which does not have a clear scope of rights.[59]

3.1.6   Design patents

In recent years, the Supreme People's Court has heard a number of difficult trials on design patent disputes, which reflect several fundamental issues concerning the design patent law.

Regarding the assessment methods and standards of similarity, the Supreme People's Court points out in *Honda Co. v. the PRB* (2010) that the examination of the degree to which the design is similar to other previous existing designs should be based on the cognitive capacities of ordinary consumers of the product incorporating the design. The consumers need to observe the existing design and the alleged design as a whole, and then determine whether the visual effect is significantly affected by the difference between the two designs.[60] In the *Midea Co.* case (2011), the Supreme People's Court further held: 'to view as a whole and to judge comprehensively' means that ordinary consumers should determine whether there are clear visual differences between the two designs as a whole, not as parts of the designs. The ordinary consumers should pay attention to both similarities and differences between the two designs, and consider the overall effect and extent of similarities and differences to the entirety of the visual effect.[61]

As for the design space of a design patent,[62] the Supreme People's Court held in the *Jinfei Co.* case (2010) that the concept of design space

---

[59]   In this case, the petitioner is Bo Wanqing and the respondent is Chengdu Goods Marketing Service Center & Shanghai Tianxiang Industrial Co. Ltd. The Supreme People's Court (2012) minshenzi, no. 1544.

[60]   *Honda Co. v. the Patent Review Board*, the Supreme People's Court (2010) xintizi, no. 3.

[61]   In this case, the petitioner is Zhuhai Gree Electric Co. Ltd. and the respondent is Guangdong Midea Electric Co. Ltd., and the second appeal to the PRB. The Supreme People's Court (2011) xingtizi, no. 1.

[62]   China's Patent Law does not specify the design space of the appearance of design patent. The design space is a discretionary factor introduced in recent years by the People's Court in China.

has a significant meaning to the ordinary consumers' knowledge and cognitive ability on the understanding and recognition of the related design products. When determining the identical nature and similarity of two designs, it is necessary to consider the design space or, in other words, the freedom of designing creativity, for accurately determining the ordinary consumers' knowledge and cognitive ability of the designs. The size of the design space is a relative concept, which varies from time to time. In the patent invalidation procedures, the consideration of design space of a particular design is subject to the state of the patent at the date of application.[63] As we know, the date of patent application is the crucial benchmark for deciding novelty, inventiveness and thus the size of the design space in a given case.

With regard to assessing the functional features of a design, the Supreme People's Court ruled in the *Zhang Dijun* case (2012) that functional design features refer to those design features that, in the opinion of ordinary consumers, are defined by their functions, rather than aesthetic features. The standard of determination of functional design features is, again, based on an objective test, namely, it does not consider whether the function is the only possible choice for functionality, but whether to the ordinary consumers the functional design's function is determined only by the specific function, which does not need to consider the aesthetic aspects of the design.[64] Functional design features usually do not have a significant impact on the overall visual effect and Chinese IP law practice is cautious of giving unreasonable monopoly to functional designs.

To summarize, as we can see from the Supreme People's Court's rulings in various typical cases in patent, there is a prudential approach to patent lawsuits, which meets the development stage of China and is similar to those of many developed countries.

3.2 Typical Copyright and Trademark Cases

With regard to the liability of the search engine service providers, the Supreme People's Court pointed out in the *Baidu* case (2009) that for the ISPs that provide services such as locating information, since they do not

---

[63]   In this case, the petitioner is the PRB, Zhejiang Jinfei Machinery Group Co. Ltd, and the respondent is Zhejiang Wanfeng Motorcycle Wheel Co. Ltd. The Supreme People's Court (2010) xingtizi, no. 5.

[64]   In this case, the petitioner is the PRB and the respondent is Zhang Dijun, and the third party is Cixi Xinlong Electronics Co. Ltd. (hereinafter Xinlong company). The Supreme People's Court (2012) xingtizi, no. 14.

directly provide content, they should be differentiated from the internet content providers (ICPs). The ISPs' liability only occurs when they are at fault for others' infringing behaviour, which occurred during the use of their web services. When determining the standards of fault, the court should consider the nature of the internet and the infringed work, the service provided and its role, and the development stage of the relevant IT technologies. Such standards are designed to prevent the ISPs from bearing an excessive level of duty of care. It is unreasonable to hold the ISPs liable simply because there is infringing content found from the search results on their websites.[65]

With regard to the copyright protection of computer character fonts, the Supreme People's Court pointed out in the *Founder Co.* case (2010) that the font file in the dispute is to support the display and output of the related fonts. Its content consists of construction instructions for font outlines and their related data, as well as the codes of dynamic adjusting data instructions of the fonts. The font is run by specific software, and should be regarded a type of computer software that is designed to obtain relevant font displays in the output devices of computers and other electronic devices. Thus, it is covered by Article 3, item 1 of Regulations for the Protection of Computer Software of China, which defines a computer program as a copyrighted work. According to the typeface (font) production process of the fonts in dispute, the printed font files, computer encrypted font files and the fonts produced by computer software are different objects. In addition, the unique structure of Chinese characters and their manifestations are subjected to certain restrictions; whether a font produced by computer software contains originality under China's Copyright Law needs to be determined by specific analyses of the relevant facts.[66]

When examining the similarity of two trademarks, the court shall consider such factors as the defendant's intention, the history of the use of the mark and the mark's present conditions. For this issue, the Supreme People's Court ruled in *Lacoste Co. v. Crocodile (Singapore) International Pty Ltd.* (2009) that the term similarity is assessed in the

---

[65]   In this case, the appellant is Zhejiang Agel Ecommerce Co. Ltd., and the defendants are Beijing Baidu Netcom Science and Technology Co. Ltd. & Baidu Online Network Technology (Beijing) Co. Ltd. The Supreme People's Court (2009) minsanzhongzi, no. 2.

[66]   Beijing Founder Electronics Co. Ltd. v. Blizzard Entertainment Co. Ltd., Shanghai Ninth City Information Technology Co. Ltd., The Ninth City Inter-active Information Technology (Shanghai) Co. Ltd. & Beijing Love Books Co. Ltd. The Supreme People's Court (2010) minsanzhongzi, no. 6.

context of confusing similarity that is sufficient to cause confusion in the market. Because each trademark dispute can be complex and difficult, apart from considering the degree of similarities of the trademarks per se, the court may also, considering the specific circumstances of each case, look at other relevant factors to decide whether the trademarks in the dispute are confused by similarities. For instance, if the two trademarks in dispute demonstrate similarities while other factors do not suggest the existence of market confusion, then trademark infringement cannot be established. In particular, the trademarks of both parties have their own separate and unique development trajectories and histories in the related market, which have resulted in the situation of independent use and coexistence. In this case, in order to determine whether the alleged person infringes the exclusive right of the registered trademark by similarity, the court will have to consider their development trajectories and histories, and the reality of independent use and coexistence. It is thus not reasonable to determine this case on the exclusive basis of trademark similarities. Rather, the court shall also take into account the intent of Crocodile (Singapore) International, other factors such as the history and the coexistence of both marks, and the related market and its conditions.[67]

It is not uncommon that in the vast Chinese market, there are Chinese enterprise names identical or similar to registered trademarks of other companies. The Supreme People's Court held in the *Wangjiang Co.* case (2010) that registered trademarks and enterprise names are both legal rights, belonging to different categories protected by the relevant laws. The people's courts are required to distinguish between different situations when deciding disputes between a registered trademark and an enterprise name, and make judgment in accordance with the principle of honesty and credibility, fair competition and prior right. For instance, if a registered enterprise name has no legitimacy (such as being a result of illegitimate registration of a relatively known trademark into the enterprise name) and sufficiently causes confusion, it may be regulated under anti-unfair competition practices, even if the name is being used properly. If the enterprise uses the name improperly in a way that the name is identical or similar to another party's registered trademark and is displayed prominently on goods identical or similar to those of that trademark, such conduct can be regarded as constituting infringement of

---

[67] *Lacoste (France) Co. Ltd. v. Crocodile (Singapore) International Pty Ltd.*, Shanghai East Crocodile Garment Co., Ltd Beijing Branch. The Supreme People's Court (2010) minsanzhongzi, no. 3.

the trademark right, if the name easily causes confusion among the consumers. If the use and registration of the enterprise name is legal, but the prominent use of the name infringes the exclusive right of a registered trademark, the court shall request the party to use the name properly. If stopping the prominent use can cease the infringement, the court shall not order the party to stop using or change the enterprise name.[68]

Some companies use descriptive foreign words, which are not used in the Chinese language, as their trademarks in China. The Supreme People's Court held in the *BEST BUY* case (2011) that when deciding a case of the confirmation of registered trademark rights, the court shall determine whether the trademark has distinctiveness as a whole based on the public recognition of the goods carrying the trademark. If the descriptive elements contained in the trademark do not influence the trademark being distinctive as a whole, and the relevant customers are able to identify the origin of goods, the court shall recognize the distinctiveness of the trademark. In the present case, the trademark comprises the English word 'BEST', 'BUY' and a yellow box. Although the worlds 'BEST' and 'BUY' are descriptive to the service that the mark is designated, the trademark overall has distinctiveness with its graphics and bright colours, and can easily be identified. At the same time, the trademark is already internationally well known and has acquired a certain level of reputation through its use in China. Therefore, the Chinese general public can identify the origin of the service of the trademark.[69]

CONCLUSION

As this chapter has demonstrated, in recent years the judicial protection of intellectual property in China has made significant progress through Chinese courts' steady efforts in the area. China's IP tribunals now play an active and leading role in China's construction of innovation-based economy. This is achieved by a variety of approaches. The judicial system in China is not closed to itself.

---

[68]   In this case, the petitioner is Wangjiang dumplings (Dalian) Co. Ltd., and the respondent Li Huiting (infringement of the exclusive right to use a registered trademark dispute). The Supreme People's Court (2010) mintizi, no. 15.

[69]   In this case, the petitioner is Best Buy Enterprise Service Co. Ltd, and the respondent is Adjudication Board. The Supreme People's Court (2011) hangtizi, no. 9.

One of the essential conclusions of this chapter is that the efforts, progress and decisions of the Supreme People's Court and its IP Tribunal clearly reflect the judicial understanding of the relationships between innovation, the protection of intellectual fruits and the public interest. This is reflected in many judicial interpretations issued by the Supreme People's Court, the relevant judicial polices and many typical cases. It is expected that with the enforcement of the innovation-driven development strategy proposed by the 18th National Congress of the Communist Party of China, the judicial protection of intellectual property in China will have a greater role in promoting China's innovation activities, protecting innovative achievements, and providing an innovative environment of fair and equal legal protection.

It should be noted that although there is an administrative law enforcement model available within China's intellectual property system, the judicial protection of intellectual property is still the most important implementation approach in China. With the influence of China gradually extending in the world and the strengthening of international protection of intellectual property, the Chinese judicial protection of intellectual property has attracted more and more attention, both from foreign companies in China and Chinese domestic enterprises.

Finally, it is important for our foreign readers to know that although China's IP protection is not perfect, we care very much about its continuous development and ongoing reflections. We apply rational, forward-looking principles in guiding our progress. As a famous Chinese poet and statesman Wang Anshi (1021–1086) wrote in the year 1050, 'No flowing clouds may block my eyes'. We believe that we have the wisdom and steadfastness to achieve further. There should be no unrealistic dreams in the world; nor should there be realities without dreams. We understand that there are strong demands of intellectual property protection in both foreign and Chinese communities and there are always challenges of new technologies and various other complexities to the dimensions of intellectual property protection. Therefore, we will not stop here.

6. The cluster effect in China: Real or imagined?

Michael Keane

INTRODUCTION

Policy makers, urban planners and economic geographers readily acknowledge the potential value of industrial clustering. Clusters attract policy makers' interest because it is widely held that they are a way of connecting agglomeration to innovation and human capital to investment. Urban planners view clustering as a way of enticing creative human capital, the so-called 'creative class',[1] that is, creative people are pre-disposed to live where there is a range of cultural infrastructure and amenities. Economists and geographers have contrived to promote clustering as a solution to stalled regional development.[2]

In the People's Republic of China, over the past decade the cluster has become the default setting of the cultural and creative industries, the latter a composite term applied to the quantifiable outputs of artists, designers and media workers as well as related service sectors such as tourism, advertising and management.[3] The thinking behind many cluster

---

[1]   In 2002 Richard Florida coined this term, noting a 'super creative core', a composite of scientists, engineers, academics, poets, actors, novelists, entertainers, artists, architects and designers, 'cultural worthies', think-tank researchers, analysts and opinion formers. See Richard Florida, *The Rise of the Creative Class,* New York: Basic Books, 2002.

[2]   Michael Porter, 'Clusters and the New Economics of Competition', *Harvard Business Review* Nov–Dec 1998, pp. 77–90; Michael Porter, 'Competitive Advantage, Agglomeration Economies and Regional Policy', *International Regional Science Review* 19(1), 1996, pp. 85–94; for a critical view see R. Martin, and P. Sunley, 'Deconstructing Clusters: Chaotic Concept or Policy Panacea?', *Journal of Economic Geography*, 3(1), 2002, pp. 5–35.

[3]   The national government mandates the use of term cultural industries in policy documents whereas city and regional governments opt for the creative industries or the composite term 'cultural creative industries'. The use of the

projects is to 'pick winners'. In this sense the rapid expansion in the number of cultural and creative clusters in China over the past decade is not so very different from the early 1990s, a period that saw an outbreak of innovation parks, most of which inevitably failed to deliver measurable innovation and ultimately served as revenue-generating sources for district governments via real estate speculation.[4]

Since the early years of the first decade of the new millennium the cluster model has been pressed into the service of cultural development. Prior to the 1990s culture was primarily about national security and the glorious achievements of Chinese civilization. With China's entry into the World Trade Organization (WTO) in December 2001 culture was rapidly elevated to the status of an 'industry' (*chanye*). Cultural clusters soon became the default setting for economic development; meanwhile the 'culturalisation of the economy' escalated as more and more everyday commodities were listed as exhibiting cultural attributes.[5] While the definition of a cultural cluster is somewhat elastic, encompassing media bases, districts, precincts, corridors, cultural quarters, and even theme parks, there is little doubt that the logic of agglomeration and the potential of 'attracting talent' has appeal to central and local governments looking for strategies to fast track development. But do such clusters, however defined, connect agglomeration to innovation? More specifically, do workers in such cultural projects feel inclined to share ideas?

In this chapter, I look at the relationship between clustering in China's cultural industries.[6] I begin with the proposition that clusters provide enabling conditions for the emergence of a 'strong cultural China', a recent theme to emerge within Chinese national cultural policy. The

term cultural by the central government is deliberate to distance China's development path from Western nations. *See* Michael Keane, *Creative Industries in China: Art, Design, Media*, London: Polity, 2013.

[4]   For a discussion of this *see* Jici Wang, 'Industrial Clusters in China: The Low Road Versus the High Road in Cluster Development', in A. Scott, and G. Garofoli (eds), *Development on the Ground: Clusters, Networks and Regions in Emerging Economies*, London: Routledge, 2007, pp. 145–64.

[5]   Scott Lash and John Urry, *Economies of Signs and Space*, London: Sage Publications, 1993. The term 'culturalisation of the economy' refers to how cultural and creative capabilities are mainstreamed in contemporary work practices. In China the incorporation of furniture manufacturing, theme parks, hairdressing and restaurants into cultural industry reports shows how scholars expediently expand while at the same time collapsing economic categories. For a discussion of this trend globally *see* George Yudice, *The Expediency of Culture*, Durham: Duke University Press, 2003.

[6]   Sometimes cultural industries are referred to as the creative industries.

second section provides background on the genesis of cultural industries clusters in China and their rapid uptake, both nationally and regionally. I then turn to examine processes by which projects are conceived, incubated and come to fruition. Following this, I examine the relationship between clustering and innovation by drawing on findings from cluster projects across a range of industry sub-sectors. My aim is to shed light on the efficacy of clusters in generating co-learning. I ask the question: do cultural and creative industries clusters promote trust and stimulate inter-firm collaboration? I conclude with a discussion of China's 'cultural innovation timeline' and the problematic role of cultural and creative industries clusters in making China a strong cultural nation.

1. A STRONGER CULTURAL CHINA

In 2011, then President Hu Jintao made a significant admission of China's cultural weakness when he said: 'The overall strength of China's culture and its international influence is not commensurate with China's international status. The international culture of the West is strong while we are weak.'[7] These words were widely reported, reverberating in the Ministry of Culture (MoC) as a call to action. Hu's anointed successor, Xi Jinping, was quick to take up the challenge, while not reconciling from his well-known admiration of Hollywood's creative achievements. Within months of assuming control Xi Jinping coined the 'Chinese Dream' (*Zhongguo meng*), setting the wheels of think tanks moving to identify what the dream might actually entail. Within the MoC a number of terms were put forward including 'soft power' (*ruan shili*) 'revitalization' (*zhen xing*) and 'strong cultural nation' (*wenhua qiang guojia*). Did Chinese soft power mean a head-to-head engagement with Hollywood, more cultural troupes going abroad, more investment in tourism, or a greater focus on developing creative talent? Did revitalization entail traditional culture or contemporary popular culture? And what would make China's culture strong?

Of these the strong cultural nation discourse is most embedded within the Chinese Dream. It offers a patriotic slogan for public dissemination, more palatable to the public than Hu Jintao's articulation of a 'strong

---

[7] Hu Jintao, 'Developing a Strong Socialist Culture in China'. See text of Hu Jintao's report at the 18th Party Congress, available at <http://news.xinhuanet.com/english/special/18cpcnc/2012-11/17/c_131981259_7.htm>, Beijing: The Communist Party of China. <http://www.china.org.cn/english/congress/229611.htm> Accessed 30 April 2013.

socialist culture' with its Marxist-Leninist legacy of heroic struggles and self-sacrificing role models. But how could Chinese culture revitalize itself? Many Chinese dreamers in the Politburo noted the success of Japanese and Korean culture in China. East Asian pop culture was washing over China; it was creative, modern and alluring. Chinese culture needed to 'go out' to the regions and especially to the world just as its business enterprises were doing. In March 2011 the Minister of Culture, Cai Wu, announced that cultural industries would become 'pillar industries' (*zhizhu chanye*),[8] contributing 5 per cent of GDP by 2016 (the estimated value in 2010 was 2.78 per cent[9]).

Aspirations of becoming a 'stronger' cultural nation need to be viewed in the broader context of the global creative economy. The creative economy is a terminology widely used within national and regional policy circles. This globalizing economy is characterized by a developmental agenda encompassing a broad spectrum of goods and services. According to the United Nations Conference on Trade and Development (UNCTAD) the creative economy promises gains of trade in cultural products and services especially for developing countries.[10] This new economy is often characterized as a green economy, a reassuring image in China where city skies have turned brown due to industrial development. Accordingly, scholars and consultants promote creative indexes[11] which are put into service to rank nations, regions and cities. Districts contend for the kudos of being creative, tolerant, cultural, entrepreneurial and open to investment. Behind much of this frenetic competition lies culture-led urban development. Internationally such projects include neighbourhood regeneration, the provision of public cultural services, the construction of hubs for cultural, social and economic development, and attractions for tourists.[12]

---

[8] Xinhua 'China's cultural industry predicted to become a pillar of the economy by 2016: Speech by minister, 11 March 2011, <http://news.xinhuanet.com/english2010/indepth/2011-10/22/c_131206627.htm>. Accessed 29 April 2013.

[9] Michael Keane, *Creative Industries in China*, London: Polity, 2011.

[10] United Nations Conference on Trade and Development (UNCTAD), *The Global Creative Economy Report 2010*, Geneva: UNCTAD, 2010.

[11] Peng Yi, *Report on Development Index of Cultural Industries in Chinese Provinces*, Autonomous Regions and Municipalities (Zhongguo shengshi wenhua chanye fazhan zhishu baogao), Beijing: Zhongguo Renmin Daxue Chubanshe, 2012.

[12] *See* John Montgomery, 'Cultural Quarters as Mechanism for Urban Regeneration. Part 1 Conceptualising Cultural Quarters', *Planning Practice and Research* 18(4), 2003, pp. 293–306; Graeme Evans, 'Creative Cities, Creative Spaces and Urban Policy', *Urban Studies* 46(5), 2009, pp. 1003–40; Graeme

In China the cluster has become the default for urban development. The cluster effect exerts great sway over policy makers in China. Even before Xi Jinping enunciated his dream, national cultural policy makers had endorsed the importance of clusters. In the 17th National Congress Report of 2007, Hu Jintao had spoken of the twinning of cultural creativity and soft power, noting in particular the importance of 'accelerating the construction of cultural industry bases and regional cultural industry clusters, cultivating key cultural industry enterprises and strategic investors, enriching the market and achieving international competitiveness'.[13]

There is no doubt that the cluster model offers advantages. In many countries and regions companies take advantage of spatial co-location within clusters to exploit external economies. Michael Storper describes these external economies as 'complex outcomes of interaction between scale, specialization, and flexibility in the context of proximity'.[14] External economies can accrue in several ways. The pooling of human capital is one of the principal factors. Successful clusters provide a variety of employment and opportunities for career development; for instance, Hollywood attracts technical workers (programmers, animators and film crews), core intellectual property creators (artists, writers, designers) and cultural intermediaries (entrepreneurs, entertainment industry lawyers, business facilitation services).

Few clusters have the scale and reputational effect of Hollywood. Ideally, a cluster will attract workers with specific and specialized skills, lowering the human capital search costs of firms. The presence of similar firms produces incentives for other business to establish specialist

Evans, *Cultural Planning: an Urban Renaissance?*, London: Routledge, 2001; Simon Roodhouse, *Cultural Quarters: Principles and Practice*, Chicago: University of Chicago Press, 2006; Roger Sugden, Ping Wei and James Wilson, 'Clusters, Governance and the Development of Local Economies: A Framework for Case Studies', in Christos Pitelis, Roger Sugden, James R. Wilson (eds), *Clusters and Globalisation: the Development of Urban and Regional Economies*, Cheltenham: Edward Elgar, 2006, pp. 82–95; Fiorenza Belussi and Silvia Sedita, 'Industrial Districts as Open Learning Systems: Combining Emergent and Deliberate Knowledge Systems', *Regional Studies*, 2010, pp. 1–20; Jason Potts, *Creative Industries and Economic Evolution*, Cheltenham: Edward Elgar, 2011.

[13] The 17th National CCP Congress Report, cited in Xiang Yong, '2011–2015: Principles of National Cultural Strategy and Cultural Industries Development in China', *International Journal of Cultural and Creative Industries* 1:1, 2013, pp. 75–6.

[14] Michael Storper, *The Regional world: Territorial Development in a Global economy*, NY: Guilford, 1997, p. 27.

services to these enterprises,[15] complementing the value chain of production and in many cases facilitating marketing and distribution. In turn this enables enterprises to concentrate on core capabilities, which improves average productivity and the competitive advantage of all enterprises within the cluster. From an economy of scale perspective, infrastructure, utilities, transport and other business requirements can be more efficiently supplied to a cluster, lowering average costs and reinforcing global competitiveness.[16]

In open economies clusters form naturally: successful ones drive innovation through heightened competition and the ability of enterprises and actors to observe and learn from each other. Organic 'inter-actor networks' are a much-sought-after 'cluster effect'.[17] In clusters with mature technology this effect may be less important but in industries characterized by the never-ending search for novelty – the creative industries – it is likely to be the rationale of the cluster.[18] Hollywood is a classic example of strong inter-actor networks. However while replicating the success of Hollywood is a branding strategy of a number of would-be global film production centres in China such as Zhejiang's Hengdian World Studios, sometimes called Chinawood, and Chinese billionaire Wang Jianlin's ambitious 'dream' known as the Qingdao Oriental Movie Metropolis,[19] these projects currently rely on government intervention and largesse.

2. WHAT IS A CULTURAL CLUSTER IN CHINA?

China's experience with cultural and creative clusters can be best understood within the framework of urban development. Gentrification impacts heavily on the transformation of China's cities. The cultural industries discourse with its extensive articulation in national and

---

[15] I use the term 'enterprises' rather than firms. In China, *qiye* (enterprise) is the preferred description of cultural and creative business activity.

[16] For discussion of how cultural and creative clusters attract talent, *see* Hans Mommaas, 'Cultural Clusters and the Post-industrial City: Towards the Re-mapping of Urban Cultural Policy', *Urban Studies* 41, 2004, pp. 507–32.

[17] Jane Zheng and Roger Chan, 'A Property-led Approach to Cluster Development: "Creative Industry Clusters" and Creative Industry Networks in Shanghai', *Town Planning Review* 84(5), 2013, pp. 604–32.

[18] Jason Potts, *Creative Industries and Economic Evolution*, Cheltenham: Edward Elgar, 2011.

[19] <http://www.theverge.com/2013/9/23/4763386/billionaire-wang-jianlin-hollywood-china-qingdao>.

regional Five Year Plans provides incentives for investment in projects. Many projects, however, are more appropriately described as 'property-led clusters'[20] and function as a mechanism for transforming land use. With urbanization absorbing people from rural regions, the transformation of land use regulations has assumed great commercial significance – from agricultural to industrial and from industrial to commercial. Land use regulation is often motivated by developers who are key players in 'growth coalitions'. From a broad perspective a growth coalition includes national economic policy bureaus and relevant policy advisory committees, national and international business interests and communities. More locally, growth coalitions comprise representatives of district governments who engage with developers, financiers and entrepreneurs.[21]

In previous work I have argued that the development of clusters has advanced through several distinct, although overlapping stages. The first stage is epitomized by Shanghai's initial wave of clusters in the early 2000s, workspaces dedicated to industrial design, antiques, jewellery, animation, painting and sculpture. Disused industrial space provided opportunities for artisans and resources for people with similar skills. The logic of specialization combined with agglomeration is seen in 'industrial cities' in Zhejiang which are given over to mass production of cheap artefacts. These large-scale city and township projects with extensive horizontal and vertical linkages are quite different from cultural clusters, the latter producing products and services that are subject to the vagaries of consumer trends and tastes. The weakness of specialist clusters over time with respect to innovation is the lack of integration into and complementarity with related industries; that is not to deny, however, that enterprises will not move forward by observing one another's business practices. However, the desire to experiment is often curtailed by the fact that others *are* observing. The lack of a strong sense of intellectual property in effect reduces people's desire to experiment and share.

A second expression of the cluster is a 'related variety' model. The key difference from the specialist cluster is a mix of sectors: often including animation, design, media consulting, media production, fashion, painting, photography and sculpture. On the surface the related variety model offers better opportunities for inter-actor networks, which ideally work to

---

[20]   Zheng and Chan, 'A Property-led approach to Cluster Development'.
[21]   For an extended discussion, *see* Michael Keane, *China's New Creative Clusters: Governance, Human Capital and Investment,* London: Routledge, 2011.

engender trust, collaboration and knowledge exchange.[22] Qingdao's Creative 100 represents an example of this model, a mix of multimedia, software, animation and art. Further north in Dalian, the Xinghai Creative Island advertises itself as a new creative space: the cluster enterprises produce oil painting, graphic design, media content, animation, porcelain and reproductions of traditional artefacts from the Shang dynasty. In Shanghai, the 1933 Old Mill Factory is a reconverted abattoir that showcases design, fashion and new media. The idea of cultural regeneration here is palpable, from feeding the masses to satisfying their consumer demands for contemporary brands.

Other related variety examples in Shanghai are No. 8 Bridge, the Media Culture Park, and the Modern Industry Mansion Park. Hangzhou is represented in this format by Loft 49 and the A8 Art Commune, while nearby Nanjing has Nanjing 1912 and the Creative East No. 8 District. In South China, Shenzhen has the successful OCT Loft and the F518 Creative Fashion Park, while south-east of Beijing the city of Tianjin has established the No. 6 Warehouse, the Hualun Creative Factory and the Lingao Creative Industries Park. In central Chongqing, the Tank Loft is a reconverted munitions factory once used by Chiang Kai-shek (Jiang Jieshi). In Guangdong Province, the Foshan Creative Industries Park is a large-scale development that combines elements of various media and folk cultural production, one site given over to porcelain and the other to a mix of related design, branding and software businesses. In effect, there are now countless examples of such clusters, many officially recognized, others appearing sporadically in demolished factory sites.

Meanwhile, an earlier phase of clustering projects had witnessed the genesis of art zones and cultural districts, developments combining strong tourist pull with consumer services. Zones and districts emerged organically in China's large coastal cities, often on the edges of central business districts, providing milieus in which artists and media workers could sense greater autonomy even if this fell short of Western-style freedom of expression. In Beijing, the most well-known art space is 798 Art Zone, the reconverted East German switching factory in Dashanzi. Not far away is Caochangdi, which has absorbed spillovers from 798, which many feel is overtly commercialized. Beijing's Nanluo guxiang hutong precinct in central Dongcheng district is an example of an innovative milieu closer to the centre. Situated in the proximity of art

---

[22] *See* Zheng and Chan, 'A Property-led Approach to Cluster Development', p. 606.

colleges, galleries and media schools, and with the locale having historical legacies such as the Confucius temple and the house of the famous
writer Lao She, Nanluo guxiang attracts designers, writers and artists,
and crafts persons, generating an informal economy of coffee, pasta and
local beer.[23]

Another stage is the formation of media content 'bases', often within
existing industrial zones, notably in the field of animation, mostly
concentrating on outsourcing. As part of the content development strategy of the State Administration of Press, Publications, Radio, Film and
TV (SAPPRFT), animation and video games are key targets. The
conferral of national base status is much sought after. Since 2005 China
has established more than 30 accredited 'national animation bases'; some
are accredited by the SAPPRFT and others by the MoC. The main
centres, often situated within an existing industrial area, are in Shanghai,
Beijing, Hangzhou, Suzhou, Shenzhen, Dalian, Suzhou, Changzhou and
Wuxi. Local governments offer a range of industry sweeteners, such as
preferential policies enabling start-up firms to enjoy tax holidays and to
obtain housing and educational services for employees and their children,
as well as financial incentives if content is successful. In the main, this
entails content being purchased by China Central Television (CCTV).

On a larger industrial scale stand-alone cinema and television production centres have appeared, servicing the domestic audio-visual market,
engaging in co-productions, or outsourcing production from Taiwan,
Korea and the United States. To compensate for the cyclical nature of
audio-visual production, some of these centres offer a theme park
function that cashes in on the success of cinematic and TV drama output.
In the north of Beijing, the Huairou Film production centre has established itself in recent years in competition with more established film
studios. The largest film base is Hengdian World Studios in Zhejiang
Province where tourists can see re-enactment of movies and be taken on
a tour of the set of *Hero* (Zhang Yimou) and *The Emperor and the
Assassin* (Chen Kaige). The land-locked nature of Hengdian puts it at a
disadvantage to the large urban centres of Shanghai and Beijing. To
offset this, Hengdian absorbs a great deal of low-cost television drama
production, particularly dynastical costume dramas. The most recent
addition to this model is the Qingdao Oriental Movie Metropolis,
financed by a Chinese billionaire able to entice foreign studios and

---

[23]   For a discussion, *see* Wang Jici, Zhang Chun, Wang Ching-Ning and Chen
Ping, 'Local Milieu in Developing China's Cultural and Creative Industry: the
Case of Nanluoguxiang in Beijing', *International Journal of Asian Business and
Information Management* 1(1), 2010, pp. 10–22.

celebrities. In Shanghai the construction of Shanghai Oriental Dream-works on the West Bund promises to attract investment and creative skills to the Xuhui District.[24]

Finally, yet another model is the incubator model, often with a purported emphasis on R&D, and often with the declared intention of making science parks more 'creative'. The proximity of many science and technology parks – also called innovation parks – to prestigious universities and development zones reflects a national desire to incubate something above and beyond standardized products. Proclaimed 'creative incubators' are now to be found in Chongqing (the Ideas Industry Centre), Tianjin (the Heping District Creative Animation Park; the Taida Science and Technology Park), Dalian (the Creative Incubator Garden), Hangzhou (The Hangzhou Innovation and Creative Industry New Base), Beijing's Zhongguancun Creative Industries Pioneer Base and Shanghai's Zhangjiang Hi-tech Zone in Pudong, and the KIC (Knowledge Innovation Community) in Yangpu District.

3. PROCESSES AND PLAYERS

Cultural cluster projects emerge sporadically contingent on investment opportunities and local government assistance. The principal rationale behind cluster projects is business development: in policy reform language this is usually referred to within 'cultural development' (*wenhua jianshe*). Whereas cultural industries reform is ultimately conducted by Party officials, aided by scholars in government affiliated thinks tanks such as the Chinese Academy of Social Sciences (CASS), much thinking about reform happens in epistemic communities. Government-sponsored think tanks take advantage of a range of professionals already engaged in creative endeavours, many of whom have experience of overseas projects or linkages to well-known foreign scholar-consultants.[25] Developers, entrepreneurs, investors, artist-entrepreneurs, officials, intellectuals and residents offer templates, some borrowed from afar, others local versions of existing projects elsewhere in China. Many epistemic communities are embedded within growth coalitions that have emerged to exploit the

[24] Shanghai Oriental Dreamworks is a joint venture with the US company Dreamworks and local Chinese media companies including Shanghai Media Group. Geographically it represents a small part of a designated mega cultural project called the West Bank in Xuhui District, covering a total of 70 hectares.
[25] See Xufeng Zhu, *The Rise of Think Tanks in China*, London: Routledge, 2013.

interest in 'creative estate', a felicitous term for real estate speculation. Academics with credentials in the cultural or creative industries make a good side income from consulting on local projects. Foreign experts, sometimes with little or no expertise, are co-opted into this process as well as into the process of influencing government thinking. In China, it often suffices to present a foreign expert who will support the proposal.

Local government is the key player in the development of most major urban cultural projects. According to McGee et al local governments function 'not only as the chief decision-maker but also the largest investor directly responsible for investment, development and operation of key industrial, transport and urban projects'.[26] Local governments compete to position their locality to capture the benefits of development. This is where scholars and consultants play a role, offering tender plans for consideration, plans that synthesize elements of creative class attraction with bottom-line real estate development. McGee et al note four ways to attract investment for projects in China: state budgetary allocation, foreign investment, bank loans and local fund raising. With devolution of power to provinces and municipalities over the past decade, the main sources of capital for projects is local fundraising and bank loans; this may entail strategies to set up 'seemingly independent' companies or institutions aligned with government that can receive bank loans.[27]

Local governments learn from each other very quickly. When a successful model appears it is soon copied although many unsuccessful projects are also replicated in the rush for investment and public subsidies. In practice clustering has become a modality of urban expansion. Having connections with high-level government departments adds a seal of approval that can drive up real estate value. An example is the Qujiang district of Xi'an, a large city in north-west China famous as the Imperial capital of the First Emperor, Qinshi Huangdi. Situated outside the city centre, Qujiang was a decaying district. Although it had a long history there were few remaining historical sites. With land prices low, the Qujiang New District government saw an opportunity; it rezoned land and designated a large area as a cultural cluster. In August 2007 the Xi'an Qujiang New District was awarded the title, National Cultural Industry Model Park by the National Ministry of Culture. Cultural facilities were built in the middle of the district and artists were invited to set up lofts

---

[26] T. G. McGee, C. S. Lin, A. M. Marton, Y. L. Wang, and Jiaping Wu, *China's Urban Space: Development under Market Socialism*, London: Routledge, 2007, p. 114.
[27] *Ibid.*, p. 19.

and studios. The development was then publicized as Xi'an's exemplary creative cluster. When the land price doubled the government sold the real estate.

An example of urban expansion founded on clustering is Shenzhen's north-western Longhua New District. The district was officially founded in 2011. In November 2013 the district government was the principal sponsor of an international conference. The rationale was to focus attention on the development of Longhua New District, a composite of eco-tourism, art, fashion, auto industry, electronic information enterprises, and low carbon (clean energy) demonstration bases. The fledgling district was already home to 15 Foxconn Technology Group factories. Local government saw this hi-tech venture, albeit a low-wage processing centre for Foxconn, as a springboard to develop a 'strategic emerging industries' profile, including cultural creative industries. Among the latter are the Guanlan Landscape and Idyll Tourism Cultural Park, which claims the China (Guanlan) Landscape Painting Industry Base, which is home to artists. Unlike the Dafen Oil Painting Village in the north-east of Shenzhen where thousands of copy artists ply their trade, this 'base' trades off its landscape – and its 'authentic' landscape painting. Another example of a creative estate cluster is Qipanshan district in Shenyang. Like Longhua New District, the Qipanshan 'cultural creative industries model district' is a new district in which government increased land values by building and branding cultural infrastructure. While investors have made profits by selling villas, few of the cultural projects in the district have been successful.

New urbanism strategies are common in many fringe clusters. Affluent Chinese with apartments in inner city locations are keen to acquire a country 'retreat' in less crowded, more open areas. Local governments oblige by planting trees and building new roads. However, for many of the locals the conversion of their land to a cluster means that they have no clear means of subsistence; they have to learn new skills. Alternatively they might provide low-cost services to the new creative classes or move somewhere else. With the resettlement of artists and white collar workers, the land values rise and the tax benefits to the local district bureau (*dishuiju*) increase. Because local tax revenue derives from registration of businesses, the cluster management prefers to seek out small local companies rather than businesses registered in other jurisdictions. This localism policy, however, inevitably constrains the injection of new life and cross-province linkages.

The strategy employed by local governments is captured in the apt phrase 'attracting business and investment' (*zhaoshang yinzi*). Governments have resources and wherewithal to provide land and infrastructural support below cost; they can provide special subsidies and tax privileges and they can circumvent formal rules and regulations on labour use and environmental protection.[28] While proposals are generally initiated by local governments, land transactions require approval by central or municipal governments. At the end of the day local government invests in upgrading the infrastructure and then makes it available for users. Philip Huang contends that these practices taken together represent an 'informal economy'. There is generally a lack of transparency and few people are privy to the scale of transactions.[29] Certainly there is a stark contrast with the processes at play in Mainland China compared with high-profile projects such as the West Kowloon Cultural District in Hong Kong SAR which has engaged heavily with stakeholders and civil society.[30] Such public engagement practices are deemed superfluous in China because local government takes ultimate responsibility for success or failure and makes the running by reducing obstacles (red tape) to development. Furthermore, as mentioned above local governments are willing to absorb losses to attract investment and profits down the line. Huang notes: 'most important are the chain reactions to follow: services and smaller businesses that will emerge to support the new enterprises and generate new sales and income tax revenues (*yingyeshui* and *suodeshui*), which go 100 percent to local government'.[31]

The blueprint for this cluster-led cultural development is set by the national government though its support for national champions, now a key element of the Chinese Dream. However, whereas national policy is inherently conservative and broad-brush, municipal and district policy making is flexible and forward looking. This does not imply necessarily that local cluster projects are well managed. Rather than legislating for effective market and social institutions to nurture and reward creativity the policy momentum is directed towards constructing physical spaces that can be carefully managed, and which hopefully will produce

---

[28]   Philip Huang, 'The Theoretical and Practical Implications of China's Development Experience: the Role of Informal Economic Practices', *Modern China* 37(1), 2011, pp. 3–43.

[29]   The lack of transparency is an issue for researchers of such projects. Anecdotal evidence is plentiful about who is participating but officials are reluctant to go on record about the specific details of investment.

[30]   The West Kowloon project has taken more than 10 years to get approved and much of this delay is due to feasibility studies and protracted engagement with stakeholder groups.

[31]   *See* Huang, 'The Theoretical and Practical Implications of China's Development Experience', p. 18.

economic value. Management is more concerned with the bottom line than with creativity. This, however, does deliver social benefits, notably greater degrees of liberalization. The current governance of creative space is relatively tolerant compared with previous regimes in which cultural workers were closely monitored. Prior to the 1990s cultural workers had very little autonomy. Today's cultural and media enterprises, and workers, have mobility and independence and local and regional clusters are keen to attract emerging talent through advertising campaigns.[32] Liberal management is more likely to be the case the further the project is from Beijing. Accordingly commercial culture is the prime driver of most activities and commercial development is recognized as a positive influence on people's lives as long as boundaries of expression are not transgressed.

4. ATTRACTING BUSINESSES AND INVESTMENT (*ZHAOSHANG YINZI*)

With a greater diversity of models now available the question of what kinds of enterprises will occupy a cluster is important when making a pitch to government. While establishment costs are not necessarily prohibitive (depending on the nature of the project), return on investment is important to the officials who ultimately wear responsibility for failure. Investors with good connections can prevail upon local officials. Depending on the strategy of the cluster human capital may be less important than the rent that is paid to the investors over time. For start-up companies location is an important consideration. Although registration costs vary from city to city, district to district, it is relatively easy to establish a private media or cultural enterprise in China. Obviously, the closer to the central business district the higher the premium, for instance the cost of registering a commercial business or obtaining a licence. Cheaper spaces are available out of town and in prescribed industrial zones and for this reason cluster projects are an attractive proposition for new companies. Clusters often emerge on the fringes of cities as agricultural land use regulations and relevant zoning by-laws are modified to allow commercial operations (examples are The White Horse

---

[32] For a discussion of worker mobility in the animation industry, *see* Juncheng Dai, Shangyi Zhou, Michael Keane and Huang Qian, 'Mobility of the Creative Class and City Attractiveness: a Case Study of Chinese Animation Workers', *Eurasian Geography and Economics* 53(4), 2012, pp. 649–70.

Lake Eco-Village on the fringe of Hangzhou and the aforementioned Qujiang New District project in Xi'an).

In urban centres the clustering effect is simpler to bring about. State-owned enterprises with factory assets are keen to turn these over to new forms of knowledge-based labour. An example of this reconversion model is the Shanghai Textile Group (Shangtex), a state-owned enterprise that manages several of Shanghai's high-profile creative clusters including M50, Huifeng Creative Park, Huizhi Creative Park, and Xinlin Creative Park. State-owned enterprises like Shangtex claim to be transforming and diversifying their business model while preserving industrial heritage sites. In comparison with other models of economic development, the 'cluster-led' urban economy does not require massive investments from government. It is convenient, low cost and is generally seen as low risk even if the returns are not high.

Low risk also applies to management but at the same time there is often a sense that there might be a new breakthrough, a local replica of Beijing's 798 for instance. After all creative industries are construed as 'strategic emerging industries' and 'pillar industries' and there is a great deal of support for projects. Many cluster operators thus seek out enterprises engaged in design, software and animation to populate premises. A large percentage of these enterprises are engaged in fee-for-service work; in other words they provide outsourced labour for larger enterprises and transnational companies. The focus on outsourcing in these sectors is understandable but it also reinforces the core problem of China as a processing site.

One of the conundrums of clustering in China is that the model is advanced as a mechanism to understand the arcane workings of the creative economy. The cluster is *ipso facto* a manifestation of the creative economy – or at least the government's redesignation of culture as a 'pillar industry'. Cultural officials in China are often well read in the literature on international cultural and creative industries, the creative class, and creative quarters, topics which have proliferated in the past several years; they obviously will be conversant with Chinese Communist Party pronouncements on the importance of 'cultural development'. However, the difficulty of nurturing original creative products in a political system dogged by conservatism and policy ambiguity leaves many uncertain about how to best encourage creativity. For local government at least an immediate payoff of clustering is being able to identify and aggregate creative companies, or at least enterprises that self-identify as creative. The enterprises might have decorative 'creative' names in keeping with the mood of the times and their branding strategies.

However, this does not necessarily translate into inspiring outputs especially if the enterprises are locked into outsourcing contracts. Much is therefore made of the task of identifying human capital, which in comparison with the politicized cultural workers of previous decades is younger and more mobile.

In relation to the challenge of attracting and aggregating human capital three development strategies in the clustering of cultural production in China are worth noting. The first strategy is where a growth coalition proposes a cluster plan or responds to a government initiative with the hope the local authorities will assist in making it sustainable. In most cases a municipal or district government 'promotion office' or 'leading group' will designate a certain area for development, often a disused industrial space or reclaimed land. Following this a budget will be allocated and policies will be formulated to attract cultural enterprises or culture-related enterprises. The government will provide land and infrastructural support at low cost anticipating higher returns as the cluster generates momentum. However, the key value proposition invariably resides in real estate: that is, land can be resold to developers at a considerable profit.

The next step is to establish a cluster management committee to oversee the occupancy of the spaces. In many instances local governments provide sweeteners. Enterprises would be exempt from tax and rent, or at least would have considerable reductions in taxes and rent. Such incentive policies extend for between three years to five years: in many instances, three years of no tax and free rent, then two years of low tax and rent. In this stage, the core business model of the cluster management is to secure a building or space from government and funds from local government every year to operate the infrastructure. Both the government and the cluster management want to see full occupancy; that is, the objective is to have companies coming in so the management company can apply for funds allocated by municipal governments for such projects. The outcome is realized as long as the clusters have enough registered companies and the government has allocated its budget. However, these policies are essentially designed to attract enterprises: they are not industry-promotion initiatives.

In the second stage the cluster management committee might establish a development company (*kaifa gongsi*). If the management committee has secured land from the government rather than premises they will then have to build the cluster from ground up. The development company in this instance will most probably be a land developer. If the building already exists, then the development company is a commercial operations institution (*shangye yunying jigou*). In this stage, the government is likely to reduce the amount of financial support; the development company compensates by providing professional services in the cluster, such as human resource training, information service, or marketing, even brand promotion. Once established, businesses will be prevailed upon to purchase professional services; if businesses are unsuccessful or dissatisfied they will often relocate to a different cluster looking for more concessions. Because most of the companies in clusters are SMEs with limited knowledge of cultural markets, most need help in relation to commercialization. The cluster management committee develops services and charges accordingly. If the services are appropriate, the service fee earned compensates for the money that might have been collected through rent. If the service provided is not good enough or if they are unable to provide such a service, then the cluster might be forced to seek more financial support from government. In effect, the business model is to use business services income to offset the cost of running the cluster, thereby keeping the rents relatively low.

Most clusters remain in the first stage; that is they remain dependent on government funding. The problem here is that admitting failure is likely to be a blot on the record of local officials. But there are few success stories. The Shenzhen City of Design, managed by the Sphinx Cultural Industry Investment Company is well known. The Shenzhen City of Design has been operational for almost ten years: it has the advantage of being surrounded by clients and companies engaged in manufacturing. While essentially a production cluster, the profit gained by professional business services is enough to be sustainable, turn a reasonable profit and attract an international reputation in line with Shenzhen's designation as a UNESCO Creative City. The management company, Sphinx offers its services in the management of 'domestic cultural creative clusters'; in addition to the City of Design it currently operates ten sites including Shenzhen Yantian International Creative Harbor, Hainan International Creative Harbor, Jiangsu (Taicang) LOFT Industrial Design Park, Shunde Industrial Design Park, Jiangyin Pujiang No.23 Creative Park, Shenzhen Design Center, SZ-HK Design Center and College of Industrial Design, Shenzhen University.

Sphinx represents a development in the clustering of culture whereby companies specialize in the development of clusters. Such professional companies or entrepreneurs acquire funds including bank loans or investment from listing on the stock market. The aim is to attract enough investment to form a network of clusters. In this regard running a cluster is effectively property management except it requires specialized services. There are only two real outcomes of this model: success and failure. While money from rent and services is some compensation under this professional franchising model the cluster will most likely die if enterprises are unsuccessful; at the same time if the management does not provide good services the enterprises will find it hard to grow. The cluster will then ask for government funding to continue. The problem is that the government's tax revenue is not increasing because the businesses are not successful.

When companies in the cluster are robust, the services provided by the cluster improve, as in the case of the Shenzhen City of Design. The end result is that the cluster, companies, as well as central and local government all win. In a version of creative destruction Chinese-style best practice wins the day and the weak drop off. More operators will emerge as cluster development companies. However the basic business model will be similar to real estate. A more important success scenario is human capital. How do clusters recruit talented people and how do these people function in such artificially constructed environments?

5. *ZHAO CHUANG* (ATTRACTING CREATIVITY)

The question of human capital (*rencai*) raises issues including educational backgrounds, capacity to originate ideas, and willingness to share. Of these the wiliness to share is perhaps most germane to the rationale for clustering. According to a study of China's Town and Village Enterprises (TVE) Chinese people are more predisposed to cooperate because there is a greater degree of trust among Chinese people as a result of traditional Confucian value systems. The author argues that if a low degree of trust exists there is a higher reliance on well-defined rights and contracts; the contrast is made with the international IP system.[33] Of course arguments promoting 'weaker' intellectual property rights as a well-spring of innovation in the creative industries have been common in recent times. The success of creative regions like Hollywood and Silicon Valley is to a large extent due to the mobility of ideas despite the ubiquity of IP lawyers. One might then expect China's creative clusters to be places where ideas spill over and where people cooperate in different ways.

A study conducted by Zheng and Chan between 2008 and 2010 identified superficial forms of cooperation in Shanghai's creative clusters. In particular they found that inter-company cooperation was limited: where it occurred it largely involved 'buyer-supplier relations, business

---

[33]   John Marangos, 'Why is China a High-lambda Society?', *Journal of Economic Issues* 39(4), 2009, pp. 933–50.

introduction within friends' circles and working separately on different parts of a product without intellectual interactions …'.[34] Whereas successful clusters drive innovation through heightened competition and the ability of firms and actors to observe and learn from each other, as in the example of Silicon Valley, this does not translate so easily into the Chinese context despite scholarly discourse and policy hype of the benefits of 'spillover' effects. Furthermore this research found that the extent of connections was affected by physical conditions including the image of the cluster as well as management styles and rents. A second finding was that while respondents acknowledged the importance of cooperation in fact a stronger sense of competition prevailed 'embedded in protective measures to prevent business ideas and plans being disclosed'.[35]

These results are supported by my own research findings. From 2009 to 2013, I conducted surveys, both online and written, from enterprises in five clusters ranging from mixed enterprise (i.e. related variety) to single industry (animation).[36] I was assisted in making contacts thanks to my contacts in Chinese research institutions, particularly the CASS. In addition I interviewed academics and scholars working in the field of the cultural industries, attended conferences, forums and workshops on clusters, and was co-opted in several cluster tenders, sometimes unwittingly as an 'international expert'. The clusters where I was able to conduct my surveys were in Beijing, Suzhou and Qingdao: business activities included media content, photography, industrial design, architectural services, media consulting and graphic design.[37] Respondents were owners and employees ranging from CEOs, business owners, managers), secretarial (human resources), technical (programmers) and creative (scriptwriters). Getting people to fill out surveys was facilitated by assistance of park officials in one cluster and in a second instance with the help of a cluster management company. Elsewhere, I knew persons working in the clusters who assisted in passing the online survey. I also had the assistance of a Chinese research assistant who collated hard copy surveys. While the surveys reveal interesting findings I wish to provide the caveat that they were conducted over a period of time during

---

[34]   Zheng and Chan, 'A Property-led Approach to Cluster Development', p. 619.

[35]   *Ibid.*, p. 627.

[36]   In all the total number of completed valid surveys was 251 (166 hard copy, 85 online) out of a total of 400 distributed.

[37]   Fangjia 46, Shijingshan Cyber Recreation Park (Beijing): Suzhou Industrial Park (Suzhou); Creative 100 (Qingdao).

which the cluster fever peaked.[38] The sense of participation in a new kind of 'creative' industry may have coloured people's responses.[39] In my first survey of animation enterprises in Suzhou Industrial Park I found that respondents identified positively with the word 'creative' such that in future iterations of the survey in Beijing I opted to avoid this term, choosing instead more neutral terms such as communication, cultural knowledge, sharing of ideas, and learning.

Moreover, the types of industry sector reflected people's confidence. Persons entering into early-stage clusters, particularly animation, were more inclined to be enthusiastic about their work prospects and the future of their sector. For instance, in response to a question 'what is your main reason for coming to work in this company', 44.4 per cent of animation park respondents chose the option 'I love to work in this growing industry'; the second most popular choice was 'great creative environment and opportunities for learning' (28.57 per cent).[40] Workers in animation bases also nominated financial remuneration as being less important than those in related variety parks; of course, the kind of work style in animation bases was more project based and the employees were younger overall, whereas the respondents from the related variety enterprises were generally small enterprises of less than five people. The respondents in these cases were managers and persons charged with business development. The bottom line was survival.

The workforce of these clusters reflects the description of Florida's creative classes. Survey responses revealed that over 95 per cent of persons working in China's clusters, media parks and bases had attained

---

[38]   The initial hard copy survey on animation was conducted in May 2009 (96 respondents); subsequent surveys were done in 2010 with modifications to wording, cognizant that people positively identified with being creative. The animation surveys were different also in that they included specific questions about attitudes towards the animation industry.

[39]   Surveys were multiple choice (choose one of five statements to best represent your view) as well as standard Likert scale responses (Disagree strongly, Disagree, Neutral, Agree, Agree strongly). This methodology has its limits and as such was supplemented by interviews with companies about the nature and challenges of their businesses. *See* Michael Keane, *China's New Creative Clusters: Governance, Human Capital and Investment* for discussion of this.

[40]   1. I love to work in this growing industry; 2. It has a great creative environment and opportunities for learning; 3. Better financial incentives than where I was; 4. It has a strong organizational culture; 5. The work hours are flexible.

tertiary degrees; over 54 per cent of the respondents had an undergraduate degree while Masters degrees varied between 11 and 24 per cent
across different sectors with animation parks recording the lower score
and 'related variety' clusters the upper score. Animation parks also
recorded double the number of workers with non-university diplomas or
certificates, which is to be expected considering the high proportion of
mundane technical work in animation parks. The background of persons
working in animation was predominantly from fine arts or literature
majors (53 per cent) whereas less than 20 per cent had specialist IT or
animation industry qualifications.

Echoing the research conducted in Shanghai by Zheng and Chan,
surveys showed that participants in clusters positively identified with the
environment. Working in a cluster was deemed to be more important in
career development in mixed enterprise clusters (76.78 per cent) than in
animation bases (46.04 per cent). Moreover animation base results
illustrated less enthusiasm for knowledge sharing (39.68 per cent) than in
mixed enterprise clusters where 55.36 per cent recorded positively that
they freely shared ideas.[41] Again this can be explained by the nature of
the industry and the high degree of outsourced work and competition for
contracts in animation.

CONCLUSION: READING THE CULTURAL INNOVATION TIMELINE

My perspective on China's cultural and creative clusters has been as an
observer of this important development phase of the nation's nascent
creative economy. As the first international scholar to write about China's
emergent claims to becoming a creative nation,[42] I was invited to visit
clusters, parks and bases. Like some of my interviewees and respondents
I experienced a sense of anticipation, even optimism. In the period from
2007 to 2011, there was a growing sense that clustering was a means to
an end, that is it would deliver the benefits of pooling of labour and
reduced transaction costs, and 'attract creative talent'.

To place these clusters developments into context I have identified
what I call the Chinese 'cultural innovation timeline' (see Table 6.1) in
order to show how Chinese artists, media producers and designers are

    [41] On a Likert scale this represents the values agree, agree strongly.
    [42] Michael Keane, *Created in China: The Great New Leap Forward*, London:
Routledge, 2007.

ascending the value chain.[43] In comparison with the transnational cultural and entertainment industries of developed Western economies China's industries only began to form after the country opened up in the 1980s. Beginning in the early 1990s the cultural market in China progressed through a series of structural reforms.[44] In the first decade or more after Deng Xiaoping opened up China's cultural markets to competition following the Southern Tour of Shenzhen in 1992, actors moved rapidly into cheap production of artefacts and especially imitation of successful ones, frequently shunning the need to comply with intellectual property rights. In this 'made in China' stage we see minimal originality or novelty. Participants opted to produce whatever the market (or the state) wanted; that is, they waited for others to determine the form and prescribe the content.

A second stage saw producers imitating and a 'follow the leader' pattern ensued. Following China's ascension to the WTO in 2001, concerted attempts began to be made by some to generate novelty, to accelerate creative and technological exchange, and to seek out overseas markets. Following the pattern of other industrial sectors, the cultural domain engaged in large-scale copying, routinely ignoring copyright. This practice was exacerbated by the nature of media markets whereby duplication was encouraged under a system that until the late 1990s did not allow national distribution. In effect, local and regional administrative boundaries meant there were multiple local versions of TV shows, newspapers, and magazines cannibalizing each other's output. In addition to this cannibalization a great deal of foreign content IP was plundered.

The third and fourth stages saw Chinese producers entering into co-production and knowledge-sharing arrangements with foreign players. This occurred more rapidly in non-sensitive media such as advertising and video games as China entered the WTO in 2001. The rapid rise of the Korean Wave alerted Chinese media players and policy makers that their true markets were in Asia, not the West.

If the fourth stage was recognition of overseas markets, the final move was the establishment of media bases, cultural clusters and arts zones, often co-opting investors and personnel from East Asia. Clusters, zones

---

[43]   For a more comprehensive treatment *see* Michael Keane, *Creative Industries in China: Art, Design, Media*, London: Polity, 2013.
[44]   This is generally referred to as the reform of the cultural system (*wenhua tizhi gaige*). *See* Michael Keane and Elaine Zhao, 'The Reform of the Cultural System: Culture, Creativity and Innovation in China', in Lorraine Lim and Hye-Kyung Lee (eds), *Cultural Policies in East Asia: Dynamics Between the State, Arts and Creative Industries*, London: Macmillan, 2014.

and quarters proliferated, led by the high-profile success of a few such as the 798 Art Zone in Beijing and Shanghai's Tianzifang. Meanwhile the government's emphasis on building an animation industry to compete with Japan and Korea generated a sense of confidence that 'industrial bases' were the best fast-track strategy. A similar sense of optimism occurred in film and software industries: 'build the infrastructure and they will come'.

However, the clustering phenomenon inevitably generated an innovation trap. Many participants found themselves in cultural parks because these offered the cheap premises and other ancillary services. As I have discussed elsewhere these parks have adopted a variety of strategies to manage clients while showing that they are contributing to national and regional strategies.[45] But the fact that clustering might 'attract creativity' (*zhao chuang*) is less valued than the capacity to attract business (*zhao shang*).

Table 6.1   The cultural innovation timeline

Theme	Mode	Timeline
Low-cost processing	Place competition for local and international contracts	Static: sometimes viewed as 'backward'
Imitation	Import substitution and cloning	Increase in domestic variety but audience/consumer rejection
Collaboration	Co-production and sharing knowledge	Acceleration of creative and technological exchange
Market differentiation	Breaking out of domestic market constraints (markets, regulations)	Movement into adjacent market as a result of collaboration
Clusters	Attempts to industrialize production (labour, management, organizational structure)	Fast tracking stages of development

The enthusiasm for cluster projects is now diminishing. In the main clusters have not succeeded in raising the quality of Chinese cultural output. Most of the 'evidence' for cluster failure is, however, anecdotal: performance, or lack of it, is hard to quantify and government officials who preside over urban developments are averse to open scrutiny of

[45]   Michael Keane, *China's New Creative Clusters: Governance, Human Capital and Investment*, London: Routledge, 2011.

projects. In particular, government officials are not well placed to understand how flows of tacit knowledge lead to innovation effects. In most successful clusters and quarters internationally, participants self-select; in other words participants are drawn to a locale by the cultural atmosphere, opportunities for interaction and the suitability of work and exhibition spaces; hence the term 'cluster'. Creative clusters therefore require creative space: these may be creative workshops and studios or market spaces. However, this also implies a mental space and an entrepreneurial space – willingness to experiment with new ideas. In addition, creative space entails competitive cooperation across networks of businesses, some degree of interactive learning and sharing of successful ideas.

In general, however, cultural and creative industries cluster projects have been led by real estate developers. Gentrification, together with consumer service functions, has served the bottom line. In a sense, it is not the creativity or the networks of interaction that have funded this wave of construction: it is the production and sale of tourist commodities. While one could argue that the commercial focus has conspired to produce competition, there has been a concomitant effect on cooperation in learning. Many have bemoaned a loss of authenticity and crass commercialization. The end result has been an increase in land value and rents, not enhanced creativity.

To suggest that clusters have failed in this regard maybe drawing too fine a line. As I have shown these projects do have outcomes, some of which are intended (increased rents, consumption of services) and some of which are unintended and which in turn may generate knowledge and innovation over time. However the nature of China's cultural innovation timeline suggests that creative inspiration is more likely to come from online networks than inter-firm networks. These online creative networks engage in a different modality of sharing epitomized by open source software and hacker spaces.

7. Determinants of product innovation in Chinese private small and medium-sized enterprises

Peter S. Hofman, Alexander Newman and Ziliang Deng

INTRODUCTION

In the increasingly competitive and fast-moving global market small and medium-sized enterprises (SMEs) have been an important engine behind economic growth, job creation and technological progress.[1] In particular they have made a significant contribution to the economic development in transition economies which have witnessed the movement from centrally planned to free-market economies in which the private sector dominates. In China private SMEs play a crucial role in the transition towards a more market-oriented economy and are the main source of new jobs and productivity improvements.[2] Much of the initial success of Chinese SMEs has been attributed to their ability to engage in low-cost production of relatively mature products.[3] Continuation of their success, however, will depend more and more on their ability to engage in new

[1] Michael Fritsch and Pamela Mueller, 'The Effects of New Business Formation on Regional Development over Time', *Regional Studies*, 2004, vol. 38, p. 961.

[2] Jia Chen, 'Development of Chinese Small and Medium-Sized Enterprises', *Journal of Small Business and Enterprise Development*, 2006, vol. 13, p. 140; Xiaohong He, 'The Development of Entrepreneurship and Private Enterprise in the People's Republic of China and its Relevance to Transitional Economies', *Journal of Developmental Entrepreneurship*, 2009, 14, p. 39.

[3] OECD, *OECD Review of Innovation Policy: China Synthesis Report*, Paris: OECD Publishing, 2007.

product innovation.[4] This has important implications regarding their performance, growth potential and long-term survival, given that without the development of new products it is difficult for SMEs to gain a competitive advantage over rival firms.

Although a growing body of empirical work has been conducted on what determines the propensity of SMEs to innovate in mature economies,[5] few studies have begun to investigate these issues in the rapidly emerging economy of China.[6] While these studies are valuable in helping us to understand the innovation process in SMEs they predominantly focus on a small number of firms in one geographical area or industrial sector. There is a need to complement these studies with empirical work using a bigger sample of firms from a wider range of industries to provide more representative findings and to strengthen the foundation for policy advice.

In this chapter we use data drawn from the annual reports filed by industrial firms with the National Bureau of Statistics over the period 2005–2006 to examine the main factors determining product innovation in private Chinese SMEs. In doing this we seek to examine the relative importance of internal and external factors in determining their propensity to innovate. Other factors we take into account include firm size, ownership structure and the nature of the industries involved. Previous

---

[4]   Tilman Altenburg, Hubert Schmitz and Andreas Stamm, 'Breakthrough? China's and India's Transition from Production to Innovation', *World Development*, 2008, 36, p. 325.

[5]   Mark Freel, 'Barriers to Product Innovation in Small Manufacturing Firms', *International Small Business Journal*, 2000, 18, p. 60; Mark Freel, 'Sectoral Patterns of Small Firm Innovation, Networking and Proximity', *Research Policy*, 2003, 32, p. 751; Mita Bhattacharya and Harry Bloch, 'Determinants of Innovation', *Small Business Economics*, 2004, 22, p. 155; Mark Rogers, 'Networks, Firm Size and Innovation', *Small Business Economics*, 2004, 22, p. 141; Jeroen De Jong and Patrick Vermeulen, 'Determinants of Product Innovation in Small Firms: A Comparison across Industries', *International Small Business Journal*, 2006, 24, p. 587.

[6]   Zonglin Xu, Jiali Lin and Danming Lin, 'Networking and Innovation in SMEs: Evidence from Guangdong Province, China', *Journal of Small Business and Enterprise Development*, 2008, 15, p. 788; Chunlin Zhang, Douglas Zhihua Zeng, William Peter Mako and James Seward, *Promoting Enterprise-Led Innovation in China*, Hemdon VA: World Bank, 2009; Saixing Zeng, Xuemei Xie and CM Tam, 'Relationship between Cooperation Networks and Innovation Performance of SMEs', *Technovation*, 2010, 30, p. 181.

empirical work in Western economies indicates that such factors may influence the extent to which SMEs introduce new products.[7]

1. PRODUCT INNOVATION AND THE RESOURCE-BASED VIEW

Product innovation refers to the process by which new products are created and brought to market.[8] It has been shown to be a critical factor in economic development and impacts on the growth and survival of firms.[9] New product ideas can come from sources as diverse as formal research and development, new technologies, creative employees and suggestions from customers and suppliers. The resource endowments (knowledge and skills) possessed by a firm are critical to its ability to engage in new product development. The resource-based view of the firm (RBV) proposes that the long-term competitiveness of any organization depends on its ability to develop and organize its resources in such a way that will allow it to distinguish itself from and maintain a competitive advantage over its rivals.[10] To achieve this, companies need to develop resources that are valuable, rare, inimitable and non-substitutable.[11] SMEs may enjoy some advantages over larger firms such as their flexibility to respond quickly to potential technological and market opportunities and refocus the firm towards these opportunities.[12] However, SMEs typically control fewer resources than large firms and therefore need to cope with constraints in advancing product innovation

---

[7]   Freel, 'Sectoral Patterns of Small Firm Innovation, Networking and Proximity', p. 751; Rogers, 'Networks, Firm Size and Innovation', p. 141; De Jong and Vermeulen, 'Determinants of Product Innovation in Small Firms: A Comparison across Industries', p. 587.

[8]   Zoltan Acs and David B. Audretsch, *Innovation and Small Firms,* Cambridge: MIT Press, 1990.

[9]   Joseph Alois Schumpeter, *Capitalism, Socialism and Democracy.* New York: Harper and Row, 1950.

[10]   Joseph Mahoney and J. Rajendran Pandian, 'The Resource-Based View Within the Conversation of Strategic Management', *Strategic Management Journal*, 1992, 13, p. 363.

[11]   Margaret A. Peteraf, 'The Cornerstones of Competitive Advantage: A Resource Based View', *Strategic Management Journal*, 1993, 14, p. 179.

[12]   Nina Rosenbusch, Jan Brinckmann and Andreas Bausch, 'Is Innovation Always Beneficial? A Meta-Analysis of the Relationship between Innovation and Performance in SMEs', *Journal of Business Venturing*, 2011, 26, p. 441.

based upon internal sources.[13] One way to overcome these constraints is by developing capabilities to leverage knowledge from outside business partners in a way that complements internal capabilities and the firm's learning orientation.[14] This may be particularly the case for firms in high-tech industries, where the complexity of technologically advanced products requires collaboration with specialized firms that possess technological expertise.

2. IMPACT OF INSTITUTIONAL FACTORS ON PRODUCT INNOVATION

In transition economies institutional factors play an important role in shaping the strategic behaviour of SMEs.[15] Institutional constraints impact on the ability of SMEs to engage in new product development, which in turn has consequences regarding their long-term growth and survival. In China, where private enterprises were only given equal legal status to state-owned enterprises over the course of the last five years, private enterprises continue to face significant regulatory discrimination against them.[16] They face ongoing difficulties in accessing bank financing due to a lending bias towards the public sector which results from continued government interference in the financial markets.[17] A further institutional factor that may constrain product innovation is the weak framework for protection of intellectual property rights. Both legally and normatively (replicating innovations from others as an accepted practice) this provides disincentives for firms to innovate. Moreover the strong

---

[13]   Frans J. H. M. Verhees and Matthew T. G. Meulenberg, 'Market Orientation, Innovativeness, Product Innovation, and Performance in Small Firms', *Journal of Small Business Management*, 2004, 42, p. 134.
[14]   Bruce Kogut and Udo Zander, 'Knowledge of the Firm, Combinative Capabilities, and the Replication of Technology', *Organization Science*, 1992, 3, p. 383.
[15]   Mike Peng, Dennis Wang and Yi Jiang, 'An Institution-Based View of International Business Strategy: A Focus on Emerging Economies', *Journal of International Business Studies*, 2008, 39, p. 920.
[16]   Andrew Atherton, 'From "Fat Pigs" and "Red Hats" to a "New Social Stratum": The Changing Face of Enterprise Development Policy in China', *Journal of Small Business and Enterprise Development*, 2008, 15, p. 640.
[17]   Alexander Newman, Sailesh Gunessee and Brian Hilton, 'The Applicability of Financial Theories of Capital Structure to the Chinese Cultural Context: A Study of Privately-Owned SMEs', *International Small Business Journal*, 2012, 30, p. 65.

reliance on foreign direct investment (FDI) and the perception that the role and competitive advantage of Chinese firms is in imitating these practices, and in making them more cost-effective, can be detrimental to the creation of innovative domestic firms.

3 HYPOTHESIS DEVELOPMENT

In the following sections we develop hypotheses based on the existing theoretical and empirical literature. A conceptual framework for this research study is presented in Figure 7.1.

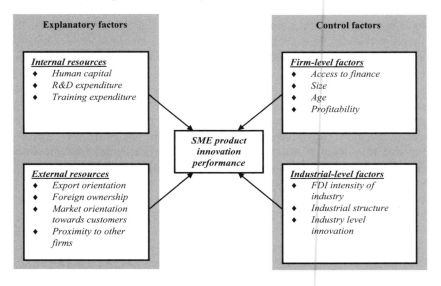

Figure 7.1   Conceptual framework

4. INTERNAL FACTORS INFLUENCING PRODUCT INNOVATION

Traditionally, empirical studies investigating the determinants of product innovation typically focused on the internal characteristics of the firm. These both impact on product innovation directly, and indirectly help it to absorb knowledge from external sources. Investment in research and development (R&D) is one of the key inputs into the innovation process.

It is a direct input to the innovative process in firms but also enhances product innovation through its effect on absorptive capacity, defined as the ability of firms to identify, assimilate and exploit new, external knowledge to their commercial advantage.[18] Empirical studies confirm a strong relationship between investment in R&D and product innovation for SMEs in Australia, Italy and the UK.[19] Research on larger Chinese firms also finds a positive link between investment in R&D and product innovation,[20] leading us to the following hypothesis:

H1: Investment in research and development will have a positive effect on product innovation.

Next to R&D, the skill set and knowledge level of employees form an important input into the innovative process. Research has confirmed that firms that develop and invest in employee skills and knowledge tend to have greater innovative outputs.[21] Investment in human capital is essential for firms looking to innovate, especially in the early stages of new product development.[22] Attracting skilled labour is not easy for SMEs as they face difficulties in competing with the salaries and career development opportunities provided by larger firms. In China in particular there is strong competition in the labour market between SMEs, larger

---

[18] Wesley M. Cohen and Daniel A. Levinthal, 'Absorptive Capacity: A New Perspective on Learning and Innovation', *Administrative Science Quarterly*, 1990, 35, p. 128.

[19] Freel, 'Sectoral Patterns of Small Firm Innovation, Networking and Proximity', p. 751; Bhattacharya and Bloch, 'Determinants of Innovation', p. 155; Bronwyn H. Hall, Francesca Lotti, and Jacques Mairesse, 'Innovation and Productivity in SMEs: Empirical Evidence for Italy', *Small Business Economics*, 2009, 33, p. 13.

[20] Jing Li, Dong Chen and Daniel Shapiro, 'Product Innovation in Emerging Economies: The Role of Foreign Knowledge Access Channels and Internal Efforts in Chinese Firms', *Management and Organization Review*, 2010, 6, p. 243.

[21] Stephen Roper, 'Product Innovation and Small Business Growth: A Comparison of the Strategies of German, U.K. and Irish Companies', *Small Business Economics*, 1997, 9, p. 523; Freel, 'Barriers to Product Innovation in Small Manufacturing Firms', p. 60.

[22] De Jong and Vermeulen, 'Determinants of Product Innovation in Small Firms: A Comparison across Industries', p. 587.

domestic firms and establishments with foreign investment, while turn-over of skilled employees is extremely high.[23] Firms that are able to attract and retain skilled employees are therefore likely to exhibit better innovative performance. Investment in employee training and develop-ment should also increase the skill level of employees and contribute positively to the innovative process. This leads us to the following hypotheses:

H2: The skill and knowledge of employees will have a positive effect on product innovation.

H3: Investment in employee training and development will have a positive effect on product innovation.

5. EXTERNAL FACTORS INFLUENCING PRODUCT INNOVATION

The importance of drawing upon external networks in the process of innovation has been an important topic of research. Firms are able to benefit from relations with external partners such as knowledge institutes, suppliers, government organizations, consumers and capital providers.[24] This is especially the case for SMEs and those in emerging markets in particular, where acquisition of external sources of knowledge is crucial to new product development. External sources of knowledge include co-operation with other firms, higher education institutions and research institutes. As resource limitations constrain the ability of SMEs to engage in product innovation, external networks provide them with a platform to acquire technical information and know-how and compete on a level playing field with larger firms.[25] Networking allows them to achieve economies of scale, share development risks with other firms and

---

[23]   Zhang, Zeng, Mako and Seward, *Promoting Enterprise-Led Innovation in China*.

[24]   Freel, 'Sectoral Patterns of Small Firm Innovation, Networking and Proximity', p. 751; Kuen-Hung Tsai, 'Collaborative Networks and Product Innovation Performance: Towards a Contingency Perspective', *Research Policy*, 2009, 38, p. 765.

[25]   Zeng, Xie and Tam, 'Relationship between Cooperation Networks and Innovation Performance of SMEs', p. 181.

integrate diverse skills, technology and core competencies.[26] Empirical studies find a strong relationship between the network ties of an SME with external organizations and its propensity to engage in product innovation in both Western and Chinese settings.[27]

In developing economies the relationship a firm has with foreign partners has been shown to be an important source of knowledge acquisition.[28] Foreign partners are typically willing to transfer technology and know-how which leads to improvements in product design, production techniques and quality control.[29] This transfer of knowledge does a great deal to enable SMEs to overcome the major institutional barriers to innovation. In the process of learning from their foreign partners the core competencies of SMEs are enhanced, further aiding the development of new product ideas. As a result the equitable and contractual relationships an SME has with foreign firms should contribute towards its propensity to engage in new product development. Empirical work on SMEs from mature economies and larger Chinese firms reveals that firms with an export orientation tend to be more innovative than non-exporters.[30] This leads to the following hypotheses:

H4: Foreign ownership will have a positive effect on product innovation.

H5: Export intensity will have a positive effect on product innovation.

---

[26]   Tsai, 'Collaborative Networks and Product Innovation Performance: Towards a Contingency Perspective', p. 765.

[27]   Frédéric Bougrain and Bernard Haudeville, 'Innovation, Collaboration and SMEs Internal Research Capacities', *Research Policy*, 2002, 31, p. 735; Rogers, 'Networks, Firm Size and Innovation', p. 141; Xu, Lin and Lin, 'Networking and Innovation in SMEs: Evidence from Guangdong Province, China', p. 788.

[28]   Li, Chen and Shapiro, 'Product Innovation in Emerging Economies: The Role of Foreign Knowledge Access Channels and Internal Efforts in Chinese Firms', p. 243.

[29]   Robert M. Salomon and J. Myles Shaver, 'Learning by Exporting: New Insights from Examining Firm Innovation', *Journal of Economics & Management Strategy*, 2005, 14, p. 431.

[30]   Salomon and Shaver, 'Learning by Exporting: New Insights from Examining Firm Innovation', p. 431; Li, Chen and Shapiro, 'Product Innovation in Emerging Economies: The Role of Foreign Knowledge Access Channels and Internal Efforts in Chinese Firms', p. 243.

168 Innovation and intellectual property in China

Clusters have been defined as 'geographic concentrations of inter-connected companies and institutions in a particular field'.[31] The role played by geographic clusters in the innovation process has gained increasing attention in the literature.[32] Empirical evidence suggests that SMEs located within geographical clusters tend to reach higher levels of product innovation than those outside such clusters due to their geographic proximity to supplier firms, customers, competitors and knowledge organizations.[33] Geographical proximity should increase the frequency of social interaction and thus facilitate knowledge flows between economic actors and reduce the transaction costs of inter-organizational collaboration.[34] The direct and indirect knowledge spill-overs generated through geographic clusters equip firms with industry-specific knowledge that enables them to establish a competitive advantage over rival firms in the same industry. In China, geographic clusters have grown around special economic zones that were set up by the government authorities during the 1980s in order to benefit directly from foreign investment.[35] In these zones local firms can reap benefits from knowledge spillovers that occur from their interaction with other firms, government agencies and knowledge institutes.[36] This leads us to the following hypothesis:

H6: Location in or close to a special economic zone will have a positive effect on product innovation.

---

[31]   Michael E. Porter, 'Clusters and the New Economics of Competition', *Harvard Business Review*, 1998, 76, p. 78.

[32]   Changhui Zhou and Jing Li, 'Product Innovation in Emerging Market-Based International Joint Ventures, An Organizational Ecology Perspective', *Journal of International Business Studies*, 2008, 39, p. 1114; Li, Chen and Shapiro, 'Product Innovation in Emerging Economies: The Role of Foreign Knowledge Access Channels and Internal Efforts in Chinese Firms', p. 243.

[33]   Brett A. Gilbert, Patricia P. McDougall and David B. Audretsch, 'Clusters, Knowledge Spillovers and New Venture Performance: An Empirical Examination', *Journal of Business Venturing*, 2008, 23, p. 405; Shujun Zhang and Xinchun Li, 'Managerial Ties, Firm Resources, and Performance of Cluster Firms', *Asia-Pacific Journal of Management*, 2008, 25, p. 615.

[34]   AnnaLee Saxenian, 'The Origins and Dynamics of Production Networks in Silicon Valley', *Research Policy*, 1991, 20, p. 423.

[35]   Changhui Zhou, Andrew Delios and Jing Yu Yang, 'Locational Determinants of Japanese Foreign Direct Investment in China', *Asia-Pacific Journal of Management*, 2002, 19, p. 63.

[36]   Zhou and Li, 'Product Innovation in Emerging Market-Based International Joint Ventures, An Organizational Ecology Perspective', p. 1114.

Market orientation refers to the extent to which a firm is responsive to the needs of its customers. Customer knowledge is one of the most important sources of innovative ideas as meeting the needs of customers is the foundation of success for any company.[37] Empirical work on SMEs in mature economies reveals that firms who are in tune with the needs of their customers are more likely to be successful in new product development.[38] In emerging markets the lack of credible market research institutions further exacerbates the importance of internal marketing efforts.[39] In order to gather reliable information firms have to expend greater resources on conducting market research than in mature economies. Previous work on larger Chinese firms demonstrates that the market orientation of a firm impacts on its propensity to engage in new product development.[40] This leads us to the following hypothesis:

H7: Market orientation will have a positive effect on product innovation.

6. METHODOLOGY AND DATA

This study uses a dataset from the Chinese National Bureau of Statistics (NBS) that draws on data from the Annual Survey of Industrial Enterprises from the years 2005–2006. The data covers all firms with over 5 million RMB in annual turnover and includes firm-level financial and operational information. The data collected and method used is consistent across geographical regions and industries and accuracy of the financial data provided by the firms is monitored by the NBS through regular

---

[37] Alfred M. Pelham, 'Market Orientation and Other Potential Influences on Performance in Small and Medium-Sized Manufacturing Firms', *Journal of Small Business Management*, 2000, 38, p. 48.
[38] Verhees and Meulenberg, 'Market Orientation, Innovativeness, Product Innovation, and Performance in Small Firms', p. 134.
[39] Li, Chen and Shapiro, 'Product Innovation in Emerging Economies: The Role of Foreign Knowledge Access Channels and Internal Efforts in Chinese Firms', p. 243.
[40] Yu-Shan, Su, Eric W. K. Tsang and Mike Peng, 'How do Internal Capabilities and External Partnerships Affect Innovativeness? *Asia-Pacific Journal of Management*, 2009, 26, p. 309; Li, Chen and Shapiro, 'Product Innovation in Emerging Economies: The Role of Foreign Knowledge Access Channels and Internal Efforts in Chinese Firms', p. 243.

audits of a selection of firms.[41] The study uses data for the years 2005 and 2006 as a number of important measures adopted in this study were not available before 2005, e.g. the sales of new products. The sample includes manufacturing firms from nine two-digit industries. These are food, beverage, tobacco, textile, general equipment, special equipment, electric machinery, transport equipment, and electronic products. These nine industries consist of several three-digit sectors, reaching 72 three-digit sectors. The sample covers all types of firm ownership and all 31 provinces, autonomous regions and municipalities in China.

The focus of this study is on private SMEs and therefore we limit our sample to firms with less than 300 million RMB in sales, 400 million in total assets, and fewer than 2000 employees.[42] We excluded all firms with any state ownership. Firms with incomplete records for our main regression variables were also dropped. The empirical study therefore utilizes a final balanced panel covering 43,732 firms.

7.   MEASURES

7.1   The Dependent Variable

We adopted the measure of product innovation used by the Chinese National Bureau of Statistics in their Annual Survey of Industrial Enterprises: the share of total output accounted for by new products in a specific firm. This measure provides a broad measure of product innovation in firms as it includes minor product improvements. We labelled this variable *INNO*.

7.2   Internal Resources

Three variables in the dataset were used to measure the internal sources of a firm's product innovation. First, in order to capture the human capital of the workforce, *HUMCAP* was constructed. This was measured as the average wage per employee in the firm. Second, the variable *RND* is used to indicate the research and development intensity of a firm and is

---

[41]   Zhou and Li, 'Product Innovation in Emerging Market-Based International Joint Ventures, An Organizational Ecology Perspective', p. 1114.

[42]   This way of defining SMEs is suggested by the NBS. 'Small-sized enterprises' refer to those firms with less than 30 million RMB in sales, 40 million in total assets, and fewer than 300 employees.

measured as the R&D expenditure of the firm as a percentage of its total sales. Third, *TRAIN* was measured as training expenditure per employee.

7.3   External Resources

Five variables in our dataset were used to measure the firm's external orientation. Firstly, *MARKET* was constructed to indicate the level of a firm's market orientation. This was measured by the size of advertising fees as a percentage of sales. Secondly, to capture the firm's export intensity (*EXPORT*) was constructed. This was measured as the proportion of export sales to total sales. Thirdly, we developed a dummy variable (*FOREIGN*) to measure whether a firm has capital from overseas, including Hong Kong, Macau and Taiwan. Fourthly, a dummy variable (*ZONE*) was constructed to measure whether or not the firm was located in a city with a national Economic and Technology Development Zone (ETDZ). The Chinese central government established the first ETDZs in 1982, and by 2005 there were 54 ETDZs. The purpose of establishing ETDZs was mainly to develop high-tech industries, absorb foreign funds and build up an export-oriented economy. Cities with ETDZs generally have a dynamic market environment, which offers the firms located in these cities easier access to new market information via direct and indirect contacts with the actively innovative firms located inside the zones.

7.4   Control Variables

Four firm-level factors which have been shown to influence product innovation were entered as control variables. A dummy variable, *FINANCE*, was included to measure whether or not a firm has long-term liabilities. The significant constraints faced by Chinese SMEs in accessing external financing from the banking sector should impact on their ability to fund inputs into the innovation process such as R&D and employee training. *SIZE*, measured as the log of total assets, was adopted to control for firm size. Firm size has been widely studied as a variable that may influence product innovation.[43] In general, larger firms are expected to be more innovative than smaller firms as they have greater potential to exploit economies of scale in production, marketing, finance and R&D. This should enable them to reduce the fixed costs of innovation per unit of output. They should also have better access to

---

[43]   Zoltan Acs and David B. Audretsch, 'Innovation in Large and Small Firms: An Empirical Analysis', *American Economic Review*, 1988, 78, p. 678.

external financing and are more able to attract human capital to their organization. We also controlled for firm age (*AGE*), which was measured as 2005 minus the opening year of the firm. As firms get older it might be expected that they become more innovative due to greater knowledge and efficiency and thus mature firms more routinely may generate innovations. Finally, firm profitability (*PROFIT*) was controlled for. It was measured as the proportion of net profits to total assets. It is expected more profitable firms will have more financial leeway to invest in innovative activities.

Three variables were also utilized to control for the effects of industry structure. Firstly the FDI intensity of each of the 72 three-digit industries in each of the 31 provinces was controlled for using the variable *INDFDI*. It was measured as the average proportion of foreign ownership of firms in a given industry. It is expected that firms in industries with a significant foreign presence will benefit both directly and indirectly from knowledge spillovers. Secondly, aggregate firm-level information was used to construct a Herfindahl index for market concentration, allowing us to measure the competitive intensity of the industry. The Herfindahl index gives a measure of firm sizes in relation to the size of the industry. This variable was labelled *INDCOMPETE*. The variable was defined as follows:

$$H_j = \sum_{i=1}^{N} S_{i,j}^2$$

where $S_{i,j}$ is the market share of firm i in industry j.

The higher the variable *INDCOMPETE* is, the higher the degree of market competition will be. In highly concentrated industries there are typically lower levels of product innovation due to less competition in product markets.[44] Finally, the variable *INDINN* was created to control for the intensity of innovative activity within each particular industry in each specific province. This was measured as the average share of total output accounted for by new products for firms in a given industry-province group. It is expected that industry innovation can generate knowledge spillovers to firms and hence will be positively related to the product innovation of individual firms. Appendix 1 provides a description of all the variables used in the study.

---

[44] Li, Chen and Shapiro, 'Product Innovation in Emerging Economies: The Role of Foreign Knowledge Access Channels and Internal Efforts in Chinese Firms', p. 243.

8. RESULTS

Table 7.1 presents statistics relating to the propensity of firms to engage in new product innovation across industries in 2006. Overall, the majority of private Chinese SMEs do not engage in product innovation. Firms in the electronic products industry are most likely to engage in new product innovation (22.4 per cent), and those in the textile industry the least likely (6.4 per cent). Secondly, medium-sized firms exhibit a greater propensity to innovate than small firms. Compared to OECD countries these findings indicate a much lower propensity to innovate in Chinese small-sized firms. A recent study reports that the percentage of SMEs[45] that introduced a product innovation for the period 2004–2005 ranged from 16 per cent in Japan, 32 per cent in the UK, 35 per cent in Korea, 41 per cent in Germany to 47 per cent in Switzerland, with around 30 per cent on average for all OECD countries,[46] while in our sample the share of private small-sized firms with product innovation ranged from 5 per cent to 20 per cent depending on the industry. Thirdly, single-owner firms are less likely to engage in innovation than firms with multiple owners.

Table 7.1   Share of innovators, 2006 (%)

	Industry	All	Small-sized	Medium-sized	Single owner	Multiple owners
Low-tech	Food	11.0	10.2	19.4	16.1	10.3
	Beverage	10.6	8.8	24.4	9.4	10.8
	Tobacco	18.4	10.8	26.7	0.0	18.5
	Textile	6.4	5.2	17.8	5.7	6.5
	General equipment	12.0	9.5	43.0	5.8	13.1
Hi-tech	Special equipment	15.8	13.4	42.9	10.2	16.6
	Electric machinery	13.4	10.0	40.4	8.9	14.0
	Transport equipment	13.2	10.7	40.3	8.7	13.7
	Electronic product	22.4	19.8	42.7	9.4	23.3

[45]   Within the OECD statistics SMEs are defined as companies with fewer than 250 employees, similar to the group of small-size firms in our sample.
[46]   OECD, *Innovation in Firms: A Microeconomic Perspective*, Paris: OECD Publishing, 2009.

If we focus specifically on the firms that innovate, Table 7.2 illustrates that new product sales as a share of total sales are highest in the high-tech industries. For the electronic products industry new product sales take up a dominant share in total sales (61.1 per cent), while the share of total sales is lowest for the tobacco industry (13.6 per cent). Size does not have a clear impact on the rate of new product sales in total sales, however ownership structure does. In our sample of innovative firms, single-owner businesses have much lower shares of new products in their overall sales than firms with multiple owners, with the exception of the electronic products industry.

Table 7.2   New product sales as share of total sales of innovators, 2006 (%)

	Industry	All	Small-sized	Medium-sized	Single owner	Multiple owners
Low-tech	Food	26.1	28.4	24.3	12.6	27.4
	Beverage	25.0	20.3	27.0	11.9	25.5
	Tobacco	13.6	22.4	13.1	0.0	13.6
	Textile	30.2	28.4	31.0	19.0	30.7
	General equipment	33.4	31.2	34.3	13.5	34.1
Hi-tech	Special equipment	36.8	36.2	37.1	16.1	37.6
	Electric machinery	43.0	32.7	45.8	15.7	43.7
	Transport equipment	42.6	43.0	42.5	18.3	43.5
	Electronic product	61.1	62.2	60.6	61.7	61.1

Table 7.3 provides descriptive statistics and a correlation matrix for all variables in the study.

As the propensity of firms to engage in new product innovation across the nine industries was not high, ranging from 6.4 per cent to 22.4 per cent, a Tobit model was employed to examine the determinants of innovation performance of SMEs. The model was estimated using maximum likelihood method, which generates consistent estimators for the coefficients. Table 7.4 reports the regression results of the various models that were run. Model 1 covers the data of all nine industries.

Table 7.3   Descriptive statistics and correlation matrix [C1]

Variable	Mean	S.D.	1	2	3	4	5	6	7	8	9	10	11	12	13	14	15
1 INNO	0.060	0.192	1.000														
2 FINANCE	0.262	0.440	0.082	1.000													
3 SIZE	8.088	1.561	0.143	0.291	1.000												
4 AGE	9.975	11.364	0.041	0.257	0.238	1.000											
5 PROFIT	0.031	1.547	0.004	−0.006	0.004	0.000	1.000										
6 INDFDI	0.290	0.224	−0.026	−0.074	−0.103	−0.084	−0.002	1.000									
7 MARKET	0.001	0.021	0.018	0.003	0.015	−0.002	0.000	−0.007	1.000								
8 INDCOMPETE	0.997	0.005	−0.042	0.012	−0.002	0.019	0.003	−0.060	−0.004	1.000							
9 INDINN	0.152	0.125	0.173	0.019	0.048	0.027	−0.007	−0.082	0.002	−0.113	1.000						
10 HUMCAP	14.396	26.259	0.078	0.015	0.038	0.004	0.001	0.050	0.004	−0.021	0.030	1.000					
11 RND	0.004	0.033	0.163	0.033	0.050	0.014	0.133	0.013	0.019	−0.029	0.055	0.042	1.000				
12 TRAIN	0.143	0.504	0.049	0.033	0.066	0.017	0.004	−0.001	0.015	−0.032	0.019	0.070	0.040	1.000			
13 EXPORT	0.078	0.229	0.060	−0.024	0.024	−0.035	0.000	0.091	0.001	−0.026	−0.004	0.004	−0.005	0.006	1.000		
14 FOREIGN	0.010	0.098	0.022	0.026	0.071	0.008	−0.005	0.042	0.000	−0.009	0.004	0.009	0.001	−0.001	0.053	1.000	
15 ZONE	0.447	0.497	0.070	−0.055	−0.019	0.034	0.003	0.018	0.006	−0.031	0.155	0.047	0.045	0.030	0.014	−0.015	1.000

Table 7.4 *Regression results*

	Model 1 All	Model 2 Small	Model 3 Medium	Model 4 1 owner	Model 5 >1 owner	Model 6 Low-tech	Model 7 Hi-tech	Model 8 FOREIGN2
Control variables								
FINANCE	0.105 (0.012)***	0.100 (0.014)***	0.057 (0.018)***	0.034 (0.036)	0.108 (0.012)***	0.096 (0.017)***	0.108 (0.015)***	0.105 (0.012)***
SIZE	0.100 (0.004)***	0.057 (0.005)***	0.066 (0.009)***	0.031 (0.012)***	0.099 (0.004)***	0.101 (0.006)***	0.097 (0.004)***	0.100 (0.004)***
AGE	0.002 (0.000)***	-0.001 (0.001)	0.002 (0.000)***	0.005 (0.002)***	0.001 (0.000)***	0.002 (0.001)***	0.002 (0.001)***	0.002 (0.000)***
PROFIT	-0.004 (0.002)*	-0.004 (0.003)	0.015 (0.015)	0.314 (0.203)	-0.037 (0.002)	0.069 (0.041)*	-0.003 (0.003)	-0.004 (0.002)*
INDFDI	-0.321 (0.024)***	-0.419 (0.029)***	-0.075 (0.038)***	-0.491 (0.080)***	-0.312 (0.025)***	-0.493 (0.046)***	-0.282 (0.028)***	-0.321 (0.024)***
INDCOMPETE	-2.979 (0.929)***	-3.474 (1.063)***	2.764 (2.740)	-3.297 (2.701)	-2.639 (0.979)***	48.414 (12.288)***	-2.513 (1.003)***	-2.983 (0.929)***
INDINN	1.007 (0.038)***	1.084 (0.047)***	0.611 (0.060)***	0.399 (0.132)***	1.017 (0.039)***	1.046 (0.094)***	0.985 (0.045)***	1.006 (0.038)***
Internal resources								
HUMCAP	0.001 (0.000)***	0.001 (0.000)***	0.002 (0.001)***	-0.003 (0.002)	0.001 (0.000)***	0.004 (0.001)***	0.001 (0.000)***	0.001 (0.000)***
RND	1.940 (0.103)***	1.933 (0.116)***	4.473 (0.398)***	11.777 (2.091)***	1.883 (0.104)***	5.282 (0.363)***	1.710 (0.112)***	1.940 (0.103)***
TRAIN	0.049 (0.008)***	0.049 (0.010)***	0.030 (0.021)	0.016 (0.025)	0.052 (0.009)***	0.020 (0.016)	0.056 (0.010)***	0.049 (0.008)***

	Model 1 All	Model 2 Small	Model 3 Medium	Model 4 1 owner	Model 5 >1 owner	Model 6 Low-tech	Model 7 Hi-tech	Model 8 FOREIGN2
External resources								
MARKET	0.455 (0.168)***	0.476 (0.188)***	5.180 (1.385)***	3.301 (3.750)	0.429 (0.170)***	0.178 (0.164)	2.236 (0.496)***	0.455 (0.168)***
EXPORT	0.364 (0.020)***	0.376 (0.024)***	0.202 (0.032)***	0.362 (0.058)***	0.358 (0.021)***	0.280 (0.030)***	0.390 (0.025)***	0.364 (0.020)***
FOREIGN	0.070 (0.045)	−0.068 (0.074)	0.060 (0.043)	0.052 (0.197)	0.063 (0.046)	0.181 (0.080)**	0.035 (0.054)	
FOREIGN2								0.142 (0.060)**
ZONE	0.046 (0.010)***	0.042 (0.012)***	0.049 (0.017)***	−0.090 (0.033)***	0.048 (0.011)***	−0.001 (0.016)	0.065 (0.013)***	0.046 (0.010)***
Pseudo R²	**0.096**	**0.058**	**0.100**	**0.062**	**0.095**	**0.123**	**0.089**	**0.096**
Observations	**43,732**	**39,657**	**4,075**	**5,149**	**38,583**	**15,003**	**28,729**	**43,732**

Notes: (1) Tobit model is employed; (2) dependent variable: share of total output accounted for by new product sales in 2006; (3) independent and control variables take their values in 2005; (4) standard errors in parentheses; (5)***, **, * for 1 per cent, 5 per cent and 10 percent significance levels, respectively; (6) constant terms are not reported.

We also ran a number of regressions as robustness checks (Models 2–7) to examine whether the determinants of product innovation differ according to the size of the firm, ownership concentration and the technological level of the industry in which it operates. These have been shown to be important factors influencing innovation in other settings.[47] Firstly, we might expect small firms to be more reliant on external factors in the innovation process than medium-sized firms due to the fact that they are subject to greater institutional biases towards them. Previous research on Australian SMEs reveals a stronger relationship between external networking and innovation for smaller SMEs and a stronger relationship between internal R&D and innovation for larger SMEs.[48] Secondly, we might expect differences in the antecedents of product innovation in single-owned and multiple owned firms. Single-owned private SMEs are often family dominated in China and generally more focused on labour-intensive production, with limited focus on product innovation.[49] We might therefore expect external resources to be less important for single-owned firms relative to internal factors. Thirdly, we would expect firms operating in high-technology industries characterized by rapid technological change to be more reliant on co-operation with external partners in the process of innovation than would be the case for firms operating in low-technology industries. Previous work on Dutch SMEs indicates that the determinants of product innovation may differ significantly across industries.[50]

The results of Model 1 suggest that access to finance, size, age and province-industry level innovation spillovers play a significantly positive role in determining the innovation performance of SMEs. Two of the control variables had a strong negative influence on the innovation performance of sampled SMEs. The first one is the province-industry level foreign presence, indicating that in provinces with industries that exhibit high levels of FDI innovative domestic private firms are crowded

---

[47]   Rogers, 'Networks, Firm Size and Innovation', p. 141; De Jong and Vermeulen, 'Determinants of Product Innovation in Small Firms: A Comparison across Industries', p. 587; Rosenbusch, Brinckmann and Bausch, 'Is Innovation Always Beneficial? A Meta-Analysis of the Relationship between Innovation and Performance in SMEs', p. 441.

[48]   Rogers, 'Networks, Firm Size and Innovation', p. 141.

[49]   Michael Carney and Eric Gedaljovic, 'Strategic Innovation and the Administrative Heritage of East Asian Family Business Groups', *Asia-Pacific Journal of Management*, 2003, 20, p. 5.

[50]   De Jong and Vermeulen, 'Determinants of Product Innovation in Small Firms: A Comparison across Industries', p. 587.

out. The second factor which seems to hamper innovation is market competition. Our findings suggest that if a firm faces overly strong competition from local rivals, it will seek to compete with its rivals through reducing operating costs rather than by engaging in product innovation.

The variables included to measure internal resources were also positively related to a firm's propensity to engage in new product innovation, including human capital level, R&D engagement and training intensity. With regard to the external resources for innovation, three variables included that measured external resources – market orientation, export intensity and location within a national Economic and Technology Zone – were found to influence new product innovation in SMEs. In contrast to what was hypothesized, foreign ownership was not significantly related to new product innovation The limited influence of FDI on domestic innovation might also result from the phenomenon of 'round tripping'. Much of the FDI coming from Taiwan and Hong Kong is not in fact FDI, but capital from mainland China that has made its way out of China and back again.[51] In order to understand in greater detail the relationship between foreign ownership and innovation a further robustness check (Model 8) was conducted in which foreign investment from Hong Kong, Macao and Taiwan was removed from analysis. The new variable, FOREIGN2, had positive effects on innovation, albeit at the 5 per cent level of significance, suggesting that foreign capital from non-Chinese sources had a positive influence on innovation.

In Models 2 to 7 we estimated the determinants of product innovation by dividing our sample based on size, ownership, and technological level. Overall the results are in line with those obtained in Model 1, which reflects the robustness of Model 1, but some interesting variation can be noted. Access to finance is seen to be a significant antecedent for product innovation in firms with multiple owners, but not for those with single owners. Also, whereas firm age positively influenced innovation in Model 1, its effects on innovation were insignificant for small-sized firms in Model 2. The variable industry competition shows variation across all dichotomous groups of firms. While industry competition is negatively associated with innovation in small firms, it is not a significant factor impacting innovation in medium-sized firms. Industry competition has a significant negative impact on firms with dispersed ownership but does

---

[51]   John Whalley and Xian Xin, 'China's FDI and Non-FDI Economies and the Sustainability of Future High Chinese Growth', *China Economic Review*, 2010, 21, p. 123.

not significantly affect firms with single ownership. The most striking outcome is that market competition has a significant negative impact on product innovation in hi-tech firms, but is positively associated with low-tech firms.

With regard to the variables measuring internal resources for product innovation, R&D impacts significantly on product innovation in all models, whereas human capital positively impacts product innovation in all models except for firms with single owners. Training expenditure is positively associated with product innovation in small-sized firms, firms with multiple ownership and hi-tech firms, but has no significant association in medium-sized firms, firms with single owners and low-tech firms.

The three variables measuring external resources exhibit a positive relationship with product innovation. Export intensity has a positive influence on product innovation to a high degree of significance for all groups of firms in all models. Market orientation had a significant impact on product innovation in all firms, except for those with a single owner and in low-technology industries. The role of location in or near to a national Economic and Technology Zone is somewhat more ambiguous. Being located in a city with a national Economic and Technology Zone has a negative impact on single-owned firms while it positively impacts firms with multiple owners.

9. DISCUSSION AND IMPLICATIONS

This chapter sought to understand the main determinants of product innovation in Chinese private SMEs. A number of hypotheses were developed based on various internal and external resources that are expected to provide key inputs to product innovation in firms. Its findings suggest that both internal and external resources play an important role in the process of innovation in private Chinese SMEs. Key internal factors include R&D investment, the level of skill and knowledge level of a company's human capital and investment in training. Key external factors are a company's market orientation, export intensity and location in or near to an Economic and Technology Zone. The determinants of product innovation were also found to differ significantly depending on the individual characteristics of the firm (size, ownership and technological level). We will focus on the most salient findings and discuss some of their implications. Table 7.5 summarizes the results.

Table 7.5   Overview of tested hypotheses and results

Hypothesis	Expected relationship	All firms	Small firms	Medium firms	Single owned	>1 owner	Low-tech	High-tech
Investment in R&D	+	+	+	+	+	+	+	+
Skill level	+	+	+	+	0	+	+	+
Training	+	+	+	0	0	+	0	+
Foreign ownership	+	0	0	0	0	0	+	0
Export intensity	+	+	+	+	+	+	+	+
Location in ETZ	+	+	+	+	-	+	0	+
Market orientation	+	+	+	+	0	+	0	+

Our findings indicate the relevance of key tenets of the resource-based view for innovation in Chinese SMEs. The results also show that from a comparative perspective the share of private Chinese SMEs that develop product innovations is low,[52] and therefore there is a continuing need to strengthen the human capital and R&D base within Chinese SMEs. Moreover, the results also indicate that Technology Zones offer a way for SMEs to access external knowledge and information resources, particularly for those in high-tech industries.

If we move beyond the resource-based view there is clear evidence that institutional factors significantly impact product innovation in Chinese private SMEs. Access to finance has a significant positive effect on product innovation, while product innovation is constrained by industries with higher levels of FDI at the provincial level. Also market competition is negatively associated with product innovation.

The finding that higher levels of FDI in industries at the provincial level impact negatively on product innovation in SMEs is especially intriguing, given that the negative relationship is significant across all our models. The general belief that FDI creates knowledge spillovers needs to be adjusted and refined based on our results. Various studies have

---

[52]   OECD, *Innovation in Firms: A Microeconomic Perspective.*

found that FDI into China has positive spillover effects on the performance and productivity of local firms,[53] suggesting that FDI facilitates the
transfer of advanced technologies and managerial know-how to local
firms. Although these studies demonstrate that FDI has contributed
greatly towards the success of Chinese private firms, especially those in
export-oriented sectors, our findings demonstrate that high levels of FDI
might also negatively impact on private SMEs, through reducing their
ability to innovate. Although at an individual level firms seem to benefit
from foreign investment, our findings indicate that high rates of FDI in
specific industries at the provincial level negatively affect the innovation
of Chinese private SMEs. This may be due to the fact that foreign FDI
further increases the shortage of R&D talent, reported as a barrier for
innovation in SMEs,[54] while also making it more difficult to retain
talented and high-skilled workers. Furthermore, a strong provincial
government focus on attracting FDI does not necessarily encourage
domestic SMEs to innovate, as less government resources may be
directed towards development of an indigenous knowledge infrastructure
and towards local innovation. This may result in local firms opting to
compete using a cost-reduction strategy rather than through an
innovation-oriented strategy.

The antecedents of product innovation were also found to differ
according to the size, ownership concentration and technological level of
the SME. One interesting finding is that while market competition affects
innovation in low-tech firms positively, it has a negative impact on
product innovation in firms from high-tech industries. This suggests that
in low-tech industries firms see differentiation through product innovation as a way to distinguish themselves from their competitors whereas
in high-tech industries this is not the case. Strong competition for
high-tech firms may actually provide them with a disincentive to engage
in product innovation. This may be due to the weak protection of
intellectual property in China, which does not allow companies to capture

---

[53]   Yingqi Wei and Xiaming Liu, 'Productivity Spillovers from R&D, Exports
and FDI in China's Manufacturing Sector', *Journal of International Business
Studies*, 2006, 37, p. 544; Peter Buckley, Chengqi Wang & Jeremy Clegg, 'The
Impact of Foreign Ownership, Local Ownership and Industry Characteristics on
Spillover Benefits from Foreign Direct Investment in China', *International
Business Review*, 2007, 16, p. 142; Sea Jin Chang and Dean Xu, 'Spillovers and
Competition among Foreign and Local Firms in China', *Strategic Management
Journal*, 2008, 29(5), pp. 495–518.
[54]   Zhang, Zeng, Mako and Seward, *Promoting Enterprise-Led Innovation in
China*, p. 57.

the benefits of product innovation as rivals may use illegal means to copy innovative practices.[55]

Finally, locating in designated Economic and Technology Zones was shown to have a positive impact on product innovation in both small and medium-sized firms, in firms with dispersed ownership, and in high-tech firms. Firms in high-technology industries benefit from close geographical distance to other high-tech firms and knowledge institutes, a finding reported in various studies.[56] Intriguing is the finding that single-owned firms are negatively impacted by locating close to or in such a zone. This may be due to the fact that firms with single owners, which are often family controlled, typically focus more on low-cost, labour-intensive production and non-complex technologies than firms with dispersed ownership, and are less able to co-operate with external partners due to high levels of asymmetric information.[57]

The research findings yield a number of policy and managerial implications. Continued incentives to increase levels of investment in R&D and human capital development within SMEs is crucial to spur innovation, while too much focus by government on attracting FDI may be detrimental for innovation in private SMEs, as local talent is drawn away. Provincial governments should pay attention to the nature of the industries in which FDI is concentrated, assess the technological level and nature of innovation within domestic industries, and consider the extent to which further FDI can enable the continued development of technological capabilities within domestic SMEs or constrain their innovation potential.

It is also important to consider the various ways SMEs draw on external resources in the process of new product development. Government authorities should continue to support the development of innovation clusters in economic or technological development zones and make SMEs aware of the potential benefits of locating in such a zone, especially for those operating in high-tech industries. While finance is

---

[55]   Zhang, Zeng, Mako and Seward, *Promoting Enterprise-Led Innovation in China*.

[56]   Gilbert, McDougall and Audretsch, 'Clusters, Knowledge Spillovers and New Venture Performance: An Empirical Examination', p. 405; Zhang and Li, 'Managerial Ties, Firm Resources, and Performance of Cluster Firms', p. 615; Li, Chen and Shapiro, 'Product Innovation in Emerging Economies: The Role of Foreign Knowledge Access Channels and Internal Efforts in Chinese Firms', p. 243.

[57]   Carney and Gedaljovic, 'Strategic Innovation and the Administrative Heritage of East Asian Family Business Groups', p. 5.

shown to be one of the key inputs for innovation, it is often difficult for SMEs to acquire the necessary funding for their innovative activities,[58] and therefore there is a role for government to encourage financial institutions to forward greater credit to SMEs. SMEs should also consider exporting as an effective way of accessing innovative ideas from their foreign customers.

10. LIMITATIONS AND SUGGESTIONS FOR FUTURE RESEARCH

This research has several limitations that may be considered in future research. Firstly, due to the fact that we were using a large government dataset the measures used in our study do not cover some important determinants of innovative activity and aspects of the innovative process. In future, survey research may be conducted to test the impact of variables such as the ability to retain skilled employees and the impact of informal relations and social capital on product innovation. Secondly, due to data limitations we were only able to examine the antecedents of product innovation over a short time-frame. In future research may be done over a longer period to verify the antecedents of product innovation over a longer time period.

Further comparisons between emerging economies may also shed more light on the impact of institutional factors on product innovation in SMEs and the role of relatively underdeveloped financial markets and legal systems. There is also a need for more in-depth analysis of the impact of FDI on innovation in specific industrial sectors and regions, as our research has indicated that FDI may constrain innovation in private SMEs at a more aggregate industrial level. As China now aims to expand its innovative capacity, further research is particularly necessary into the role that FDI can play in this process. More focused research is also needed to understand how and why the determinants of innovation are different for various types of SMEs in order to assist in the development of suitable strategies to promote innovation at the government and firm level.

---

[58]   Zhang, Zeng, Mako and Seward, *Promoting Enterprise-Led Innovation in China.*

APPENDIX

Table 7A.1   List of variables

	Variable	Definition of the Variables	
Dependent variable	*INNO*	the share of total output accounted for by new products	
Internal resources	*HUMCAP*	Wage/employee	
	RND	R&D expenditure/sales	
	TRAIN	Training expenditure per employee	
External resources	*EXPORT*	Export/sales	
	FOREIGN	Foreign ownership dummy (1 for non-zero foreign capital)	Firm-level variables
	MARKET	Advertising fees/sales	
	ZONE	Econ & Tech zone dummy (1 for yes)	
Control variables	*FINANCE*	Long-term liabilities dummy	
	SIZE	Size=ln(total assets)	
	AGE	Age	
	PROFIT	Profit/sales	
	INDFDI	Province-industry level share of foreign capital in total capital	Industry-level variables
	INDCOMPETE	Market concentration = 1-Herfindahl index	
	INDINN	Province-industry level share of new product in output	

8. Foreign R&D in China: An evolving innovation landscape

Seamus Grimes

INTRODUCTION

While there is a general view in the literature that despite China's very significant pace of economic growth in GDP terms since adopting its Open Door Policy in 1978, the level of innovation is still rather low. For the years 1995 to 2005, China was the fastest improving country in terms of innovation, but was still ranked only 34th globally in 2005.[1] More recent data indicates that while China continues to be considerably behind the EU27 in many indicators, it is the only BRICS country to show that it is closing the innovation gap with Europe.[2] Bearing in mind criticisms of various innovation indicators, data from *The Global Innovation Index* for various years provides some indication of China's evolving progression in relation to various indicators of innovation compared with the emerging economies of India and Brazil.[3] While India and China are of similar size in terms of population, with Brazil having less than 200 million people, GDP per capita at $12,038 is higher than that of China and significantly more than that of India (Appendix, Table 8A.1). The overall ranking of all three countries has slipped somewhat since 2009, but China remains considerably ahead of both India and Brazil. China's best performing indicator is scientific outputs, ranking number 2 globally in 2013, while its worst performance relates to institutions and creative outputs. On the other hand, China outperforms

---

[1]   Commission of the European Community, *European Innovation Scoreboard 2008*, January 2009, p. 26.
[2]   Commission of the European Community, *Innovation Union Scoreboard 2013*, p. 25.
[3]   Soumitra Dutta and Bruno Lavin, *The Global Innovation Index 2013*, Johnson Cornell, INSEAD and WIPO, 2013, available at: http://www.global innovationindex.org/content.aspx?page=GII-Home.

both India and Brazil in relation to market sophistication and human capital and research.

It is clear therefore that China has been making significant strides in science and technology, particularly in terms of growth in R&D investment. While R&D activity has been dominated by Europe, the US and Japan for the past 40 years, in 2011 China had surpassed Japan's spending. By 2018 it is expected to surpass the combined spending of Europe's 34 countries and by 2022 it is likely to exceed the R&D investments of the US in absolute terms.[4]

A major difference in R&D funding between China and the US is that while only 28 per cent of such funding in the US comes from government sources, 70 per cent of China's R&D funding is sourced from the government.[5] Boutellier, Gassmann and Von Zedtwitz predicted that within a few years China will become the second most significant location for foreign R&D labs and that already it has become an important source and provider of global technology.[6] Many interviewees of the present author, however, felt that despite the significant expenditure on R&D, China was still very much in 'catch-up' mode and that it would take many years before China reached the average level of innovation of more developed regions.

While almost 80 per cent of R&D investment comes from within China and particularly its enterprise sector, foreign investment, which has been very important in China's increasing integration into the global economy, also plays a significant role. This chapter will focus on that role, particularly in relation to R&D foreign direct investment (FDI) in Shanghai. Attention will also be given to the evolution of China's policy towards attracting FDI and particularly more recently R&D investment. China has had a very significant dependence to date on importing foreign technology. Chinese policymakers are now particularly concerned to reduce this dependency and to increase indigenous innovation. The implications for the growing significance of foreign R&D in China and the dominant role played by foreign multinational companies in high-technology sectors will also be considered.

---

[4]   R&D Magazine/Battelle, *R&D in China*, 12.9.2013, http://www.rdmag. com/articles/2013/12/r-d-china.

[5]   R&D Magazine/Battelle, *Emerging Economies Drive Global R&D Growth*, December 2009, http://www.rdmag.com/articles/2009/12/emerging-economies-drive-global-r-d-growth.

[6]   Roman Boutellier, Oliver Gassmann and Maximilian Von Zedtwitz, *Managing Global Innovations – Uncovering the Secrets of Future Competitiveness*, 3rd edition, Berlin: Springer, 2008, p. 74.

1. THE BACKGROUND

While some foreign multinational companies have been involved in China for more than a century, most were forced to leave for a period during the Cultural Revolution between 1966 and 1976, with many of them returning in 1979 with the new opening up of the economy. Most of the current foreign investment in China, however, is of recent origin. During the 1980s foreign investment in China was primarily associated with exploiting China's large supply of low-cost labour to establish a manufacturing export platform. Initially, much of the investment came from the 'Greater China region' and particularly from Hong Kong, which relocated most of its manufacturing activity to the mainland. Later Taiwan relocated much of its electronics manufacturing to the eastern urban regions of the mainland and China also became a significant location for other Asian Pacific countries, particularly Japan and Korea. Over time the overall profile of FDI in China was quite broadly based, with significant investment from the US and Europe. In addition to becoming the world's 'global factory', China's rapid economic growth over a period of almost 30 years made it a particularly attractive emerging market for the world's largest multinational companies. Investment from the key Fortune 500 companies expanded significantly over time. With China becoming the third largest recipient of FDI in 2005, European policymakers are increasingly concerned about the EU's ability to compete with China for such investment.[7]

While this initial phase of China's recent period of economic expansion succeeded in bringing hundreds of millions of formerly poor rural dwellers out of poverty, and set China on the road to becoming a major economic power, the environmental damage associated with this rapid pace of growth, and the low level of profitability associated with much of China's manufacturing activity, made it clear that major changes were required in long-term economic policy if growth was to be sustainable. The most significant change in policy in recent years has been a focus on the promotion of indigenous innovation as a means towards creating a sustainable economy. The rationale for this strategy arose from a growing concern with China's predominantly low-cost export platform, which relied on low labour costs and resulted in low profit levels from exports; China's global engagement in the last 30 years has also made China a hub for copying product development and design from other countries.

---

[7]   Lars Oxelheim and Pervez Ghauri, 'EU-China and the non-transparent race for inward FDI', *Journal of Asian Economics* 19, 2008, p. 359.

China's new approach was more focused on promoting indigenous innovation but there is also an acknowledgement of the continued role of foreign investment and the hope of increased technology transfers to the local economy. China used the attractiveness of its huge and growing market to try to leverage technology transfer from multinational companies in the initial stages, by insisting on the formation of joint ventures with local companies and building alliances with China's enterprises. With the more recent accession to the World Trade Organization (WTO) in 2001, China has been obliged to open its economy to a greater extent to outside investors and the initial emphasis on joint ventures has gradually given way to wholly owned enterprises by outside investors.[8] This pushes China to strategically think about the new role of FDI in China.

Most of the current foreign investment during their earlier period of development in China mainly focused on manufacturing and sales and marketing, with the more recent period being characterized by a growing level of R&D investment. To some extent, this changing profile of foreign investment in China reveals a fairly typical pattern of evolution, with most companies initially seeking to exploit the emerging Chinese market and in many cases using China as a significant export platform for low-cost manufacturing. Chen argues that multinational investment in China has gone beyond 'cost-driven' R&D activity and has resulted in the relocation of the whole spectrum of innovation.[9] Saxenian suggests that perhaps the greatest transfer of managerial and technical skills in human history accompanied the migration to Shanghai of the entire Taiwanese integrated circuit (IC) supply chain, including equipment manufacturers, designers, wafers and other input suppliers and packaging and test specialists.[10]

The more recent period has also seen considerable expansion of investment to the major urban centres, particularly Beijing and Shanghai, and increasingly to lower-tier cities and lower-cost locations in the western regions. Because of policy changes in relation to FDI, including tax incentives, there has been a significant push for higher-value-added investment in high-tech sectors, and the share of manufacturing FDI,

---

[8] Linda Yeuh, *The Economy of China*, Cheltenham: Edward Elgar, 2010, p. 103.

[9] Chen Yun-Chung, 'Changing the Shanghai Innovation Systems: The Role of Multinational Corporations' R&D Centres', *Science, Technology & Society*, 11(1), 2006, p. 99.

[10] AnnaLee Saxenian, *The New Argonauts: Regional Advantage in a Global Economy*. Cambridge, Mass.: Harvard University Press, 2006, p. 201.

which was 70 per cent for the period 2002 to 2004, has been rapidly declining. Foreign capital is no longer seen as a source of funding or a means of job creation but of bringing in advance technology and expertise.[11] Despite reaching a new high of US$711 billion in 2011, FDI attraction has been losing its former high priority with a greater emphasis on quality as opposed to quantity.[12]

Boutellier, Gassmann and Von Zedtwitz refer to three modes of entry of foreign R&D investments in China: as wholly owned independent labs; as R&D departments of a Chinese operation or as a joint venture with a Chinese partner; or as a form of cooperation with Chinese research universities or institutes.[13] They suggest three main objectives of these investments as acting as a link between China's market and the technology of their parent company; making an important contribution to R&D generally; or demonstrating their commitment to the Chinese government. Various authors have referred to this latter motivation arising in some cases from pressure by the Chinese government on multi-nationals to carry out R&D in China. In addition to their significantly lower cost of R&D talent in China, many foreign R&D centres in China have global mandates for products and technologies, although proximity to the Chinese market together with the plentiful supply of competent talent are also important factors. Boutellier, Gassmann and Von Zedtwitz conclude that the management of foreign-owned R&D operations in China were not that prepared to learn from Chinese science and technology, and that the general tendency was one of a short-term profit-maximizing strategy. Around 67 per cent of all foreign R&D sites are located either in Beijing or Shanghai, with more of an emphasis on research in Beijing and a greater focus on development in Shanghai.[14]

The foreign investment experience in China during the past 30 years has gone through various stages of evolution, and it has been an unusual experience compared to other regions of the world in that it has been part of the evolution of a major political economy experiment with China's one-party socialist state becoming in some senses more capitalist than societies with a more social-democratic composition. While the opening

---

[11]   Economist Intelligence Unit, *Serve the People – the New Landscape of Foreign Investment in China*, 2012, p. 6.

[12]   Ken Davies, 'Inward FDI in China and its Policy Context 2012', *Columbia FDI Profiles*, 24 October 2012, p. 1. Online at: http://www.vcc.columbia.edu/files/vale/documents/China_IFDI_final_18_Oct_0.pdf.

[13]   Boutellier, Gassmann and Zedtwitz, *Managing Global Innovations – Uncovering the Secrets of Future Competitiveness*, p. 64.

[14]   *Ibid.*, p. 67.

up of China's market presented many foreign companies with major opportunities for expanding their market share, particularly in infrastructural sectors such as telecommunications, some companies took considerable time to develop profitable operations. Some early bird investors in the telecoms sector such as Alcatel (now Alacatel-Lucent) had very high levels of profitability in the early stages of investment, with most of the competition coming from other foreign companies like Ericsson, Motorola and Nokia. More recently companies like Alcatel have been experiencing very significant competition from emerging Chinese companies, and particularly Huawei, which has become an important player in telecoms equipment internationally.

The role of the state is strongly present in relation to innovation policy in China, as it is in most countries, but the approach taken by China to date is very much a top-down model, based on a strongly technocratic belief in technology, together with the provision of very significant investment in the provision of science park and high technology infrastructure on the assumption that the clustering of high technology activity will generate higher levels of innovation in the economy. To some extent China is adopting policies that appear to have some measure of success in more developed regions of the world, but a common criticism of the approach is the over-reliance on the hardware side of the equation, while paying insufficient attention to key software factors such as the role of the university education system in innovation. Despite the limitations of the Chinese approach, some argue that emerging countries need to ensure that effective innovation policies are in place to avoid the negative effects of inward investment in R&D.[15]

One of the primary expectations of the Chinese state during the early period of foreign investment was the transfer of technology from foreign to Chinese companies, and this was an important reason for the emphasis on creating joint ventures. One of the most successful of these joint ventures was Alcatel Shanghai Bell, which became a significant manufacturing arm for Alcatel in its early period of existence. The Chinese government have not been particularly happy with the level of technology transfer from foreign companies since the opening up of China. Many technology companies during the initial stages of investment in China not only obtained huge infrastructural contracts, but also added to their

[15] Dieter Ernst, 'Indigenous Innovation and Globalization: The Challenge of China's Standardization Strategy', *UC Institute on Global Conflict and Cooperation and the East-West Center*, 2011, p. 23, http://www.eastwestcenter. org/publications/indigenous-innovation-and-globalization-challenge-chinas-stand ardization-strategy.

profitability by charging very high royalty payments for transferring technology to their Chinese subsidiaries. The more recent period, however, has seen cut-throat competition, not only between the foreign multinationals themselves, but also with Chinese companies, thus reducing significantly their margins.[16] The more recent phase of investment in China has also seen a growth in R&D investment in China by foreign multinationals, which has resulted in a reduction in the need to transfer technology from their headquarters.

2. A CLOSER LOOK AT FOREIGN R&D IN CHINA

As the above has revealed, to some extent, the changing pattern of foreign investment in China reflects an evolution in the political economy of innovation in China, with China initially leveraging its huge and growing market size to attract foreign investment, to insist on technology transfer by means of joint ventures with foreign multinationals, and more recently by insisting that foreign multinationals increase R&D investment in China. Since this most recent phase of policy development has also been accompanied by the shift from joint ventures to wholly owned foreign subsidiaries (also known as foreign-invested firms), the actual location of some of their R&D activity in China by foreign firms does not necessarily mean that China's ultimate objective of shifting its economic model from low-cost manufacturing to a greater level of indigenous innovation will be easily facilitated. There is a general perception among both Chinese and foreign actors that interaction between foreign and domestic R&D is not as strong as it might be.[17]

As mentioned earlier, the early stages of China's innovation policy were based on the assumption that the constraints placed on multinational companies requiring them to form joint ventures (JVs) would result in significant technology transfer, and since this has not happened to any great extent there are some signs that China may be re-evaluating its policy options.[18] China is no longer prepared to function as the 'world's factory', which is a model based on low levels of innovation and low

---

[16]   Loren Brandt and Eric Thun, 'The Fight for the Middle: Upgrading, Competition, and Industrial Development in China', *World Development*, 38(11), 2010, p. 1565.

[17]   Boutellier, Gassmann and Zedtwitz, *Managing Global Innovations – Uncovering the Secrets of Future Competitiveness*, p. 72.

[18]   Denis Simon, 'China's new S&T reforms and their implications or innovative performance', *Testimony before the US-China Economic and Security*

levels of profitability.[19] In place of the rather vague specifications about transferring technology from foreign companies in the earlier phase of FDI, the most recent phase associated with 'indigenous innovation' is much more specific in that only products and services with a certain level of 'indigenous innovation' will be eligible for the public procurement market. By insisting that the Chinese entity must fully own the IP or must first register the trademark in China, this creates the problem for foreign companies of being restricted to selling products in a market in which IP has been developed.[20]

Some of the early bird foreign investors in China, such as Alcatel and Motorola, showed considerable willingness to work closely with the Chinese government and to some extent become 'Chinese companies' – at least in China. In other cases, notably Microsoft, becoming profitable in China was a slower and more difficult process. Microsoft has also learned how to work very closely with the Chinese government by developing close links with major institutions and developing a significant R&D operation mainly in Beijing and Shanghai. Like many other companies, the initial approach of Microsoft was to exploit the Chinese market by selling its popular software at prices similar to those charged in other regions. During the 1980s and 1990s, however, Microsoft, together with other foreign companies in China, encountered a great level of intellectual property piracy, where there was little implementation of regulations protecting IP. This has been an ongoing problem for foreign companies in the Chinese market, and while the government has introduced more stringent regulations recently, the issue of vigorous implementation, which in the view of some is related to the absence of an independent judiciary, remains a problem. Because of their fear of losing IP to competitors in the Chinese market, some companies were only prepared to use middle-range IP in China, and their main objective was to gain market share without compromising their IP.[21] Lundvall, however,

---

Review Commission, 10 May 2012, online at: http://www.uscc.gov/sites/default/files/5.10.12Simon.pdf.

[19]   Shulin Gu, Bengt-Ake Lundvall, Ju Liu, Franco Malerba & Sylvia Schwaag Serger, 'China's System and Vision of Innovation: An Analysis in Relation to the Strategic Adjustment and the Medium- to Long-term S&T Development Plan (2006–20)', *Industry and Innovation*, 16(4–5), 2009, p. 372.

[20]   Seamus Grimes and Debin Du, 'Foreign and Indigenous Innovation in China: Some Evidence from Shanghai', *European Planning Studies*, 21(9), 2013, p. 1364.

[21]   Timothy Moran, 'Foreign Manufacturing Multinationals and the Transformation of the Chinese Economy: New Measurements, New Perspectives',

argues that companies from more developed regions who are deriving significant benefits in China as a result of Chinese investment in providing science and engineering talent, should adopt a more flexible approach to IP issues.[22]

The problem of Intellectual Property Regulation (IPR) reflects characteristics of emerging markets which are also found in other regions and in most regions in earlier stages of development. The Chinese market, like other emerging markets, is strongly segmented in tiers, with a large low-margin tier and a growing, but relatively modest, middle class tier. To overcome the problem of software piracy rates in excess of 90 per cent, Microsoft, for example, has been forced to opt for very low charges for its software packages in China. In the opinion of an interviewee from Microsoft, the only way for success in the Chinese market was to develop a partnership with a local company through a JV or through developing an alliance with a state-owned enterprise (SOE) such as China Mobile in Microsoft's case.

Although there is considerable rhetoric among foreign multinational companies about developing innovative activities in China and contributing towards making China a more innovative economy, the reality is that the multinational model of innovation is very much about controlling intellectual property within the boundaries of the corporation, while at the same time sharing knowledge creation between subsidiaries in different regions of the world, but also ensuring that there is no leakage to potential competitor companies. Traditionally, R&D investment was concentrated close to the headquarters of the corporation, but with increasing globalization and with the growing significance of emerging markets in Asia and elsewhere, corporations have been decentralizing their R&D activity to a greater extent in recent years, partly to develop products closer to their customers in increasingly important markets like China, but also to tap into the lower-cost surplus of intellectual talent in these emerging markets. Very often R&D investments in locations like China have begun being focused on more basic activities related to the local market such as technical support, localization and adaptation of products to the local market. Over time, however, with increasing experience of the growing capabilities of the local labour force, together

---

Working Paper 11-11, Peterson Institute for International Economics, Washington DC, 2011.

22   Bengt-Ake Lundvall, 'The Changing Knowledge Landscape and the Need for a Transatlantic Vision and a New Pragmatism', Presentation to Aalborg University and Sciences Po, Paris. Online at:http://transatlantic.saisjhu.edu/partnerships/Cornerstone%20Project/cornerstone_project_lundvall_paper.pdf.

with improved infrastructure and policy incentives, R&D investment has become more innovative, and in some cases has moved significantly up the value chain to the complete production of new products. In the pharma sector, for example, Roche have evolved their activity in China from an initial focus on drug development to highly innovative projects with emerging Chinese biotechnology companies.[23]

Although the growth in R&D investment which has characterized the more recent period of FDI in China is not disputed, there is considerable scepticism about the nature of the activity involved and its level of innovation. Some of this investment has resulted from government pressure on companies to move beyond the market for technology transfer stage towards making a greater contribution to local innovation. There is little doubt that China has invested hugely in growing its R&D investment in recent years, and part of this results from attracting foreign high-technology companies. A large number of science and high-technology industrial parks have been developed in the major cities in recent years and together with attractive low rates of corporation tax and other financial incentives, China has been very successful in increasing this investment. In addition to its emphasis on high technology, China's policy has also sought to cluster much of the R&D activity in science and industrial parks in the major cities.

Despite China's obvious success in attracting a significant volume of R&D foreign investment, and also increasing at a very rapid rate its own expenditure on R&D, questions remain about how successful this policy has been to date in raising the level of indigenous innovation. A major thrust of China's current policy in science and technology is to reduce its technology dependence on foreign companies, currently estimated at about 50 per cent to about 30 per cent.[24] As Chinese technology companies such as Huawei have emerged as serious competitors for foreign technology companies in China and elsewhere, there is a growing commitment by the Chinese government to implement intellectual property rights. While this is acknowledged by many foreign companies, IP infringement in China remains a major barrier towards introducing core technology to their R&D activities in China. While multinational companies who have been successfully penetrating the Chinese market have

---

[23]   Bethan Hughes, 'China Spurs Pharma Innovation', *Nature Reviews Drug Discovery* 9, (August 2010), p 581, online at: http://www.nature.com/nrd/journal/v9/n8/full/nrd3238.html.

[24]   Economist Intelligence Unit, 'Unlocking Innovation in China – An Economist Intelligence Unit Report Sponsored by Cisco', 2009, online at: http://graphics.eiu.com/marketing/pdf/Cisco_Innovation%20in%20China_English.pdf.

many reasons for extending their investment in R&D activity, a strategy of splitting various R&D operations is often used to ensure that China does not acquire access to their integrated core IP. A similar type of strategy may also be used at the local level in China in R&D operations, by not allowing researchers full access to the complete process being developed.[25] Thus, while the Chinese government and foreign-owned companies may have complementary objectives in increasing the level of R&D investment in China, there are clearly major differences and possible areas of tensions between the objectives of the two major actors involved. In general, the multinational model will seek to restrict the sharing of knowledge creation within the boundaries of the organization and between its various subsidiaries, an important objective of the Chinese government is to increase the level of indigenous innovation, which appears to give rise to a tension between these two sets of objectives. While it is difficult to quantify the contribution of multinational companies to building management and other capacities of local firms by their operations in China, the extent of actual technological spillovers does not appear to be very extensive.[26] In many cases they are testing the water and exploring what is the best way forward to fulfil what is expected of them from the state, while ensuring that they are not providing access to cutting edge technology.

In the initial phase of their investment, multinationals for the most part were competing with each other for China's expanding market in those sectors which had been opened up for competition. In the most recent phase of development, foreign multinational companies are not only competing with each other for China's market, but they are facing increasing competition from local Chinese companies. Part of their R&D strategy, therefore, is to develop products that are more suitable for China and more generally for Asia, and to retain their market position through being more innovative. This, however, is proving in many cases to be quite challenging. In the earlier stages of FDI in the 1980s and 1990s, earlybird foreign multinational companies in China had the market largely to themselves, with significant opportunities for major contracts and high profit margins. More recently, China has become a much more competitive and challenging marketplace, with foreign multinationals

---

25   Adam Segal, *Advantage: How American Innovation Can Overcome the Asian Challenge*, New York: WW Norton & Company, 2011, p. 98.

26   Yifei Sun and Debin Du, 'Domestic Firm Innovation and Networking with Foreign firms in China's ICT Industry', *Environment and Planning A*, 43, 2011, pp. 786–809; Segal, *Advantage: How American Innovation Can Overcome the Asian Challenge*, p. 88.

struggling to preserve their profit margins. Despite the more challenging nature of China's market, however, most major multinationals accept that their ability to compete in China will impact greatly on their ability to compete globally in the future. What has changed significantly is not only that China plays a key role for locating lower cost manufacturing, but that the rapid growth of the Chinese market itself is impacting greatly on the nature of the global marketplace. Gadiesh, Leung and Vestring argue that winning China's 'good-enough' segment is critical to success in China, but may also have global implications.[27]

The telecommunications sector reveals some of the important changes in the Chinese market over the past 30 years. Telecommunications services remains monopolized by three major SOEs, China Telecom, China Mobile and China Unicom. While this particular segment of telecommunications has not yet been open to competition from foreign companies, there is growing competition within the sector. Telecommunications equipment, however, was opened up to outside competition, with multinationals such as Alcatel-Lucent, Motorola, Nokia and Ericsson being early entrants in the market. Motorola made significant investments in China from the 1980s onwards and was one of the first major technology companies to develop R&D centres in China. But its success in the market was restricted mainly to the early stages of analogue technology, losing out to Huawei, one of China's most successful indigenous companies, during the more recent digital and GSM technological stages.

In the earlier stages of development China's telecommunications market, with no significant local Chinese companies present, foreign multinationals monopolized the market and obtained profit margins as high as 45 per cent. The telecommunications market in China, with an annual growth in the region of $200bn provided considerable opportunities for foreign companies. But from 2005 the main state service providers have centralized their procurement, thus significantly reducing profit levels for the multinationals by increasing competition. Thus while Alcatel-Lucent was very successful in the earlier period, succeeding in doubling its market share, that share has now fallen more recently to only 4 per cent because of increasing competition from Ericsson and Nokia, and particularly from Huawei. Alcatel-Lucent's poorer performance in recent years is also partly explained by the merger in 2006 of Alcatel and Lucent Technologies.

---

[27] Orit Gadiesh, Philip Leung and Till Vestring, 'The Battle for China's Good-enough Market', *Harvard Business Review,* 1 September 2007, p 80.

While Huawei is currently ranked the largest telecommunication equipment maker in the world after taking over the leadership position from Ericsson in 2012, and has succeeded in going international (with 60 per cent of its revenue coming from outside China), it remains one of the most successful of only a small number of Chinese companies to have emerged in recent years. There is still a very high level of technology dependence by China on imported technology, for which they had to pay high royalty fees. In 2000 foreign-invested enterprises (FIEs) accounted for more than 85 per cent of all high-technology exports. Thus the so-called 'market for technology' policy has not resulted in the level of technology spillovers from foreign to Chinese enterprises that policy-makers had hoped for. This is reflected in the fact that foreign multi-national companies were responsible for 96 per cent of all Advanced Technology Products (ATP) exports since 2002.[28]

To summarize, an understanding of the evolution of China's market during the past three decades helps to explain the context in which foreign multinational investments have developed to their most recent phase which has been associated with rapid growth in R&D activity. Just as the initial stages of the most recent phase of foreign investment in China during the 1980s and 1990s has been associated with exploiting China's lower-cost manufacturing advantages to achieve greater competi-tiveness in the global marketplace, the most recent R&D phase has also had a similar objective, particularly in terms of exploiting China's rapidly expanding talent pool of science and technology graduates. However, as China's market itself has become more integrated into the global economy, with a gradual expansion in its overall purchasing power, this has also had an impact on the focus of R&D activity of multinational companies in China.

3. STAGES OF EVOLUTION

It is clear, therefore, that over the past 30 years, both the Chinese market itself, and the nature of foreign investment in China have been evolving. The chief executive of Philips' operation in Asia Pacific, which is based in Shanghai, summarized the evolution of their activities in terms of three stages: the first was 'global to local' with global products being sold in China. This stage was characterized by a rather restricted 'high-end'

---

[28]   Timothy Moran, 'Foreign Manufacturing Multinationals and the Trans-formation of the Chinese Economy: New Measurements, New Perspectives', p. 10.

market. The second stage was 'local to local', with the development of products locally for the Chinese market, and the third stage was 'local to global', with China being used as an export base for global production. This suggested model of FDI evolution in China, while being broad based, is only suited to explain the development of some business segments, since many corporations have long been using China as a major export platform for manufactured goods.

While accepting that different sectors may be at particular stages of the evolution, it is clear that the most recent phase of development is characterized by increasing competition within the Chinese market from local companies. Global corporations are becoming aware that the future of global competition for market share will increasingly be impacted by the Chinese market itself, which is already very large and has been until the past year or so expanding much more rapidly than other regions of the world. With more sophisticated procurement strategies in China and the growing competition for market share from local companies, global corporations accept that their performance in China will have an important impact on their ability to compete internationally in the future.

Historically, China's market had two tiers. At the top was a small high-end segment, served by global corporations who benefited from high growth rates and high margins. At the bottom was a large low-end segment served by local companies offering low quality products at prices which were often 40–90 per cent cheaper than the high-end goods. The newly expanding market in recent years is the economy segment or what is referred to as the 'good-enough' market.[29] In the earlier 'global to local' phase of multinational involvement in China, companies like Philips in the healthcare sector were importing very expensive hospital equipment such as MRI and x-ray equipment. The affordability in China for such expensive equipment was restricted to top-tier hospitals. To address the rapidly growing economy segment of mid-tier hospitals, Philips established a joint venture with Neusoft, a Chinese company with greater familiarity with the local market. GE Healthcare has also used a line of reliable but less expensive machines targeted at China's remote and financially constrained second- and third-tier cities.

Thus while foreign multinational companies are gradually moving down from the top-tier market to the middle segment, they are meeting more and more Chinese companies that are moving upwards from the

---

[29] Orit Gadiesh, Philip Leung and Till Vestring, 'The Battle for China's Good-enough Market', *Harvard Business Review*, 1 September 2007, p. 80.

lowest segment of cheap products. Multinationals see this middle segment of the market as a major battle ground for capturing future market
share, and it may also play an important role in the battle for innovation
in China between foreign-owned R&D centres and attempts by the state
to promote greater levels of innovation among Chinese companies.

4. EVIDENCE FROM SHANGHAI-BASED FOREIGN MULTINATIONALS

In many cases (though not all) R&D investment in China has been the
most recent stage in the evolution of company involvement in the
country. Much of the R&D investment by foreign-owned companies has
occurred in recent years. Company case studies in Shanghai provide
some background to the evolution in these R&D investments and reveal
their efforts to carve out a role within their corporations, with a focus
primarily in many cases on the market in China. These recent investments in Shanghai also reflect some level of restructuring of activities by
the corporations within the Asia Pacific region, with a greater focus on
the more rapidly growing market in China. With increasing decentralization of investment by large corporations, including R&D activity, there
is a trend towards investment growth outside their home countries, and in
some cases this may include the decentralization of headquarter activity
as multinational companies become more globalized.

DOW Chemical Company, the third largest chemical company in the
world, opened its business and innovation complex for Asia Pacific, the
Shanghai Dow Centre, in Shanghai Zhangjiang High Tech Park in 2009.
In 2011 China accounted for $4.45 billion or 7 per cent of its global
sales.[30] With markets in other parts of Asia Pacific such as Malaysia,
Indonesia and Singapore in decline, Dow is focusing more on the growth
potential of China, which is close to becoming its second largest market.
As the Chinese government seeks to attract more high-technology
investment, locations like Singapore are losing out to the more attractive
Chinese market. In developing the Shanghai centre, part of the objective
is to build a global knowledge centre, but concentrating very much on
applications for the local market, such as paying attention to the different
texture of Asian people's hair in personal care products. In the early
stages of developing this centre, discussion centred on the extent to

---

[30] Presentation at International Advanced Coal Technologies Conference,
Xian, 4 June 2012, http://www.uwyo.edu/ser/_files/docs/conferences/2013/china/
peng%20ningke.pdf.

which Dow should become a 'Chinese' company, and how much resources should be diverted from their headquarters in the US.

Philips had been in China since the 1920s, but restarted their more recent activities in 1985, having returned after the Cultural Revolution. They began with sales activities ('global to local'), then progressed to manufacturing and sourcing in the mid-1990s ('local to local'), and have evolved more recently to an organization where all business functions are present, including marketing and R&D. Their R&D activities in Shanghai are connected with those in Bangalore.

Microsoft adopted a three-fold approach to their involvement in China, involving three stages which they describe as 'crawl, walk and run'. In a market where piracy rates for computer software have been estimated to be in the region of 90 per cent, Microsoft's early entry into China in the 1980s, which was focused on sales and marketing, was not particularly successful. It was also one of the first foreign technology companies to establish R&D activity, initially in Beijing in 1984 and more recently in Shanghai and other cities. The three-stage approach refers to initially employing relatively young and inexperienced university graduates in software engineering and helping them become familiar with product development. In the early stages, Microsoft brought expatriate managers (often returnee Chinese) from their Redmond headquarters to China to mentor the newly formed research teams and build up their expertise. After a period of two to three years they moved to the 'walk' stage where the team was more involved in a focused area, involving part of the product, and they become very immersed in the product life cycle. At this point they have a greater understanding of what it is like to be at the coalface and how the product is developed. They can now see how their own contribution feeds into the development of the product. It should be noted that most foreign companies carrying out R&D activity in China fragment the various processes to avoid problems of intellectual property theft. The last stage of development is when the company has sufficient trust in the ability of the R&D centre to produce the complete product in China, and none of the Microsoft teams have yet reached that stage.

While each company has had its own unique evolutionary path in China, associated with the company's overall fortunes both globally and regionally, each of the foreign subsidiaries in Shanghai have had to prove their capabilities to their parent company to ensure their growth and development. When the major German software company SAP established its Labs China in Shanghai in 1998, its first area of assigned tasks was related to the localization and translation of software modules for the local market and also building in local legal requirements into the software. Between 1998 and 2002 they received a lot of project-based development, including developing solutions for the Chinese and Japanese markets and to some extent for the global market. From 2002 the Shanghai lab built considerable confidence with their headquarters and moved on from project development to the development of standard products such as financial services software. In 2003 they employed only 300 people, but in the subsequent period of boom they have grown to 1,200.

While the China market is and will continue to be a major focus of this operation, they have in more recent years being making a significant contribution to the global activities of SAP, creating cost-effective solutions for a range of markets, including the US, Brazil, Japan, the Philippines, Thailand, India, Pakistan, Russia, France and Germany. In the early stages of the Labs China, competence in the English language was an issue for global activity, and while there is still dependence on help from other subsidiaries in the area of documentation, the overall competence has improved considerably. The Shanghai lab has also the advantage of access to talent which can deal with other Asian countries such as Japan and Korea.

With the establishment of Labs China, SAP now had 10 R&D labs worldwide, and with this trend towards decentralizing R&D activity to regional centres, corporations like SAP are faced with the task of managing the sharing of knowledge created by these different centres. SAP together with other companies interviewed, however, made it clear that the emphasis within the corporation was more on collaboration than competition. Each centre was expected to develop its own area of expertise and to avoid overlapping with other centres. Rather than having a bidding process for projects, SAP had a systematic approach towards allocating projects based in the specific expertise of different centres. Thus SAP, like other globalizing corporations were evolving towards a network form of organization of R&D centres around the headquarters, with headquarters being mainly focused on more advanced technologies.

The Fortune 500 US company 3M has been in China since 1984, but it was only in 2005 that it established a $40m R&D centre, already having six manufacturing plants in Shanghai, Suzhou and Guangzhou. Since its establishment, the R&D centre, which employs 400, has produced 950 inventions, 110 Chinese patents, and 60 global patents, which is unusual because of the general reluctance of multinationals to file patents in China. Its activities evolved from lower-level tasks, including technical support, localization and product modification, to producing new products for the Chinese market. Activities to date range from fundamental research, and product development and commercialization across 45 technology platforms, with the lab achieving self-sufficiency in certain areas, which means that that they are capable of piloting technology in these areas. Partly because of China's world leadership in high-voltage technology, 3M in Shanghai are becoming a world class centre in electrical cable capacity within the corporation. Another interviewed R&D centre, established by the French energy company, Areva (now part of Alstom), is also building on local Chinese expertise in long-distance electricity transmission, indicating that such niche areas of technological expertise provide an additional attraction for such companies together with the rapidly growing and potentially very large Chinese market in this sector. Synergies have also been developed with world leadership in coal-gassification technology and GE's R&D centre in Shanghai.

CONCLUSION

Although China is still in the 'catch-up' phase of investment in R&D, there is little doubt about the state's commitment to providing the necessary conditions, both in terms of infrastructure and skills, to facilitate rapid growth in innovation in China. The private sector, including major successful companies such as Huawei and BYD, are major investors in R&D. Yet, questions remain about the overall level of outputs in China from the rapid growth in R&D investment. Much of this has been recent and bringing about major shifts in levels of innovation usually takes decades. Some suggest that the dynamic nature of China's strong economic growth creates a market where short-term innovations based around cost and affordability are rewarded more than the longer-term strategies based on basic research.

It is clear that the first 30 years of foreign investment in China after its opening, when China became the primary centre for manufacturing offshoring from the developed world, has created a very significant level of dependence on foreign technology, costing China major payments in licences and royalty fees. This model is no longer satisfactory for China, and the current policy of 'indigenous innovation' shows a determination to reduce this technology dependence significantly. It is both understandable and admirable that China would also want to shift its development model away from the environmentally destructive phase of basic manufacturing offshoring to a more sustainable and environmentally friendly one. The low level of added value accruing to China from its significant high-technology exports is also a major factor driving the new policy to seek to have greater local ownership of intellectual property production.

The urgent environmental challenges facing China because of its predominant focus on being an offshore location for manufacturing are creating a significant push for the development of greener technologies in a wide range of sectors, from the electric car and other more environmentally friendly forms of transport, to the development of solar and wind energy technologies. The scale of the challenge is resulting in a very concentrated level of state and private sector investment in these new technologies, which could give China some edge in these important areas of innovation.

It is likely, however, that China will depend to a considerable extent for some time to come on foreign technology, and that foreign R&D centres in China can make an important contribution to solving many challenges associated with the future development of this enormous country. The evolving innovation policy is placing increasing pressures on foreign companies to increase their level of local innovation as a prerequisite for gaining greater access to one of the most promising markets in the world. Depending on the sector, China is rapidly moving upwards in terms of its ranking for many multinational companies for revenue generation and market growth. Most multinationals are acutely aware that they must grow with China and learn to compete in a market where there is considerable emphasis on affordability. The challenge for multinational companies with their established model of proprietary intellectual property creation will be to develop ways of raising local capabilities without compromising their core IP. The evolution of this unprecedented relationship between the dominant Western multinational IP model and the powerful bargaining position of a state with a huge market presents a fascinating topic for ongoing research. With the growing significance of China's rapidly developing market, China is in a very strong bargaining position in relation to multinational companies who are determined to be part of China's future growth, and despite their traditional experience of determining the shapes of markets globally, in most cases they will be willing to negotiate some level of compromise with a state that is firmly in control of its own destiny.

APPENDIX

Table 8A.1   Innovation index for China, India and Brazil

	China		India		Brazil	
	Score	Rank	Score	Rank	Score	Rank
Global Innovation Index 2013	44.7	35	36.2	66	36.3	64
2011	46.4	29	34.5	62	37.7	47
2009		37		41		50
Institutions 2013	48.3	113	51.9	102	53.8	95
2011	51.7	98	52.3	94	87	87
Human capital & research 2013	40.6	36	21.7	105	30.3	75
2011	39.9	56	26.9	104	33.9	76
Infrastructure 2013	39.8	44	27.5	89	37.2	51
2011	35.4	33	27.7	63	32.2	45
Market sophistication 2013	54.2	35	49.5	49	44.9	76
2011	54.1	26	44.6	45	35.7	80
Business sophistication 2013	42.9	33	28.3	94	38.0	42
2011	49.3	29	30.8	84	41.5	46
Knowledge & Technology 2013 Scientific outputs	56.4	2	34.5	37	26.5	67
2011	52.7	9	24.8	60	25.2	58
Creative outputs 2013	31.9	96	38.6	65	37.2	72
2011	40.9	35	40.3	38	46.9	12
Population (millions) 2013	1,374.0		1,267.6		201.5	
GDP per capita $ 2013	9146		3851		12038	
GDP (US$ bns) 2013	8250		1946		2425	

Source: S. Dutta and B. Lavin, *The Global Innovation Index 2013*, Johnson Cornell, INSEAD and WIPO, available at: http://www.globalinnovationindex.org/content.aspx?page=GII-Home.

9. Intellectual property, innovation and the ladder of development: Experience of developed countries for China

Wei Shi

INTRODUCTION

The reasons for which protection is afforded to intellectual rights are twofold. One is to give expression to the moral sentiment that a creator, such as a craftsman, should enjoy the fruits of their creativity; the second is to encourage the investment of skills, time, finance, and other resources into innovation in a way that is beneficial to society.[1] This is usually achieved by granting creators certain time-limited rights to control the use made of those products.[2]

However, the tension between stimulating creation and disseminating its benefits to society at large is delicate.[3] Intellectual Property Rights (IPR) as a concept has been debated throughout history and, with a global economy, this debate has become increasingly controversial and confrontational.[4] Scholars from different backgrounds have often debated

---

[1] *See* 'WIPO Intellectual Property Handbook: Policy, Law and Use', WIPO Publication No. 489, http://www.wipo.org/about-ip/en/ iprm/pdf/ch1.pdf.

[2] *Ibid.*

[3] *See, e.g.*, Thomas Cottier, *Intellectual Property: Trade, Competition, and Sustainable Development*, University of Michigan Press, 2003. *See* also, Philippe Cullet, *Intellectual Property and Sustainable Development*, New Delhi: Lexis/ Nexis Butterworths, 2005.

[4] *See* Brigitte Binkert, 'Why the Current Global Intellectual Property Framework under TRIPs is Not Working', *Intellectual Property Law Bulletin* 143 (Spring 2006).

the validity and legitimacy of IPR from different perspectives.[5] In this chapter, the author attempts to review IPR through a prismatic lens in order to justify the correlation between IPR and economic growth and examine the implications of the existing IPR regime. By tracing development trajectories of different economies, this chapter draws on the experience of such developed countries as the United States and Japan, which have developed a similar development strategy for implementing and enforcing intellectual property rights, and provide a penetrating insight into the economic and social foundation needed to enable development of an effective IPR enforcement mechanism. Such a comparative focus may be constructive to China's designing of its innovation system.

1. INTELLECTUAL PROPERTY AND ECONOMIC GROWTH: DOES PROTECTION OF INTELLECTUAL PROPERTY AFFORD INCENTIVE FOR INNOVATION?

Economic growth, in the sense attributed to this concept in contemporary macroeconomics, is a natural phenomenon of industrialization.[6] Economic growth depends, in large part, on technological change (*e.g.* innovation) and reflects the increase and accumulation of technological and other knowledge of commercial value.[7] From its early days, scholars,

---

[5]   *See* L. Bently and B. Sherman, *Intellectual Property Law*, Oxford University Press, 2001, p. 3.

[6]   The contemporary concept of economic growth has distant origins, since it stems back from the early days of the Industrial Revolution and is constantly evolving. In the 1950s, following the publication of papers by Robert Solow and Nicholas Kaldor, growth theory became a dominating topic until the early 1970s. The 'new growth theory' that emerged (also known as endogenous growth theory) asserts that new ideas are the root source of economic growth since they promote technological innovation and hence stimulate productivity improvements. For a substantive introduction, *see*, e.g., Neri Salvadori, 'Introduction', 54 (2–3) Metroeconomica, 2003, pp. 125–28; Michael Borrus and Jay Stowsky, 'Technology Policy and Economic Growth', Berkeley Roundtable on the International Economy, Paper BRIEWP97, p. 3; *see* also, Charles I. Jones, *Introduction to Economic Growth* (2nd edn), New York, London: W. W. Norton and Company, 2002.

[7]   *See* Gene M. Grossman and Elhanan Helpman, 'Endogenous Innovation in the Theory of Growth', *The Journal of Economic Perspectives*, 1994, vol. 8, pp. 25–27.

in particular economists, have attempted to address issues concerning economic growth and its correlation with technological advancement, since these issues concern human welfare in the long run.[8] As one of the most popular fields in contemporary macroeconomics, economic growth is not only essential to theorists but also valuable to policy makers and the practitioners,[9] as it is alleged that a strengthened IPR regime acts as an important catalyst of economic growth.[10] In order to maintain economic growth, countries have endeavoured to establish varied mechanisms to foster innovation and facilitate the transfer of technology. The creation and protection of IPR exemplify a central part of this strategy.

1.1   IPR: Intellectual Property in a Knowledge-driven Economy

Over the past two centuries or so, the acceleration of technological advancement has radically changed the landscape of human lives and demonstrated values of innovation in creating our everyday reality. The design of IPR has thus evolved quietly in a manner that has emphasized the value of ideas and knowledge. In a modern society, an increasing number of companies have found their creative knowledge one of their most valuable assets as it determines their future capacity to generate profit. The perpetual exponential advance of technology has rendered increasingly visible the intellectual content to innovation at a time when the globalization of world markets creates global opportunities for the products of innovation. In a knowledge-driven economy, the effective protection of IPR is emerging as a critical element of commercial success.[11] With increasing levels of international trade, the amount of trade involving IPR also increases, causing significant resources to be devoted to effective protection.

As a consequence of significant economic growth and explosive technological development, world trade now has more knowledgeable and technological content than ever before and the intellectual assets have become major value drivers in our modern business community. A case in point is the United States. According to Professor Juan Enriquez, the leading authority on the economic and political impacts of the life

---

[8]   *See* Jones, *supra* note 6, at pp. 3–16.
[9]   *Ibid.*
[10]   Steven P. Reynolds, 'Antitrust and Patent Licensing: Cycles of Enforcement and Current Policy', *Jurimetrics Journal*, vol. 37, 1997, p. 138.
[11]   Grossman and Helpman, *supra* note 7, pp. 25–27.

sciences, the United States generates the most patents per capita.[12] As shown in Table 9.1, it takes about 3,000 Americans to generate one US patent, compared to 4,000 Japanese, 6,000 Taiwanese, 1.8 million Brazilians, 10 million Chinese and 21 million Indonesians.[13] IPR has been carefully refined over the past decades to meet the challenges of countries as they developed an industrial base and post-industrial service economies. With ever increasing levels of international trade, the question arises as to whether IPR as it has evolved will be up to the challenge of levelling the per capita levels of innovation between the developed and developing countries or whether they will merely reinforce the existing levels of difference.

Table 9.1   Patents per capita/U.S.

Nation	Population/per patent
United States	3,000
Japan	4,000
Taiwan	6,000
Brazil	1,800,000
China	10,000,000
Indonesia	21,000,000

Source: Professor Juan Enriquez, available at http://www.technology.gov/Speeches/ p_BPM_020503_Wealth.htm.

The illustration and interpretation of the economic rationale and function of IPR as a necessary policy-making instrument that stimulates innovations might seem abstruse and obscure. As a matter of conceptual design, IPR legislation confers on the holder of the right an exclusive 'monopoly ' for a limited period of time.[14] This enables them to control commercial exploitation by setting the level of revenue arising from their use and safeguarding it by excluding others from making, selling or using

---

[12]   Bruce P. Mehlman, 'The Changing Wealth of Nations: Intellectual Property in the Age of Innovation', Licensing Executives Society Spring Meeting, United States Department of Commerce, 3 May 2002, Washington, DC, www.technol-ogy.gov/ Speeches/p_BPM_020503_Wealth.htm.

[13]   *Ibid.*

[14]   *See* W. R. Cornish, *Intellectual Property: Patents, Copyright, Trade Marks and Allied Rights*, London: Sweet and Maxwell, 1999, p. 38.

it.[15] Ensuring that social benefit derived from knowledge-based innovation outweighs the social cost is at the core of balancing the factors to be considered. However, in high-technology sectors such as pharmaceuticals, the risk of failure of expensive research to bear fruit is high and entrepreneurs must have good reason to expect that the cost of failure can be recaptured from the profits of future business endeavours. Otherwise the incentive to undertake innovative activities will dry up.

1.2   Geographical Limitation on the Coverage of IPR

It is pragmatically important to investigate whether an IPR regime is the appropriate vehicle for stimulating enabling, rather than applied technologies, or whether industry-funded research and development (R&D), government-funded awards, or the public sector are more effective vectors.[16] IPR plays a big role in human society as the decision to grant property rights in intangibles impinges on both competitors and the public.[17] As noted by Nancy Gallini and Suzanne Scotchmer, 'if the balance between private gain and public good slips too far beyond what is necessary to spur innovation, it will instead become a drag on innovation and impede creating further innovations'.[18]

How the proper balance is established and whether the same balance is capable of universal adoption has engaged much academic debate. Ishac Diwan and Dani Rodrik, on the one hand, conclude that developing countries may embark on protecting IPR of developed countries to facilitate the invention of technologies that are indigenously appropriate to the developing world.[19] On the other hand, recent economic analysis

---

[15]   *Ibid.*

[16]   Randall Kroszner, 'Economic Organization and Competition Policy', *Yale Journal on Regulation*, 2002, vol. 19, pp. 541–97 (arguing that 'on the one hand, it is impossible for IPR regime to provide profound protection without exception. On the other hand, some innovation may be too difficult to imitate that, even without IPR protection, the innovator can enjoy a substantial cost or quality advantage over its competitors for some period. In either case, other characteristics of some dynamically competitive industries are important in making it likely that a successful innovation will yield a firm the leading position in a market, and profits that are essential to encourage such innovation').

[17]   Bently and Sherman, *supra* note 5, p. 4.

[18]   *See* Nancy Gallini and Suzanne Scotchmer, 'Intellectual Property: When Is It the Best Incentive System?', *UC Berkeley Department of Economics Working Paper*, 2001.

[19]   *See* Ishac Diwan and Dani Rodrik, 'Patents, Appropriate Technology, and North-South Trade', 30 *Journal of International Economics*, 1991, pp. 27–47.

offers a somewhat different interpretation from the traditional views. Judith Chin and Gene Grossman analysed a 'static' model of symmetric duopoly whereby all innovation takes place in developed countries and all imitation takes place in developing countries and discovered that developing countries have little incentive to go for positive IPR protection because their competitive position in the output market would be weakened after paying a higher wage.[20] Similarly, Alan Deardorff designed another static model and indicated that the welfare effect of worldwide patent coverage could have an 'offsetting effect', in the event that 'all innovation originates in one part of the world', since 'on one hand, permitting inventors to earn monopoly profits on their inventions and thus stimulating inventive activity and, on the other hand, distorting consumer choice by monopoly pricing'.[21] He subsequently suggested that there would be geographical limitation on the coverage of patents as to how far IPR should be extended internationally.[22]

Elhanan Helpman applies a more intrinsic approach to examining the benefits and costs of stronger IPR enforcement in a general equilibrium model where innovation originates in the developed world while the developing world relies upon the imitation of the innovation produced by the former.[23] Helpman advocates incremental improvement of IPR standards and demonstrates in his model that it is feasible for the innovation of developed countries to slow down the speed of the unification process of the IPR protection in the developing world lest the stricter IPR protection may undermine the social foundation on which innovation relies and ultimately hurt both developed and developing countries. Helpman concludes that, in general, the developing world has little to gain from stronger IPR protection due to the terms of trade deterioration from an

---

[20]   Judith Chin and Gene Grossman, 'Intellectual Property Rights and North-South Trade', 1988 *NBER Working Paper*, No. 2769, http://www.nber.org (the authors show in their model that there are certain circumstances where a less-developed country may be better off with weak IPR protection. In their model, a northern firm and a southern firm have divergent access to patent protection and produce the same good in the same market. In the first instance, the Southern firm can benefit from weak protection of IPR; however, after achieving a high global share of production output and gaining adequate technological advance, the protection of IPR becomes authentic).
[21]   A. V. Deardorff, 'Welfare Effects of Global Patent Protection', *Economica*, 1992, vol. 59(233) p. 49 (demonstrating the 'offsetting effects' of the patent protection and their implications for the less-advanced countries).
[22]   *Ibid*, pp. 35–36.
[23]   Elhanan Helpman, 'Innovation, Imitation, and Intellectual Property Rights', *Econometrica*, 1993, vol. 61(6), pp. 1247–80.

initial position of equilibrium.[24] Similarly, Stephen Richardson and James Gaisford also argue that in a country where the knowledge gap is significant and domestic invention is scarce, a heightened protection of IPR could impair the overall welfare of that country and result in reduced world welfare.[25] Some commentators go even further. Michele Boldrin and David Levine argue that 'while awarding a monopoly to an innovator increases the payoff to the original innovator, by giving her control over subsequent uses of the innovation, it reduces the incentive for future innovation'.[26] They emphasize that '[f]rom the perspective of the functioning of markets, [...] what is ordinarily referred to as "intellectual property" protects not the ownership of copies of ideas, but rather a monopoly over how other people make use of their copies of an idea'.[27]

A rather recent contribution in this area is the book *The Economic Structure of Intellectual Property Law* contributed by William Landes and Richard Posner.[28] By identifying and testing the interaction patterns of intellectual property law and economics, Landes and Posner argue that 'expanding IPR can actually reduce the amount of new IPR that is created by raising the creators' input costs, since a major input into new intellectual property is existing such property'.[29] The key insight of their economic approach is to demonstrate that overprotection of IPR undermines the traditional balance between right proprietors and society at large. Paradoxically, over-extended protection of IPR may have a counteraction effect to the innovation.[30]

---

[24]   *Ibid.*
[25]   *See*, e.g., Stephen Richardson and James Gaisford, 'North-South Disputes over the Protection of Intellectual Property', 29 *Canadian Journal of Economics*, 1996, (Special Issue, April), pp. 376–81. *See* also James Gaisford and Stephen Richardson, 'The Trips Disagreement: Should GATT Traditions Have Been Abandoned', *Estey Centre Journal of International Law and Trade Policy*, 2000, vol. 1, pp. 137–69.
[26]   *See* Michele Boldrin and David K. Levine, 'Perfectly Competitive Innovation', Working Paper Archive from *UCLA Department of Economics*, 2003, SSCNET, UCLA, http://levine.sscnet.ucla.edu/papers/pci23.pdf, p. 4.
[27]   *See* Lewis Kornhauser, 'The Economics of Ideas and Intellectual property', http://levine.sscnet.ucla.edu/papers/pnas18.pdf, p. 1.
[28]   William Landes and Richard Posner, *The Economic Structure of Intellectual Property Law*, Cambridge, Mass: Belknap Press of Harvard University Press, 2003.
[29]   *Ibid*, p. 422.
[30]   *See* Daniel Levine, *'05, Profiles: The Economic Structure of Intellectual Property Law*, http://www.law.uchicago.edu/alumni/record/landes-posner-book. html.

1.3 Intellectual Property, Market Equilibrium and the Ladder of Development: Secrets That Developed Countries Are Trying to Hide

As the above passage has demonstrated, IPR is based on the notion of balance in that it must optimize benefit for both innovators and society,[31] and countries ought to be able to have IPR standards that line up with their economic strengths and comparative advantages. While human capital plays a key role in promoting economic growth in the developing world, technological competitiveness has not yet been established and it has been insufficient to produce desirable inventions.[32] In other words, the pirating of intellectual property fuels economic development until the country reaches the stage where IPR protection becomes economically advantageous to a sufficiently strong set of domestic vested interests.[33] Contrastingly, if the establishment of an IPR legal system lacks social foundation on which adequate economic values of the system have been fully realized, the incentives of innovation may recede and the underpinnings that sustain creativities may collapse. In other words, if a country has not obtained an endogenously generated impulse to change their economic behaviour, any radical strategy for stronger demands of IPR protection will serve as destructive enthusiasm and only turn into a legal failure.[34]

The emergence of counterfeiting and piracy is a natural consequence of market equilibrium, where demand meets supply. In such a market, authorities lack genuine enthusiasm and native intelligence to enforce IPR, since providing substantial IPR protection does not render immediate economic benefits to the national economy.[35] For many companies

---

[31] Cornish, *supra* note 14, pp. 11–12.

[32] Mikhaelle Schiappacasse, 'Intellectual Property Rights in China: Technology Transfers and Economic Development', *Buffalo Intellectual Property Law Journal*, 2004, vol. 2, p. 166 (stating that the long-term beneficial effect from strengthened IPR protection in developing countries is dependent on various factors, such as increasing human capital).

[33] *See*, e.g., Stefan Kirchanski, 'Protection of U.S. Patent Rights in Developing Countries: US Efforts To Enforce Pharmaceutical Patents in Thailand', *L.A. International & Comparative Law Review*, 1994, vol. 16, p. 598; Frederick M. Abbott, 'The WTO TRIPs Agreement and Global Economic Development', in *Public Policy and Global Technological Integration*, 1997, pp. 3, 4–12.

[34] *See* Robert E. Hudec, *Enforcing Intellectual Property Law: The Evolution of the Modern GATT Legal System*, 1993, p. 364.

[35] J. Cheng, 'China's Copyright System: Rising to the Spirit of TRIPs Requires an Internal Focus and WTO Membership', *Fordham International Law Journal*, 1998, vol. 21, p. 1979.

lacking independent home-grown intellectual property, strengthened IPR protection implies that domestic enterprises are obliged to pay a colossal sum of royalties to foreign proprietors, thereby resulting in escalating production costs and shrinking profit margins.[36] Correspondingly, most enterprises are typically content with making imitation products and have invested little capital and made little effort to develop their own creative and innovative technologies.[37] Understandably, in order to harness the weak purchasing power of low-income citizens, and also to maintain the national revenue generated from imitation, authorities of developing countries often turn a blind eye to counterfeiting and piracy because it is a 'legitimate grey market' in the early stages of development,[38] as they know they need time to phase in effective policies.

Nurturing and rewarding innovative talent is the beginning of intellectual property. Construction of a system balancing protection and exploitation is therefore indispensable for the establishment of an intellectual creation cycle. An economy must reach a certain stage of overall development before it can commit substantial resources to R&D and embark on a genuine effort to protect IPR.[39] For example, within the global pharmaceutical companies, R&D funds are in excess of one billion dollars.[40] On health-related R&D, the United States federal government invested more than 25 billion US dollars in 2005.[41] By contrast, the largest amount spent on pharmaceutical R&D in China was only 100 million Chinese Yuan in 2003,[42] which is just equivalent to 12 million US dollars. China's R&D expenditure as a percentage of its GDP was 1.34

---

[36]   *See* 'Changes in China's IPR System, Business Alert – China', Publication of Hong Kong Trade Development Council, 2000, Issue 10, www.tdctrade.com/alert/cba-e0010b.htm.

[37]   *Ibid.*

[38]   *See* e.g., Seth Faison, 'China Turns Blind Eye to Pirated Disks', *N.Y. Times*, 28 March 1998, at D1 (noting that Chinese custom officials pose little threat to copyright pirates).

[39]   John R. Allison & Lianlian Lin, 'The Evolution of Chinese Attitudes toward Property Rights Invention and Discovery', *U. Pa. Journal of International Economic Law*, 1999, vol. 20, p. 775.

[40]   Cui Ning & Qin Jize, 'IPR Strategy to Define Government's Role', *China Daily*, 14 June 2004, p. 5.

[41]   *See* 'Research and Development in the Pharmaceutical Industry', The Congress of the United States of Congressional Budget Office, October 2006, Pub. No. 2589, http://www.cbo.gov/sites/default/files/cbofiles/ftpdocs/76xx/doc7615/10-02-drugr-d.pdf.

[42]   'IPR Strategy to Define Government's Role', *supra* note 40.

per cent in 2005.[43] Since 2006 China has become one of the top three spenders on R&D and this again supports the above economic argument.

Looking back at national economic development in the international balance of payments structure, countries are normally technological followers of more industrialized countries, and usually pass through a stage of cycle in the balance of payments.[44] The primary stage of development is largely characterized by *imitation* rather than *innovation*, given the fact that the divergence between the 'haves' and 'have-nots' in the information age is still significant.

The above perceptions may be well interpreted as the 'ladder of development' towards underlining demand of IPR, which developing countries have to step on and come through. Apparently, IPR can either trigger or thwart innovation; it can either promote or hinder economic growth, depending on how it is oriented on the 'ladder of development'. However, developing countries are attempting to 'hide the secrets of their success,' and 'kick away the ladder'.[45]

1.4 The International Architecture of IPR and the Dilemma of the Global IPR Regime

The protection of IPR has been an international issue since the second half of the nineteenth century.[46] The variety of international business transactions in which IPR forms a part is significant and the design of global strategies to manage intangible assets has become increasingly

---

[43] China's R&D investment in 2005 accounts for 1.34 percent GDP, China Supply Chain Council, 18 September 2006, http://www.supplychain.cn/en/art/?1043.

[44] R. J. Ruffin and P. R. Gregory, *Principles of Macroeconomics*, Reading, Mass., Harlow: Addison Wesley, 2001, p. 729.

[45] Ha-Joon Chang, *Kicking Away the Ladder: Development Strategy in Historical Perspective*, 2002, p. 128 (questioning the legitimacy of Neo-Liberal policies and demonstrating how the developed countries are '"kicking away the ladder" by which they climbed up to the top beyond the reach of the developing countries').

[46] The first conventions concerning international protection of intellectual property are the Paris Convention for the Protection of Industrial Property (1883) and Berne Convention for the Protection of Literary and Artistic Works (1886). As a result of these two conventions, the IPR issues were converted from a national forum to an international arena. For a detailed account of this conversion, *see generally*, Vincenzo Vinciguerra, 'A Brief Essay on the Importance of Time in International Conventions on Intellectual Property Rights', *Akron Law Review*, 2006, vol. 39, p. 635.

fashionable to the extent that the interests of international trade are safeguarded by a stable IPR system.[47] However, as developed economies have become increasingly knowledge based and thus have far more comparative advantages than developing countries, the position of the latter is considerably marginalized. In this context, IPR protection has become a key issue involved substantially in both international law and development policy.

The strengthening of the global marketplace with the WTO Agreement and the compelling trend of intensified globalization have generated increasing pressure on the WTO members from the developing world to liberalize their trading regimes by providing foreign nationals with national treatment. Whilst for the most part this means dismantling the protection afforded to domestic industry, in the case of IPR, the TRIPs Agreement operates to increase standards of domestic protection.

One of the significant characteristics of national law on IPR is territoriality.[48] If the IPR proprietors wish to extend recognition of their rights to other countries, they will have to make an application to the countries concerned. In this context, the 'universal protection' of IPR is granted by individual countries. The lengthy and costly application process, as well as the considerable risks of procedural differences made it essential to find ways to ensure that protection obtained in one country could be extended to another.[49]

Attempts towards eliminating these obstacles were subsequently initiated in the last quarter of the nineteenth century with the main three pillars being the Paris Convention for the Protection of Industrial Property signed in 1883, the Berne Convention for the Protection of Literary and Artistic Work in 1886, and the Madrid Agreement Concerning the International Registration of Marks in 1891.[50] However it was not until 1967 that the World Intellectual Property Organization (WIPO) was established to coordinate and oversee the protection of IPR generally

---

[47] *See* Adam I. Hasson, 'Domestic Implementation of International Obligations: The Quest for World Patent Law Harmonization', *B.C. International & Comparative Law Review, 2002*, vol. 25, p. 374.

[48] *See* Cornish, *supra* note 14, at 26 (stating that one way of expressing the close association of national policy and legal rights lies in the principle of 'territoriality', and this characteristic is often attributed to the major form of intellectual property).

[49] *Ibid*, at p. 747 (noting that intellectual property 'forms a central barrier along the boundary between the fair and unfair competition, and ideas where the boundary should be drawn undoubtedly vary').

[50] For the full text of these three conventions, *see* Andrew Christie & Stephen Gare, *Statutes on Intellectual Property*, 2003, pp. 354–8, 490–98.

within the member states.[51] WIPO, a United Nations specialized agency, has been particularly promoting worldwide protection of various forms of intellectual property and assisting its members to meet their obligations for the protection of IPR.[52]

However, neither the Conventions nor the WIPO prescribed specific levels of IPR protection, only the processes by which such protection can be accessed. To enable this change, the issues of IPR had to find a place on the agenda of international trade talks where it could be part of a negotiated package. The justification was that 'weak protection of IPR distorts natural trading patterns and acts as an impediment to free trade'.[53]

More to the point, the particular voting system of WIPO fell short of the interests of developed nations and impeded the efforts of developed countries to seek harmonized standards.[54] Accordingly, IPR protection was added to the agenda of the Uruguay Round of GATT negotiations at the request of developed countries in 1986. Since then, developed countries have started to 'pull the debate away from WIPO', trying to integrate the issue of IPR with that of free trade.[55] In practical terms, this meant that negotiations over IPR were integrated into the GATT/WTO based on multilateral negotiations coupling free trade with IPR, leading to the TRIPs Agreement in Marrakesh in 1994.[56] By then, the United States and other developed countries had at last 'achieved their objective

---

[51]   *See* Robert J. Pechman, 'Seeking Multilateral Protection for Intellectual Property: The United States "TRIPs" Over Special 301', *Minnesota Journal of Global Trade*, 1998, pp. 179, 181 (stating that the Paris Convention left the enforcement of IPR up to each member state).

[52]   While WIPO administers most of the international conventions concerning IPR, some other agencies are also playing specific roles. For example, the UN Educational, Scientific and Cultural Organization (UNESCO), which administers Universal Copyright Convention, is a UN institution that has been playing an essential part in the broad areas concerning cultural diversity and pluralism.

[53]   *See* Jacques Olivier and Aiting Goh, *Free Trade and Protection of Intellectual Property Rights: Can We Have One Without the Other?* http://www.hec.fr/ hec/fr/professeur_recherche/cahier/finance/CR730.pdf.

[54]   J. Van Wijk and G. Junne, *Intellectual Property Protection of Advanced Technology-Changes in the Global Technology System: Implications and Options for Developing Countries*, United Nations University, Institute for New Technologies, Maastricht, Working Paper No. 10 (1993).

[55]   Joshua J. Simons, 'Cooperation and Coercion: The Protection of Intellectual Property in Developing Countries', *Bond Law Review*, 1999, vol. 11, p. 60.

[56]   *Ibid.*

of incorporating internationally enforceable IPR norms into the world trading system'.[57]

Upon its establishment, the TRIPs Agreement was hailed as the 'milestone' in the development of international IPR regime at the end of the twentieth century,[58] and 'the most far-reaching and comprehensive legal system ever concluded at the multinational level in the area of IPR',[59] which 'revolutionized international intellectual property law'.[60]

Although the TRIPs Agreement does not impose substantial provisions and create a unitary framework for IPR protection,[61] it does impose minimum international standards for the protection of IPR by which WTO members are obliged to demonstrate full compliance with the substantive obligations of the primary international intellectual property conventions, including the Berne Convention and the Paris Convention.[62] In its preamble, TRIPs specified as one of its objectives 'to reduce impediments to international trade, to promote effective protection of IPR, and to ensure that measures to enforce IPR do not become barriers to legitimate trade'.[63] In other words, although TRIPs does not introduce a uniform set of substantial rules, by explicitly underlining the obligation of each member to take measures to eliminate abuses of IPR, it potentially and indirectly establishes leverage against different member states.

The establishment of TRIPs within the WTO framework of the multilateral agreement is perhaps the most ambitious and adventurous

---

[57]   Laurence R. Helfer, 'Regime Shifting: The TRIPs Agreement and New Dynamic of International Intellectual property Lawmaking', *Yale Journal of International Law*, 2004, vol. 29, p. 2.

[58]   *See* Vincent Chiappetta, 'The Desirability of Agreeing to Disagree: The WTO, TRIPs, International IPR Exhaustion and a Few Other Things', 21 *Michigan Journal of International Law*, 2000, vol. 21, pp. 333, 335–6, 368.

[59]   *See*, e.g., Carlos M. Correa and Abdulqawi A. Yusuf, *Intellectual Property and International Trade: The TRIPs Agreement*, London: Kluwer Law International, 1998, p. 17; Charles McManis, 'Intellectual Property and International Mergers and Acquisitions', *University of Cincinnati Law Review*, 1998, vol. 66, pp. 1283, 1286.

[60]   Helfer, *supra* note 57, p. 23.

[61]   Eric Allen Engle, 'When is Fair Use Fair?: A Comparison of E.U. and U.S. Intellectual Property Law', *Transnational Law*, 2002, vol. 15, p. 187.

[62]   Article 1 of TRIPs Agreement.

[63]   *See* preamble of TRIPs, Annex 1C of The Uruguay Round Final Act.

attempt to harmonize IPR on a worldwide scale,[64] not least because TRIPs enables enforcement by private parties at the national level,[65] and where this fails to provide an effective remedy, it enables enforcement by states at an international level,[66] using the 'WTO's comparatively hard-edged dispute settlement mechanism in which treaty bargains are enforced through mandatory adjudication backed up by the threat of retaliatory sanctions'.[67] For these reasons it exercises a profound influence on domestic legislation and trade policy and in this regard has increasingly marginalized the international IPR agreements negotiated under the auspices of the WIPO.

Faced with the dilemma of the current global IPR system, more and more commentators and policy makers have discerned a tendency towards overprotection of IPR leading to anti-competitive effects that are pernicious to both developing and developed countries by diluting important liberties and freedoms.[68] In the political realm, the harmonization of the universal TRIPs standards has been in some way depicted as a lever that allows developed countries to maximize their interests in the global marketplace. While TRIPs has established a new international IPR arena based on the minimum standards in contrast to previous flexibility to afford differentiated protection, no distinction has ever been made to accommodate the varied circumstances of the countries, except for the length of transition periods.[69] Without a natural consistency

---

[64] Paul Demaret, 'The Metamorphoses of the GATT: from the Havana Charter to the World Trade Organization', *Columbia Journal of Transnational Law*, 1995, vol. 34, p. 162.

[65] Articles 41–60 of TRIPs provide civil and administrative procedures and remedies, as well as provisional measures to prevent IPR infringement. Article 61 provides criminal procedure. *See* TRIPs Articles 41–60; Article 61.

[66] Donald P. Harris, 'TRIPs Rebound: An Historical Analysis of How the TRIPs Agreement Can Ricochet Back Against the United States', *Northwest Journal of International Law and Business*, 2004, vol. 25, p. 116.

[67] Helfer, *supra* note 57, p. 2.

[68] Harris, *supra* note 66, p. 101 (arguing that 'TRIPs' focus on private interests will not only harm developing countries, but also will rebound back against the United States, thereby inflicting significant harm').

[69] *See* Martin Khor, 'How Intellectual Property Rights Could Work Better for Developing Countries and Poor People', A Remark at the Conference of the Commission on Intellectual Property Rights, 21–22 February 2002.

between IPR and the level of domestic adaptation, enforcement is likely to be sporadic.[70]

Taking copyright as an example, implementing a stronger IPR system in the short run should be judged not only by its ability to protect the interests of owners of copyrights and related rights, but also by its commitment to avoid pitfalls caused by overprotection that may lead to cultural appropriation and hinder the pace of global civilization. This is apparently inconsistent with the long-term goal set out by the TRIPs Agreement. However, it is very interesting to note that developed countries have attempted to hide the secrets of their success and, by introducing the TRIPs regime, have kicked away the ladder through which the emerging economies wish to climb up to become industrial countries.

2. FROM IMITATION TO INNOVATION: EXPERIENCE OF DEVELOPED COUNTRIES

All countries pass through a stage of development where imitation of foreign products is strategic business practice.[71] All the industrial countries, including the European countries, the United States and Japan, had inherent deficiencies of intellectual property protection. Teresa Watanabe demonstrated that the United States passed through a stage of development in copying European technology in its early years of economic growth.[72] The development of the United States in the nineteenth century was largely based on adoption of technological, economic and legal policies from England and France.[73] In the case of Japan, Watanabe pointed out that 'the total price Japan had to pay for the Western technology it needed to transform itself from a nation of "rice paper and

---

[70]   Stefan Kirchanski, 'Protection of US Patent Rights in Developing Countries: US Efforts to Enforce Pharmaceutical Patents in Thailand', *Loyola of Los Angeles International and Comparative Law Review*, 1994, vol. 16, pp. 569, 598.

[71]   Assafa Endeshaw, 'A Critical Assessment of the US-China Conflict on Intellectual Property', *Albany Law Journal of Science and Technology*, 1996, vol. 6, pp. 295, 300 (demonstrating the fact that industrializing countries usually 'borrow, often without public acknowledgment, policies, technologies, as well as legal concepts' from industrialized countries). *See* also Douglas Clark, 'IP Rights Will Improve in China – Eventually', *The China Business Review*, May–June 2000.

[72]   Teresa Watanabe, 'Japan Sets Sights on Creativity', *L.A. Times*, 10 June 1990, at A1.

[73]   Endeshaw, *supra* note 71, pp. 266, 300.

bamboo" to "transistors and skyscrapers" was a bargain-basement 9 billion dollars'.[74] American domestic entrepreneurs were 'notorious pirates of British works of intellectual property',[75] as were the Japanese.

2.1 Experience of the United Kingdom

Patent law did not come into being in England until 1624 with the Statute of Monopolies, lagging far behind the first-known written law of patent, which was introduced in Venice in 1474, granting ten years' monopoly to the crafts guilds.[76] Most of the early English patent legislation, including the Statute of Monopolies and the following acts passed in the nineteenth and early twentieth centuries, was rather 'purpose-made', intending to solve specific problems,[77] and the patent as a term was less restrictively used than it is today.[78] In addition, early modem patents are understood to be policy oriented.[79] For example, the patent system of the time includes Sir Edward Dyer's control over the tanning industry and a patent to John Martin as 'informer and prosecutor' for the Crown on penal laws.[80] The enactments of the Patent Acts of 1835, 1852, 1883 and 1902 'went beyond a codification of existing case law or well-established administrative practice, [and] utterly lacked the boldness of civilian-style draftsmanship'.[81] Patent law at the time 'lacked disclosure requirements,

---

[74] *See* Watanabe, *supra* note 72.

[75] Eric M. Griffin, 'Stop Relying on Uncle Sam! – A Proactive Approach to Copyright Protection in the People's Republic of China', *Texas Intellectual Property Law Journal*, 1998, vol. 6, p. 187.

[76] Ha-Joon Chang, *supra* note 45, p. 83.

[77] Thomas M. Meshbesher, 'The Role of History in Comparative Patent Law', *Journal of the Patent and Trademark Office Society*, 1996, vol. 78, p. 600.

[78] Chris Dent, 'Generally Inconvenient: The 1624 Statute of Monopolies as Political Compromise', 33 *Melbourne University Law Review*, 2009, vol. 33, p. 417.

[79] *Ibid*, at 418 (summing up that '[e]arly modem patents can be seen to contribute to the fulfilment of three policy goals: the increase in the level of employment in England; the improvement of the balance of trade between England and its trading partners; and the delegation of governance'). *See* also Frank D. Prager, 'Historic Background and Foundation of American Patent Law', *American Journal of Legal History*, 1961, vol. 5, p. 313 ('A significant attitude toward patents was expressed by the British statute of 1624, which limited itself to the showing of an awareness that patents can be lacking in novelty, or contrary to law, or mischievous to the state … , or hurt of trade, or generally inconvenient').

[80] Dent, *supra* note 78, p. 418.

[81] Meshbesher, *supra* note 77, pp. 600–601.

incurred very high costs in filing and processing patent applications, and afforded inadequate protection to the patentees'.[82]

More significantly, patenting by British nationals of foreign inventions was unequivocally considered legitimate.[83] Moreover, the process of ruling on petitions or applications for patents was subject to royal discretion and was beyond the reach of the English judiciary until 1932, when the Patent Appeals Tribunal (PAT) was established.[84] As a consequence, '[t]he beneficial aspects of the patent system, however, did not prevent its occasional abuse by patentees and their servants'.[85] Even the Patents and Designs Act of 1907, the most comprehensive patent legislation by far, marking a significant step toward modernizing patent law in Great Britain, 'failed to address major legal issues that were hardly even recognized, much less litigated until 150 years later'.[86]

Britain did not adopt a trademark law until 1862, when the Merchandise Mark Act was introduced to deal with 'commercial thievery', such as the forging of trademarks and the labelling of false quantities.[87] This Act, however, failed to be enacted.[88] This led to the subsequent amendment of the Act in 1887, in an effort to ban patently false descriptions and misleading descriptions, notably the then widespread German practice of selling counterfeit Sheffield cutlery with fake logos.[89]

British copyright law has been seen as the 'most significant of the early salvos in the formalization of copyright'.[90] However, copyright at that time was barely in embryo, as '[t]he putative recipients of any benefit to intellectual development from copyright were, rather, the small coterie of "learned men" who, according to the Statute, needed exclusivity to "compose and write useful books", presumably for one another's consumption'.[91] Unsurprisingly, in the mid-eighteenth century, 'copyright theory was torn among inconsistent and conflicting suppositions about its purpose, about the relative importance to it of the natural rights claims of

---

[82] Ha-Joon Chang, *supra* note 45, p. 84.

[83] *Ibid.*

[84] Meshbesher, *supra* note 77, p. 608.

[85] Dent, *supra* note 78, p. 420.

[86] Meshbesher, *supra* note 77, p. 601.

[87] Ha-Joon Chang, *Globalization, Economic Development and the Role of the State*, London: Zed Books, 2003, p. 282.

[88] *Trademark Timeline, Trademark Report*, 1992, vol. 82, p. 1026.

[89] Ha-Joon Chang, *supra* note 87, p. 282.

[90] Dianne Leenheer Zimmerman, 'The Statute of Anne and Its Progeny: Variations. Without a Theme', 47 *Houston Law Review*, 2010, vol. 47, p. 966.

[91] *Ibid*, p. 972 (quoting Statute of Anne, 1710, 8 Ann., c. 19).

authors, and about the strength of society's claim to greater freedom to share in and utilize new expression and ideas'.[92]

2.2 Experience of the United States

The term 'intellectual property' did not appear in the United States until the second half of the nineteenth century.[93] Of all forms of IPR, copyright has been viewed as 'the most positive, and as critical to the development of local culture',[94] 'and has emerged as one of the most important means of regulating the international flow of ideas and knowledge based products.'[95] It is thus of significance to examine the history of the copyright law of the United States in order to have a glimpse of the development trajectories of intellectual property.

As Barbara Ringer, the former Register of Copyrights in the United States and one of the principal architects of the Copyright Act of 1976,[96] commented four decades ago, '[u]ntil the Second World War the United States had little reason to take pride in its international copyright relations; in fact, it had a great deal to be ashamed of. With few exceptions its role in international copyright was marked by intellectual short-sightedness, political isolationism, and narrow economic self-interest.'[97]

As has been demonstrated, tolerant IPR national policies are almost inevitable at the early stages of economic development. Indeed, as has been critically observed, '[t]he U.S. was long a net importer of literary

---

[92] Zimmerman, *supra* note 90, p. 981.

[93] Edward C. Walterscheid, 'Early Evolution of the United States Patent Law: Antecedents (Part 1)', *Journal of the Patent and Trademark Office Society*, 1994, vol. 76, p. 702.

[94] Stas Burgiel and Lisa Schipper, 'A Summary Report of the Conference on How Intellectual Property Rights Could Work Better for Developing Countries and Poor People', *Sustainable Developments*, 2002, vol. 70(1), p. 4.

[95] 'World Information Report 1997/98', UNESCO, Paris (1998), p. 320.

[96] *See* official bibliography of Barbara Ringer from the U.S. Copyright Office, http://www.copyright.gov/history/bios/ringer.pdf.

[97] Barbara A. Ringer, 'The Role of the United States in International Copyright – Past, Present, and Future', *Georgia Law Journal*, 1968, vol. 56, pp. 1050, 1051. *See* also Pat Choate, *Hot Property: The Stealing of Ideas in an Age of Globalization*, New York: Knopf, 2005 (arguing that the United States, the major promoter of establishment of the world intellectual property regime, 'is not blameless in the realm of idea theft' in a historical perspective).

and artistic works, especially from England, which implied that recognition of foreign copyrights would have led to a net deficit in international royalty payments'.[98] In the period before the Declaration of Independence, individual American states embarked on the process of promotion and reorganization of patent rights, but copyright protection was more or less neglected.[99] As observed by Peter Yu, shortly after independence, the domestic market was flooded with imported newspapers, periodicals and books, and 'copyright laws were virtually nonexistent'.[100] As noted by Zorina Khan, '[d]espite the lobbying of numerous authors and celebrities on both sides of the Atlantic, the American copyright statutes did not allow for copyright protection of foreign works for fully one century'.[101]

As a result, American publishers and producers felt it more than legitimate to pirate foreign literature, art and drama.[102] It was not until 1783 that the first legislation made its debut in Connecticut.[103] Even at that time, the piracy of foreign authors' works was still not regarded immoral.[104] As a consequence, in the period 'between 1800 and 1860, almost half of the bestsellers in the U.S. were pirated, mostly from English novels'.[105] It was surprising that the United States was not interested in the formation of and the participation in the international IPR regime until after the Second World War whilst the foundation stone of the system was laid by the end of the nineteenth century, implying that the American IPR system was established rather late, lagging largely behind its economic capacity.[106] Today, with its rapidly growing

---

[98]   B. Zorina Khan & Kenneth L. Sokoloff, 'History Lessons: The Early Development of Intellectual Property Institutions in the United States', *Journal of Economic Perspectives,* 2001, vol. 15(3), p. 237.

[99]   *See* B. Zorina Khan, 'Intellectual Property and Economic Development: Lessons from American and European History', Study Paper 1a, Commission on Intellectual Property Rights, 2002, p. 36, www.iprcommission.org/papers/word/ study_papers/ sp1a_khan_study.doc.

[100]   Peter K. Yu, 'The Copyright Divide', *Cardozo Law Review*, 2003, vol. 25, p. 337.

[101]   Khan, 'Intellectual Property and Economic Development', *supra* note 99, p. 40.

[102]   *Ibid.*

[103]   In 1783 Connecticut became the first state to approve an 'Act for the encouragement of literature and genius', followed shortly by Massachusetts and Maryland. *See* Yu, 'The Copyright Divide', *supra* note 100, p. 338.

[104]   Yu, p. 341.

[105]   *Ibid.*

[106]   *Ibid*, p. 421.

economic strength and technological sophistication, the United States has long since moved away from its notorious past and turned over a new leaf. Furthermore, it has converted 'from the most notorious pirate to the most dreadful police'.[107]

2.3 Experience of Japan

Although Japan has enjoyed the longest tradition of IPR in Asia, it only serves to illustrate the early development of the Japanese economy.[108] In fact, it is not surprising that Japan's IPR legal regime had long been characterized as a diffusion of knowledge rather than a facilitating innovation.[109] The first Director-General of the Japanese Trademark Registration and the Patent Office, Korekiyo Takahashi, who became Prime Minister in 1921, wrote in his autobiography when visiting the United States Patent Office in Washington DC, around the year 1900: 'We have looked about us to see what nations are the greatest, so that we can be like them. We said: "What is it that makes the United States such a great nation?["] And we investigated and found that it was patents and so we will have patents.'[110] Interestingly, the major driving force for developing a Western-style IPR legal system in Japan during the *Meiji* period was to promote Japan to becoming 'an advanced nation', as Emperor Meiji wished, or facilitate it into 'a greatest nation', as Premier Takahashi expected. The nationwide transplantation of an exotic intellectual property system in Japan was virtually a massive copying activity reflected by an ingrained habit of imitation.

---

[107] *Ibid*, p. 353.

[108] Christopher Heath, 'Intellectual Property Rights in Asia – Projects, Programmes and Developments', Online Publication of Max Planck Institute for Intellectual Property, Competition and Tax Law, http://www.intellecprop.mpg.de/Online-Publikationen/Heath-Ipeaover.htm.

[109] Koichi Hamada, 'Protection of Intellectual Property Rights in Japan', Working Paper, April 1996, Council of Foreign Relations (maintaining that Japan's IPR-related legal system emphasized the 'diffusion of foreign knowledge rather than creating its own').

[110] David Vaver, 'The Future of Intellectual Property Law: Japanese and European Perspectives Compared' (Working Papers of Oxford IP Research Centre, Working Paper No. 09/99), www.oiprc.ox.ac.uk/DVWP0999.pdf. *See* also 'Intellectual Property Policy Outline', Strategic Council on Intellectual Property, 3 July 2002, www.kantei.go.jp/foreign/policy/titeki/kettei/020703 taikou_e.html. (demonstrating that the ambitions and strategies of the Japanese government are to make Japan 'a nation built on intellectual property').

Due to the lack of economic underpinnings for a strong IPR protection, during the early phase of economic development, compulsory licensing was frequently required for a patent holder and, until 1938, a patent was liable to expire in practice if it was not in use by the patent holder.[111] In the 1960s, the United States Patent Office normally approved or dis-approved an application for patent within 18 months.[112] By contrast, it took the Japanese Patent Office (JPO) an average of five to seven years,[113] with the Kilby patent case being a typical example.[114] Also, the JPO required 'full disclosure of the technology submitted in the application for the accommodation of imitation'.[115]

In addition, although Japan had joined the Paris Union on 15 July 1899, as recently as in the 1990s, the duration of patents in Japan was less than 20 years, which is the minimum duration set out in the TRIPs Agreement.[116] It was not until 1994 that the patent law was amended and improved to guarantee at least 20 years after the application for the patent.[117] Strong IPR protection only came into being in Japan when external pressure was created by the United States and a lobbying pressure was raised by the domestic industrial sectors. In this sense, it was only recently that Japan substantially came into harmony with the international standards and embarked on a national undertaking with a view to the construction of a nation built on intellectual property.[118]

---

[111]   Hamada, *supra* note 109.

[112]   *See* Richard E. Vaughan, 'Defining Terms in the Intellectual Property Protection Debate: Are the North and South Arguing Past Each Other When We Say "Property"? A Lockean, Confucian, and Islamic Comparison', 2 *ILSA Journal of International & Comparative Law*, 1996, vol. 2, p. 347.

[113]   *Ibid.*

[114]   In 1961 the electronic giant Texas Instruments obtained the basic patent in Japan covering the integrated circuit, known as the 'Kilby patent' under the name of Nobel laureate Jack St. Clair Kilby. Texas Instruments was then required by the JPO to divide the application into 14 segments of which 12 were ultimately rejected. It took approximately 17 years for the first patent to be granted after it was filed, 'during which time the Japanese semiconductor industry copied and exported large quantities of chip products, earning billions of dollars in profit'. For a substantive introduction to and comment on the Kilby case, *see* Dana Rohrabacher and Paul Crilly, 'The Case for a Strong Patent System', *Harvard Journal of Law & Technology*, 1995, vol. 8(2), pp. 263, 265.

[115]   Vaughan, *supra* note 112, p. 70.

[116]   Hamada, *supra* note 109.

[117]   *Ibid.*

[118]   Since 2002 the Japanese government has initiated various institutional reforms in the area of intellectual property rights. The work has been promoted in accordance with the 'Intellectual Property Policy Outline' in July 2002 and the

In this context, the Japanese government applied a relatively tolerant intellectual property enforcement policy and, as a result, counterfeiting and piracy were very common. Counterfeit products were usually protected by the Registered Trade Mark and Design Law.[119] It was during this period that Japan seized a valuable developmental opportunity. In 1953, less than a decade after the Second World War, the Japanese were able to overcome the devastation of the war, and exceed pre-war levels of prosperity.[120] At the beginning of the 1960s the Japanese Prime Minister Hayato Ikeda launched his ambitious 'doubling the income' plan.[121] Then, at the centennial of the Meiji restoration, when China was under a violent storm of Cultural Revolution, Japan's GNP climbed dramatically to become the second largest in the world, surpassing West Germany.[122] It comes as no surprise that Japan did nothing different from the United States in copying European technology in its early years.[123]

The era of Japan's economic miracle led to a transition towards stronger IPR protection in response to lobby groups within specific domestic sectors.[124] As a major example, Yoshida Kogyo KK, famous maker of YKK zippers, discovered counterfeit YKK imported from Korea and initiated a protracted six-year lawsuit against the copiers.[125] Although the Japanese plaintiff lost the case, the setback aroused enthusiasm for

---

'Strategic Program for the Creation, Protection and Exploitation of Intellectual Property' in July 2003, which defined concrete measures the government should take and priorities in establishing a 'nation built on intellectual property' where intellectual property is used to create high-value added products and services with the aim of revitalizing the economy and society. *See* 'Intellectual Property Outline', Strategic Council on Intellectual Property, available at www. kantei.go.jp/foreign/policy/titeki/kettei/020703taikou_e.html; 'Strategic Programme for the Creation, Protection and Exploitation of Intellectual Property', Intellectual Property Policy Headquarters, 8 July 2003, http://unpan1.un.org/intradoc/groups/public/ documents/APCITY/UNPAN017539.pdf.

[119] *See* Michio Morishima, *Why Has Japan 'Succeeded'? Western Technology and the Japanese Ethos*, Cambridge University Press, 1982 (stating that, since the Meiji Restoration, Japan has had extensive contacts with the European countries, through which Japan 'broke with a long history of isolationism and paved the way for the adoption of western technologies').

[120] Hamada, *supra* note 109, p. 4. *See also* Shotaro Inshinomori, *Japan Inc.: An Introduction to Japanese Economics*, Betsey Scheiner trans., 1988 (introducing the post-war Japanese economic miracles).

[121] *Ibid*, p. 7.

[122] *Ibid*.

[123] Vaughan, *supra* note 112, pp. 316–17.

[124] *See* Inshinomori, *supra* note 120, pp. 3–4.

[125] *See* Vaughan, *supra* note 112, p. 349

enhancing IPR protection. Since then, the Japanese Ministry of Finance has organized the 'Customs Information Centre', a 'watchdog unit to monitor illicit copying' and to 'combat IPR infringement.'[126] This gradually became more pervasive, and counterfeits of Japanese origin had almost entirely disappeared by 1970 due to the stringent efforts of the Japanese government to crack down on counterfeit goods and the steady growth of the local economy.[127] However, a period of reversal was noticeable in the mid-1970s when Japan 'faced a resurgence of counterfeit goods that flooded into the Japanese market'.[128] It is interesting to observe that the rebound phenomenon occurred during the recession, on the heels of the oil crisis in the 1970s.

3.   FAIR USE, OPEN ACCESS AND THE DIGITAL DIVIDE

Of all forms of IPR, copyright has been viewed as 'the most positive, and as critical to the development of local culture',[129] 'and has emerged as one of the most important means of regulating the international flow of ideas and knowledge based products'.[130] However, the actual positions that developed and developing countries have within the global copyright system are divergent. The United States is the world's dominant producer of copyright-protected products,[131] and industrialized countries are the main beneficiaries of the copyrights.[132] By contrast, developing and less-developed countries are primarily consumers of copyrighted works.[133] As suggested in the UNESCO Information Report, 'copyright ownership is largely in the possession of the major copyright corporations'.[134] By maintaining monopoly status, the rights-holders 'place low per capita income countries and smaller economies at a significant

---

[126]   *Ibid.*
[127]   Masashi Kurose, 'Law Strengthened to Fight Flow of Counterfeit Goods', in *Managing Intellectual Property*, 2004, p. 12.
[128]   *Ibid.*
[129]   Burgiel & Schipper, *supra* note 94, p. 4.
[130]   'World Information Report 1997/98', UNESCO, Paris, 1998, p. 320.
[131]   Alan Story, 'Burn Berne: Why the Leading International Copyright. Convention Must be Repealed', *Houston Law Review,* 2003, vol. 40, p. 766 (concluding that 'the United States is the main producer, seller, and beneficiary of intellectual property exports').
[132]   *Ibid*, p. 769.
[133]   *Ibid.*
[134]   UNESCO World Information Report, *supra* note 130.

disadvantage'.[135] Various solutions are being considered in an effort to remedy this imbalance, among which the fair use of copyright may be a plausible and feasible option.

3.1 'Fair Use' Doctrine in the Realm of International Law

'Fair use', as a doctrine of national law,[136] is based upon the fact that 'every book in literature, science and art, borrows and must necessarily borrow, and use much which was well known before', and it alleviates the 'inherent tension in the need to simultaneously protect copyrighted material and to allow others to build upon it'.[137] As a common exception of the exclusive right granted by copyright law, fair use attempts to balance the rights of copyright owners and society's interests as a whole.

'Fair use' in the realm of international law still lacks sufficient legitimacy and calls for justification. As the most influential agreement in international intellectual property law, the TRIPs Agreement is playing a role that is unique in the international law arena. TRIPs on the one hand reinforces the protection of copyright and the neighbouring rights; on the other hand, however, the copyright provisions do not go as far as was envisaged by other provisions such as that of patents, in light of developing new international standards of protection which are considered to be beneficial for developing countries.[138] In this sense, developing countries have found themselves in an embarrassing position of being unable to find a legal basis to challenge the defective copyright regime. Some commentators attempted to link the claim of developing countries to theory of fair use, but the opponents argued that, while it stands as a common law doctrine, the doctrine of fair use is not justified in international law.[139]

---

[135] *Ibid.*

[136] 'Fair use' was a unique common law doctrine until it was incorporated into the Copyright Act of 1976. This doctrine exists as 'fair dealing' in some other common countries such as the United Kingdom and Australia.

[137] *Luther R. Campbell v. Acuff-Rose Music, Inc.*, 510 U.S. 569, 575, 29 U.S.P.Q.2d (BNA) 1961, 1964 (1994); Acuff-Rose, 510 U.S. at 575, 29 U.S.P.Q.2d at 1964 (quoting Filippo M. Cinotti, '"Fair Use" of Comparative Advertising under the 1995 Federal Dilution Act', 1996, 37 *IDEA* 149.

[138] Carlos M. Correa, 'Public Health and Patent Legislation in Developing Countries', *Tulane Journal of Technology & Intellectual Property*, 2001, vol. 3, p. 6.

[139] Eric Allen Engle, 'When is Fair Use Fair?: A Comparison of E.U. and U.S. Intellectual Property Law', *Transnational Law*, 2002, vol. 15, p. 222.

However, as Ruth Okedji has suggested, '[a]lthough the status of fair use under current international law is at best, uncertain', international law should nevertheless specify such a standard.[140] The TRIPs Agreement represents a significant compromise among the copyright laws of many countries and reflects the treatment of exceptions to copyright owners set out in the Berne Convention. In practice, TRIPs permits an individual member to exercise its discretions and make its own determinations as to the adaptability of TRIPs to the local circumstances.[141] One possible option could be to adopt the doctrine of fair use standard internationally, but this process may take time and 'it will not happen without pressure from international community through TRIPs'.[142]

In this context, it is reasonable and acceptable for developing economies to seek to develop solutions that 'encourage use of digital technology and promote access to information while preserving the rights of copyright owners'.[143] In other words, at the catching-up stage of the economy, every effort should be made to reconcile the interests between private and public. In fact, many communities in the developing world have 'more pressing concerns than copyright rules', such as poverty, illiteracy, unemployment, poorly resourced schools and libraries and so on.[144]

Attention should therefore be paid to contrast realities between developed, technologically proficient societies and less-developed, rural areas. Special attention should be given to the tension between meeting the public need and respecting commercial interests.[145] If no measures are to be taken, the increasing information gap will exacerbate the disparities in the digital realm.[146] As some scholars have suggested, temporary arrangements, such as appropriate exemptions in copyright regulations and affordable licensing, should be put in place so that the world economy can be developed in a more sustainable and integrated manner.[147]

---

[140]   Ruth Okedji, 'Towards an International Fair Use Doctrine', *Columbia Journal of Transnational Law*, 2000, vol. 39, pp. 87–9.

[141]   *Ibid*, p. 142.

[142]   Engle, *supra* note 139, pp. 222–23.

[143]   Burgiel & Schipper, *supra* note 94, p. 4.

[144]   *Ibid.*

[145]   *Ibid.*

[146]   *Ibid.*

[147]   *Ibid.*

3.2 Open Access: An Inevitable Trend in a Digital Society?

Following the establishment of the TRIPs regime, two international conventions on copyright law, namely the Copyright Treaty and Treaty on Performances and Phonograms, were adopted by member states of WIPO.[148] While the purpose of these conventions was to intensify copyright protection, various initiatives have been established on the basis of the concept of 'open access'.[149] These initiatives aim at making use of digital technology in a manner that promotes and facilitates freedom of sharing.[150] Some initiatives, which include themes such as free software, open content, open access and open standards, may be implemented under an open and collaborative model of R&D.[151] Meanwhile, there has been an empirical study on a new copyright licensing model, demonstrating a new approach to using dual licensing for one product, especially on the legal and economic requirements of dual licensing.[152]

While functioning as a non-profit and voluntary model, open access as a doctrine is grounded in the current legal framework of copyright law, as there is no separate legal mechanism governing open access data sharing.[153] Though still controversial, as Correa has suggested, open

---

[148] 'WIPO Copyright Treaty (WCT) and WIPO Performances and Phonograms Treaty (WPPT)', WIPO Information Resources, www.wipo.int/copyright/en/activities/wct_wppt/wct_wppt.htm.

[149] *See*, Carlos M. Correa, 'Recent International Developments in the Area of Intellectual Property Rights', ICTSD-UNCTAD Dialogue, 2nd Bellagio Series on Development and Intellectual Property, 18–21 September 2003, p. 6.

[150] *See*, e.g., Tere Vaden, 'Policy Options and Models for Bridging Digital Divides: Freedom, Sharing and Sustainability in the Global Network Society', *Global Challenges of eDevelopment*, 10 December 2004.

[151] *See* Olli Hietanen, 'Global Challenges of eDevelopment', From Digital Divides towards Empowerment and Sustainable Global Information Society, Seminar on Global Perspectives of Development Communication, University of Tampere, 28 June 2004, http://www.uta.fi/jour/global/hietanen2.pdf.

[152] Mikko Välimäki, 'Dual Licensing in Open Source Software Industry', published in Systemes d'Information et Management 1/2003, http://opensource.mit.edu/papers/valimaki.pdf.

[153] *See* 'Declaration of Principles and Plan of Action', Article 25, http://unpan1.un.org/intradoc/groups/public/documents/UN/UNPAN014246.pdf (stating that 'the sharing and strengthening of global knowledge for development can be enhanced by removing barriers to equitable access to information for economic, social, political, health, cultural, educational, and scientific activities and by facilitating access to public domain information, including by universal design and the use of assistive technologies').

access initiatives may be particularly appropriate in fields of academic research and software development.[154] As an alternative to the restricted access model, open access has gained a growing number of adherents in the software area and achieved understanding of many countries including the United States and the EU countries, who are considering measures to encourage the public procurement of open-source software, such as the Linux operating system.[155] A feasibility study conducted by the Swedish Agency for Public Management shows that 'open software in many cases are equivalent to – or better than – commercial products'.[156]

In Europe, while the European Parliament has endorsed the IPR Enforcement Directive for the prohibition of the widespread copying practice, there has been a growing demand for diversity of licensing arrangements and, in practice, varieties of licences which offer more flexibility than traditional copyright licences, have been available.[157] Among these, the launch of the Creative Commons, 'a nonprofit organization that offers artists, authors, publishers and musicians the option of creating and defining a flexible copyright for their creative works', is a promising achievement.[158] On 17 February 2013 the European Commission took concrete steps to give substance to open access to publicly funded research.[159]

More encouragingly, there have been a number of cases of landmark copyright litigation endorsing the validity of the new forms of licence. In the Netherlands, the Creative Commons licence was judged in the courts

---

[154]   Correa, 'Recent International Developments in the Area of Intellectual Property Rights', p. 6.

[155]   *Ibid.*

[156]   *See* 'Cases of Official Recognition/Adoption of F/OSS', European's Information   Society,   http://ec.europa.eu/information_society/activities/open source/cases/index_en.htm.

[157]   *See* 'The Management of Copyright and Related Rights', Consultation response from Professor Ross Anderson, University of Cambridge, and Foundation for Information Policy Research, 2004, http://europa.eu.int/comm/ internal_market/copyright/docs/management/consultationrightsmanagement/ross anderson_en.pdf.

[158]   *See* 'Creative Commons', http://creativecommons.org/.

[159]   *See* the European Commission 'Recommendation on Access to and Preservation of Scientific Information, http://ec.europa.eu/research/science-society/ document_library/pdf_06/recommendation-access-and-preservation-scientific-inform ation_en.pdf.

and the validity of this alternative copyright licence was upheld.[160] This decision was noteworthy because, as the first case about the Creative Commons licence, it reinforces the principle that 'the conditions of a Creative Commons license automatically apply to the content licensed under it, and bind users of such content even without expressly agreeing to, or having knowledge of, the conditions of the license'.[161]

A more recent development was the open access initiative released by the US White House Office of Science and Technology Policy (OSTP) on 22 February 2013. The new open access directive required that '[f]ederal agencies with more than \$100M in R&D expenditures to develop plans to make the published results of federally funded research freely available to the public within one year of publication and requiring researchers to better account for and manage the digital data resulting from federally funded scientific research'.[162] While the concepts and rationales underlined in the memorandum remain to be clarified, this initiative represents a remarkable breakthrough in the development of public access.

3.3 Bridging the Digital Divide: From Apple to Nokia and Ericsson

In order to facilitate the transformation of a state from 'copyright poor' to 'copyright rich', industries have an important role to play. A good illustration of this strategy is Apple's iTunes, which has been regarded as 'the driving force behind the digital music revolution'.[163] In April 2003

---

[160] Adam Curry, a famous internet entrepreneur, sued *Weekend*, a Dutch gossip magazine, for copyright infringement after the magazine published family photos of Curry's daughter without his prior consent. These pictures were published under a specific non-commercial Creative Commons licence. The photos also carried the notice that 'this photo is public'. Curry sued for both copyright and privacy infringements. *Weekend* defended itself, maintaining that it did not understand the reference to the Creative Commons licence. The magazine also claimed there could be no damages, since the pictures on the website were publicly accessible. On 6 March 2006 the District Court of Amsterdam ruled in summary proceedings that *Weekend* could not republish pictures as *Weekend* did not seek or obtain prior permission. For a more detailed introduction about the case and its judgment, *see* Mia Garlick, 'Creative Commons Licenses Enforced in Dutch Court', 16 March 2006, http://creativecommons.org/weblog/entry/5823.

[161] Ingrid Marson, 'Creative Commons Licence Upheld by Court', *ZDNet UK*, 21 March 2006, http://news.zdnet.co.uk/0,39020330,39258529,00.htm.

[162] *See* 'Memorandum for the Heads of Executive Departments and Agencies', OSTP, White House, www.whitehouse.gov/sites/default/files/microsites/ostp/ostp_public_access_memo_2013.pdf.

[163] 'Belgacom's Skynet Gives Up for iTunes', *Brussels Review*, 30 January 2006.

Apple unveiled its online music service, the iTunes Music Store, offering low-priced downloads from recording companies, which might possibly catch on as an alternative to the services that allowed customers to access music for free.[164] In January 2006 a major Belgian music retailer, Belgacom Skynet, announced a partnership with Apple's iTunes Music Store, further offering their customers 20 free iTunes downloads to promote the service.[165]

As reported by the media, iTunes undoubtedly offered 'the first small glimmer of hope that Hollywood and the music industry may actually avert a digital Armageddon in which perfect copies of every artist's work become instantly obtainable online for free'.[166] As Joseph Menn, author of *All the Rave: The Rise and Fall of Shawn Fanning's Napster*, commented, iTunes is so far 'the best thing that's come along for consumers who would rather not steal'.[167]

Another issue in light of open access is attributed to open standards involving information technology.[168] Digital technology makes distribution of information more affordable so that people can make full use of the opportunities to access information available throughout the world.[169] One characterization of the global network society requires the freedom to share the information on a reasonable scale.[170] In the EU, the growth of Nokia and Ericsson into global mobile phone giants is to some extent attributable to the early establishment of an open international standard in Nordic Mobile Telephone.[171] This paved way for the companies to innovate and update the standard efficiency.[172] When the wider Global System for Mobile Communications (GSM) standard was created, the

---

[164]   Laurie J. Flynn, 'Apple Offers Music Downloads with Unique Pricing', *N.Y. Times*, 29 April 2003, at C2 (mentioning that Apple plans to offer individual songs for 0.99 dollars each and most albums for 9.99 dollars each).

[165]   *Ibid.*

[166]   'Apple Tunes Out the Pirates', *Telegraph*, 11 May 2003.

[167]   *Ibid.*

[168]   Vaden, *supra* note 150.

[169]   *See* Hietanen, *supra* note 151.

[170]   *Ibid.*

[171]   Petri Rouvinen and Pekka Ylä-Anttila, 'Case Study, Little Finland's Transformation to a Wireless Giant', ETLA, The Research Institute of the Finnish Economy, in The Innovation Alliance: Succeeding in an Evolving Global Economy, 24 August 2004, Berkeley Roundtable on the International Economy (BRIE), pp. 92–96.

[172]   *Ibid.*

companies had obtained a significant advantage that enabled them to capture the market potential.[173]

The developments in freedom of sharing are of particular importance to developing countries that would like to advance the information society and leapfrog right into the latest and best available technologies.[174]

CONCLUSION

Economic factors is one of the important reasons for the IPR enforcement problems in developing countries. When economy is premature, a tolerant IPR policy helps economic blooming up. IPR protection in developing countries should not be as strong as that of developed countries in the 'catch-up' phase until they are about to come through the 'ladder of development'. While protection of IPR is essential to safeguard innovation, a tolerant IPR policy is indispensable for capacity building in the primary stage of development. To speed up this process will undermine the developmental bulwark, but beyond a certain point, allowing it to continue will also hinder economic growth. This means that the political judgment as to the appropriate balance in any state at any time moves along a continuum as a counterpart to development.

The TRIPs Agreement represents a successful culmination of several attempts by developed states to consolidate their monopoly position over the global economy. The role of developing states within the TRIPs regime has been vulnerable and the concessions they have made should be enumerated in appropriate ways, such as providing financial aid and offering technical assistance. In this context, developed countries are best advised to formulate long-term strategies and extend as much cooperation and assistance as possible in order to bridge the economic divide and help developing countries reach the 'development stage' and change their 'economic behaviour', rather than 'kicking off the ladder of development'. Today's investment in bridging the economic divide is a wise and logical step towards gaining many rewarding benefits tomorrow through the voluntarily implemented IPR policies.

---

[173]   Vaden, *supra* note 150.
[174]   *Ibid.*

10. The international enclosure of China's innovation space

Peter K. Yu*

INTRODUCTION

A country's ability to innovate depends on a wide variety of factors. Internally, it depends on the size of its economy, the availability of technological capabilities and the presence of much-needed human capital. Externally, it depends on constraints imposed by standards laid down by the World Trade Organization (WTO) and the World Intellectual Property Organization (WIPO) and in other international fora. It also depends on international relations and foreign pressures, such as those exerted by the United States Trade Representative (USTR) through the widely criticized Section 301 process.[1]

Although China has a long history of international engagement, it was largely outside the international intellectual property community until it reopened its market for foreign trade in the late 1970s.[2] In December 2001 China was finally admitted to the WTO after more than 15 years of

---

*   This chapter draws on research from the author's earlier articles in the *Campbell Law Review*, the *Drake Law Review Discourse* and the *Michigan State Law Review*.

[1]   On the USTR's Section 301 process, see Joe Karaganis and Sean Flynn, 'Networked Governance and the USTR', in Joe Karaganis (ed.), *Media Piracy in Emerging Economies*, New York: Social Science Research Council, 2011, pp. 75–98; Paul C. B. Liu, 'U.S. Industry's Influence on Intellectual Property Negotiations and Special 301 Actions', *UCLA Pacific Basin Law Journal*, 1994, vol. 13, pp. 87–117; Peter K. Yu, 'From Pirates to Partners: Protecting Intellectual Property in China in the Twenty-First Century', *American University Law Review*, 2000, vol. 50, pp. 131–243, 138–40.

[2]   On China's participation in the international intellectual property regime and its role in both the WTO and WIPO, see Peter K. Yu, 'The Middle Kingdom and the Intellectual Property World', *Oregon Review of International Law*, 2011, vol. 13, pp. 209–62.

exhaustive negotiations. Because of its then outsider status, many of the rules and standards in the existing international intellectual property regime have been established without the country's input and participation. As China's technological capabilities improve, these rules and standards have posed significant challenges to the country's ability to innovate.[3]

To highlight the external constraints on China's ability to innovate, this chapter recounts how the existing international intellectual property regime has evolved in a way that significantly encloses the innovation space of less developed countries – which, in WTO parlance, include both developing and least developed countries. The chapter begins by tracing the development of this regime from its very beginning to the establishment of the Agreement on Trade-Related Aspects of Intellectual Property Rights (TRIPS Agreement). It discusses not only the constraints the Agreement has placed on less developed countries, but also the various flexibilities it retains to their benefit.

The chapter then examines the rapid proliferation of TRIPS-plus bilateral, plurilateral and regional trade, investment and intellectual property agreements, including both the controversial Anti-Counterfeiting Trade Agreement (ACTA) and the still-under-negotiation Trans-Pacific Partnership (TPP) Agreement. It also points out that China has been slowly emerging as an innovative power, and therefore a potential beneficiary of higher intellectual property standards, just as developed countries used non-multilateral agreements aggressively to further enclose the innovation space of less developed countries. The chapter concludes by outlining four sets of challenges the international intellectual property regime will pose to China's continued effort to strengthen its innovative capacity.

1. THE BEGINNING

When the international intellectual property regime was created in the 19th century, it was designed primarily to patch up the divergent laws and customs of the participating countries.[4] The cornerstones of this

---

[3] On China's recent effort to develop its innovative capacity, see Peter K. Yu, 'Building the Ladder: Three Decades of Development of the Chinese Patent System', *WIPO Journal*, 2013, vol. 5, pp. 1–16.

[4] Paul Edward Geller, 'From Patchwork to Network: Strategies for International Intellectual Property in Flux', *Duke Journal of Comparative and International Law*, 1998, vol. 9, pp. 69–90, 70.

regime are the Paris Convention for the Protection of Industrial Property and the Berne Convention for the Protection of Literary and Artistic Works, both of which were established in the 1880s.

Consider the Paris Convention. When the Convention was being negotiated, countries disagreed significantly over such issues as compulsory licences, parallel importation, working requirements and filing systems.[5] While some countries, such as the Netherlands and Switzerland, did not have a patent system,[6] others, like Germany, remained heavily influenced by the anti-patent movement.[7] To enable countries to coordinate this wide range of protection (or the lack thereof) at the international level, the Convention struck a compromise by allowing each country to decide how intellectual property was to be protected within its borders. Instead of creating a system with uniform rules and standards, the Convention embraced the anti-discrimination principle of national treatment and left considerable room for countries to experiment with different intellectual property systems.[8]

In the patent area, for example, countries could decide whether they wanted to include a local working requirement or a compulsory licensing provision. They could also explore whether the protection of patents in processes provided sufficient incentives or whether they needed to extend protection to products as well. Countries could even determine whether they wanted to protect patents in the first place. It was no coincidence that the Netherlands and Switzerland were allowed to join the Paris Convention without even offering patent protection.[9]

---

[5]   Peter K. Yu, 'Currents and Crosscurrents in the International Intellectual Property Regime', *Loyola of Los Angeles Law Review*, 2004, vol. 38, pp. 323–443, 349.

[6]   Eric Schiff, *Industrialization without National Patents*, Princeton: Princeton University Press, 1971.

[7]   Heinrich Kronstein and Irene Till, 'A Reevaluation of the International Patent Convention', *Law and Contemporary Problems*, 1947, vol. 12, pp. 765–81; Fritz Machlup and Edith Penrose, 'The Patent Controversy in the Nineteenth Century', *Journal of Economic History*, 1950, vol. 10, pp. 1–29.

[8]   Stephen P. Ladas, *Patents, Trademarks, and Related Rights: National and International Protection*, Cambridge, Mass.: Harvard University Press, 1975, pp. 9–16.

[9]   Eventually, Switzerland introduced patent protection in 1888, and the Netherlands followed suit in 1910. Before these countries introduced patent protection, both countries did have trademark laws in place. Such protection might have justified their Paris Convention memberships. Schiff, supra note 6, at 22. It is also worth noting that the United States was able to join the Paris Union even though it did not offer any protection to utility models and offered only

Although this Convention worked well for developed countries for decades, most less developed countries failed to enjoy the autonomy and innovation space countries traditionally retained through the Convention. Instead, intellectual property laws were transplanted from developed countries onto the soil of less developed countries through colonial laws. As Ruth Okediji explained:

> Intellectual property law was not merely an incidental part of the colonial legal apparatus, but a central technique in the commercial superiority sought by European powers in their interactions with each other in regions beyond Europe. Granted, intellectual property systems in Europe prior to the seventeenth century were neither fully developed nor had intellectual property protection become a systematic policy designed primarily for encouraging domestic innovation. Whatever protections existed, however, would be exerted against other Europeans in colonial territories in the process of empire building. The [early period of European contact through trade with non-European peoples] thus was characterized predominantly by the extension of intellectual property laws to the colonies for purposes associated generally with the overarching colonial strategies of assimilation, incorporation and control. It was also characterized by efforts to secure national economic interests against other European countries in colonial territories.[10]

Even after these colonies became independent, many of the intellectual property laws that were originally transplanted from the former controlling powers remained on the books. These laws either survived state succession or had been retroactively adopted as part of the post-independence national law. As Professor Okediji observed further:

> It is well-known ... that most developing countries retained the structure and form of laws and institutions established during the colonial period, including intellectual property laws. Until 1989, Lesotho operated under the Patents, Trade Marks and Designs Protection Proclamation of 1919, a United Kingdom instrument. Mauritius, a former French colony, continued to operate under its Trade Marks Act (1868) and Patents Act (1975) for over twenty years after obtaining independence in 1968. Swaziland also inherited its IP

---

limited protection to industrial designs. Pamela Samuelson, 'Challenges for the World Intellectual Property Organisation and the Trade-Related Aspects of Intellectual Property Rights Council in Regulating Intellectual Property Rights in the Information Age', *European Intellectual Property Review*, 1999, vol. 21, pp. 578–91, 579.

[10] Ruth L. Okediji, 'The International Relations of Intellectual Property: Narratives of Developing Country Participation in the Global Intellectual Property System', *Singapore Journal of International and Comparative Law*, 2003, vol. 7, pp. 315–85, 324–25.

[intellectual property] regime 'as a colonial legacy.' The same is true with respect to other laws and institutions. Indeed, prior to the compelled compliance with intellectual property rights imposed by the TRIPS Agreement, many developing and least developed countries still had as their own domestic laws the old Acts and Ordinances of the colonial era. While some developing countries had laws in place that attracted the ire of the developed countries by explicit refusals to grant patents to pharmaceutical products, or through compulsory licensing provisions, or by the failure to enforce recognized rights, many others simply had obsolete laws.[11]

Nevertheless, the decolonization effort and the subsequent emergence of less developed countries called into question the extent of protection in the international intellectual property regime. During the Intellectual Property Conference of Stockholm in 1967, India and other less developed countries demanded special concessions in the international copyright system in light of their divergent economic, social, cultural and technological conditions.[12] The revision conference eventually led to the creation of WIPO as a United Nations specialized agency and the adoption of the Protocol Regarding Developing Countries in the Berne Convention.[13] A revision of that protocol became the Berne Appendix now incorporated by reference into the TRIPS Agreement.

Since the 1960s, less developed countries had also actively engaged in the debate on the transfer of technology, which culminated in the drafting of the International Code of Conduct on the Transfer of Technology under the auspices of the United Nations Conference on Trade and Development (UNCTAD).[14] When the Paris Convention was considered for revision in the early 1980s, these countries further demanded the lowering of the minimum standards of intellectual property protection as applied to them and to expand compulsory licences available under the Convention.[15]

These demands, to which the United States vehemently objected, precipitated the famous stalemate between developed and less developed

---

[11]   *Ibid.* at 335–36.

[12]   Barbara A. Ringer, 'The Role of the United States in International Copyright – Past, Present, and Future', *Georgetown Law Journal*, 1968, vol. 56, pp. 1050–79, 1065.

[13]   Peter K. Yu, 'A Tale of Two Development Agendas', *Ohio Northern University Law Review*, 2009, vol. 35, pp. 465–573, 471–93.

[14]   *Ibid.* at 493–505.

[15]   *Ibid.* at 505–11; Pedro Roffe and Gina Vea, 'The WIPO Development Agenda in an Historical and Political Context', in Neil Weinstock Netanel (ed.), *The Development Agenda: Global Intellectual Property and Developing Countries*, Oxford: Oxford University Press, 2009, pp. 79–109.

countries in the mid-1980s over the Nairobi text of the Convention.[16] Led by the United States and heavily influenced by multinational corporations, developed countries responded to this stalemate by abandoning the intellectual property-based forum in favour of the General Agreement on Tariffs and Trade (GATT), a trade-based forum that eventually expanded into the WTO. After close to a decade of negotiations, and some threats of trade sanctions by the United States, countries finally agreed to the Marrakesh Agreement Establishing the World Trade Organization, which included in its annex a multilateral agreement on intellectual property rights known as the TRIPS Agreement.[17]

2. THE TRIPS AGREEMENT

Based on models from developed countries, this Agreement remade the international intellectual property regime by strengthening protection in at least four significant ways. First, it established minimum standards for intellectual property protection and achieved new international consensus on the protection of emerging technologies and subject matters. For example, Article 10.2 states that 'computer programs, whether in source or object code, shall be protected as literary works under the Berne Convention (1971)'. Article 23 offers special protection to geographical indications for wines and spirits. Article 27.1 stipulates that 'patents … be available and patent rights enjoyable without discrimination as to the place of invention, the field of technology and whether products are imported or locally produced'. Article 27.3(b) requires each member state to 'provide for the protection of plant varieties either by patents or by an effective sui generis system or by any combination thereof'. Article 35 offers protection to integrated circuit topographies by reference to the Treaty on the Protection of Intellectual Property in Respect of Integrated Circuits.

---

[16]   Yu, supra note 13, at 510.

[17]   On the origins of the TRIPS Agreement, see Daniel Gervais, *The TRIPS Agreement: Drafting History and Analysis*, 3rd edn, London: Sweet and Maxwell, 2008, pp. 3–27; Jayashree Watal, *Intellectual Property Rights in the WTO and Developing Countries*, The Hague: Kluwer Law International, 2001, pp. 11–47; Peter K. Yu, 'TRIPS and Its Discontents', *Marquette Intellectual Property Law Review*, 2006, vol. 10, pp. 369–410, 371–79.

These heightened standards are particularly important because they transformed the international intellectual property regime from an international framework to a global one.[18] Traditionally, treaties within this regime, such as the Paris and Berne Conventions, were introduced largely to patch up the divergent protections in various national systems. In light of this patchwork effort, countries tended to focus only on the minimum standards, or the protection floor, when they negotiated international treaties. The TRIPS Agreement, however, altered that setup by imposing a 'supranational code' on the weaker WTO member states despite their limited economic development.[19] Because the code now requires higher standards than are appropriate for these countries, the focus on minimum standards and the virtual lack of maximum standards have made it difficult for countries to respond to domestic needs.[20]

Second, the TRIPS Agreement expanded the coverage of intellectual property protection to eight different areas. In addition to copyrights, patents and trademarks, the three main branches of intellectual property, the Agreement also covers geographical indications, industrial designs, plant variety protection, integrated circuit topographies and protection of undisclosed information. Such coverage is remarkable because a number of these areas did not attain international consensus before the adoption of the TRIPS Agreement. As Jayashree Watal, the former negotiator for India and a current WTO official, pointed out, 'at least one, undisclosed information, has never been the subject of any multilateral agreement before, and another, protection for integrated circuit designs, had no effective international treaty, while others, like plant variety protection or performers' rights, were geographically limited'.[21]

Third, through complex procedures and burdensome obligations, the TRIPS Agreement significantly curtailed the ability of less developed countries to design an intellectual property system that is tailored to local needs, interests, conditions and priorities. The three-step test in Articles

---

[18]   Peter K. Yu, 'The International Enclosure Movement', *Indiana Law Journal*, 2007, vol. 82, pp. 827–907, 901–906.

[19]   Jane C. Ginsburg, 'International Copyright: From a "Bundle" of National Copyright Laws to a Supranational Code?', *Journal of the Copyright Society of the U.S.A.*, 2000, vol. 47, pp. 265–89, 267–76; Yu, supra note 5, at 354–75.

[20]   Yu, supra note 17, at 402. It is worth noting that the TRIPS Agreement does include very few maximum standards. For example, Article 9.2 denies protection to 'ideas, procedures, methods of operation or mathematical concepts as such'. Article 27.3(b) also allows for the exclusion of diagnostic, therapeutic, and surgical methods and plants and animals other than micro-organisms from patent protection.

[21]   Watal, supra note 17, at 4.

13 and 30 and a similar test in Article 17 have made it particularly difficult for countries to create new limitations or exceptions in their copyright, patent and trademark systems. Article 31 also includes a set of complex procedural rules delineating the conditions under which a country can issue a compulsory licence. Although these rules have been relaxed lately by the Doha Declaration on the TRIPS Agreement and Public Health (Doha Declaration), the Decision on the Implementation of Paragraph 6 of the Doha Declaration on the TRIPS Agreement and Public Health, and the protocol to formally amend the Agreement by adding Article 31*bis*, it remains to be seen whether two-thirds of the WTO membership will ratify the proposed amendment before 1 December 2015 – a deadline that has been extended four times already since the protocol's adoption in 2005.[22]

Finally, the TRIPS Agreement 'married' intellectual property to international trade and established a dispute settlement process that is mandatory for disputes arising under the Agreement. As a result, the Agreement has greatly improved the enforceability of international intellectual property treaties, which hitherto have been virtually unenforceable.[23] The Agreement also provided developed countries with a process through which they can induce their less developed trading partners to offer stronger intellectual property protection. This process includes such measures as consultation, good offices, conciliation, mediation and finally dispute settlement.

Indeed, many commentators have considered the dispute settlement process a crowning achievement, if not the crowning achievement, of the Uruguay Round of Multilateral Trade Negotiations.[24] Ironically, although this process was used primarily by developed countries in the first few years of its establishment, less developed countries have recently begun to use the process more frequently.[25] Despite their growing use of the

---

[22] As of this writing, more than a third of the WTO member states have already ratified the proposed amendment.

[23] Gervais, supra note 17, at 10.

[24] Rachel Brewster, 'Shadow Unilateralism: Enforcing International Trade Law at the WTO', *University of Pennsylvania Journal of International Law*, 2009, vol. 30, pp. 1133–46, 1134; William J. Davey, 'The WTO Dispute Settlement System: The First Ten Years', *Journal of International Economic Law*, 2005, vol. 8, pp. 17–50, 32; Rochelle Cooper Dreyfuss and Andreas F. Lowenfeld, 'Two Achievements of the Uruguay Round: Putting TRIPS and Dispute Settlement Together', *Virginia Journal of International Law*, 1997, vol. 37, pp. 275–333, 275; Ruth Okediji, 'Toward an International Fair Use Doctrine', *Columbia Journal of Transnational Law*, 2000, vol. 39, pp. 75–175, 149–50.

[25] Davey, supra note 24, at 17, 24.

process, the latter have had only very limited success in getting developed countries to amend their laws. Some commentators, as a result, have begun to question the effectiveness of the WTO dispute settlement process.

A case in point is *China – Measures Affecting the Protection and Enforcement of Intellectual Property Rights*, the first and only WTO case involving China in the intellectual property arena.[26] While China prevailed on the first claim concerning the thresholds for criminal procedures and penalties, the United States won the last claim concerning the denial of copyright protection to works that have not been authorized for publication or dissemination within China. The remaining claim concerning the failure of the Chinese customs authorities to properly dispose of infringing goods seized at the border was somewhat divided between the two parties. In the end, the 2–1 outcome allowed both parties to declare victory, even though the panel decision was technically a tie between the two.[27]

More importantly, because the United States lost the most important claim on criminal thresholds and had mostly academic victories in the other two claims, the panel decision did not provide US intellectual property rights holders with more meaningful protection.[28] To some extent, 'the panel's narrow focus and the limited scope of its findings clearly revealed the TRIPS Agreement's shortcomings in the enforcement area'.[29] The decision therefore helped pave the way for the future negotiation of heightened intellectual property enforcement standards – through ACTA, the TPP and other non-multilateral trade and investment agreements.

[26]   World Trade Organization, 'China – Measures Affecting the Protection and Enforcement of Intellectual Property Rights', WT/DS362/R, 26 January 2009.

[27]   On further discussions of the dispute, see Peter K. Yu, 'TRIPS Enforcement and Developing Countries', *American University International Law Review*, 2011, vol. 26, pp. 727–82; Peter K. Yu, 'The TRIPS Enforcement Dispute', *Nebraska Law Review*, 2011, vol. 89, pp. 1046–1131.

[28]   Yu, 'The TRIPS Enforcement Dispute', supra note 27, at 1081–103.

[29]   Peter K. Yu, 'TRIPS and Its Achilles' Heel', *Journal of Intellectual Property Law*, 2011, vol. 18, pp. 479–531, 511.

3. TRIPS FLEXIBILITIES

Although the TRIPS Agreement increased considerably the protection of intellectual property rights at the international level, significant safeguards, flexibilities and transition measures exist in the Agreement to protect less developed countries. For example, Article 7 explicitly states:

[T]he protection and enforcement of intellectual property rights should contribute to the promotion of technological innovation and to the transfer and dissemination of technology, to the mutual advantage of producers and users of technological knowledge and in a manner conducive to social and economic welfare, and to a balance of rights and obligations.

Article 8 also recognizes the needs of WTO member states to 'adopt measures necessary to protect public health and nutrition, and to promote the public interest in sectors of vital importance to their socio-economic and technological development, provided that such measures are consistent with the provisions of this Agreement'.[30]

In addition, the second sentence of Article 1.1, with added emphasis, stipulates that 'members may, *but shall not be obliged to*, implement in their law more extensive protection than is required by this Agreement'. The next sentence in this provision states further that member states are 'free to determine the appropriate method of implementing the provisions of this Agreement within their own legal system and practice'. As Frederick Abbott highlighted in the public health context:

The TRIPS Agreement ... does not ... restrict the authority of governments to regulate prices. It ... permits [compulsory or government use licenses] to be granted. It permits governments to authorize parallel importation. The TRIPS Agreement does not specify that new-use patents must be granted. It allows patents to be used for regulatory approval purposes, and it does not require the extension of patent terms to offset regulatory approval periods. The TRIPS Agreement provides a limited form of protection for submissions of regulatory data; but this protection does not prevent a generic producer from making use of publicly available information to generate bioequivalence test data. The TRIPS Agreement provides substantial discretion for the application of competition laws.[31]

---

[30] On the use of Articles 7 and 8 to recalibrate the balance of the international intellectual property system, see Peter K. Yu, 'The Objectives and Principles of the TRIPS Agreement', *Houston Law Review*, 2009, vol. 46, pp. 979–1046.
[31] Frederick M. Abbott, 'The Cycle of Action and Reaction: Developments and Trends in Intellectual Property and Health', in Pedro Roffe, Geoff Tansey

As if these safeguards and flexibilities were not enough, the TRIPS Agreement includes many ambiguities that have been intentionally built into the instrument through the efforts of skilful negotiators. As Carlos Correa pointed out, although developed countries would interpret the word 'review' in Article 27(3)(b) to mean 'review of implementation', less developed countries are more likely to interpret that same word to suggest the possibility of 'revising' the Agreement to meet their needs and interests.[32] Likewise, Sisule Musungu recently reminded us of the different ways of conceptualizing the transition periods built into the TRIPS Agreement:

> While giving extra time due to administrative and financial constraints was one aim, the central objective of the LDCs [least developed countries] transition period under the TRIPS Agreement is different. Article 66.1 of TRIPS read together with the Preamble of the TRIPS Agreement and its objectives under Article [7] envisage the purpose and objectives of the LDCs transition period to be to respond and address: the special needs and requirements of these countries; and the need for maximum flexibility to help these countries create a sound and viable technological base.[33]

Jayashree Watal has described these ambiguous words and phrases as 'constructive ambiguities'.[34] These ambiguities are constructive, because they provide less developed countries with a bulwark against the continuous expansion of intellectual property rights. If carefully interpreted, they will enable countries to preserve the innovation space appropriately reserved for them during the negotiation process. They may also allow less developed countries to "'claw[]" back much of what was lost in the negotiating battles in TRIPS'.[35]

Finally, the Agreement recognized the inability of less developed countries to immediately increase their levels of protection. Article 65 provided developing and transition countries with a four-year transition period, which has since expired. Likewise, Article 66 provided least

---

and David Vivas-Eugui (eds), *Negotiating Health: Intellectual Property and Access to Medicines*, London: Earthscan, 2006, pp. 27–40, 30.

[32]   Carlos M. Correa, *Intellectual Property Rights, the WTO and Developing Countries: The TRIPS Agreement and Policy Options*, London: Zed Books, 2000, p. 211.

[33]   Sisule Musungu, *A Conceptual Framework for Priority Identification and Delivery of IP Technical Assistance for LDCs during the Extended Transition Period under the TRIPS Agreement*, Geneva: Quaker United Nations Office, 2007, p. 5.

[34]   Watal, supra note 17, at 7.

[35]   *Ibid.*

developed countries with an initial 10-year transition period, which has now been extended twice to 25½ years. Article 66 further requires developed countries to provide incentives for their businesses and institutions to help create 'a sound and viable technological base' in least developed countries by promoting and encouraging the transfer of technology.

In sum, although the TRIPS Agreement has greatly strengthened intellectual property protection while significantly enclosing the innovation space of WTO member states, it includes certain safeguards, flexibilities and transition measures to help countries 'buy time' to update their intellectual property systems. It also leaves some space for less developed countries to develop policies that respond to their needs, interests, conditions and priorities. Whether countries will be able to take advantage of these benefits will depend on their capacity to interpret the Agreement, insist on their interpretations and resolve disputes before the WTO Dispute Settlement Body.[36]

4. TRIPS-PLUS AGREEMENTS

Unfortunately for less developed countries, recent years have seen even greater enclosure of their innovation space. Whatever limited space the TRIPS Agreement retained, that space has been further enclosed by the aggressive push by developed countries for TRIPS-plus bilateral, plurilateral and regional trade and investment agreements – free trade agreements (FTAs) for the United States and FTAs and economic partnership agreements (EPAs) for the European Union. As the US Trade Act of 2002 explicitly declared:

> [T]he principal negotiating objectives of the United States regarding trade-related intellectual property are … to further promote adequate and effective protection of intellectual property rights, including through … ensuring that the provisions of any multilateral or bilateral trade agreement governing intellectual property rights that is entered into by the United States reflect a standard of protection similar to that found in United States law …

There are generally three different types of provisions in the so-called TRIPS-plus agreements: TRIPS-plus provisions, TRIPS-extra provisions

---

[36] Gregory Shaffer, 'Recognizing Public Goods in WTO Dispute Settlement: Who Participates? Who Decides? The Case of TRIPS and Pharmaceutical Patent Protection', *Journal of International Economic Law*, 2004, vol. 7, pp. 459–82, 473–76.

and TRIPS-restrictive provisions. TRIPS-plus provisions increase the commitments of less developed countries by increasing the protection stated in the TRIPS Agreement. For example, although the Agreement requires patent protection for only 20 years, some recent US FTAs have required a limited extension of the patent term based on the period during which a product undergoes regulatory review.[37] Such an extension is similar to the extension provided by the US Hatch-Waxman Act of 1984.

TRIPS-extra provisions, by contrast, add new commitments that are not covered by the TRIPS Agreement. Examples of these provisions include those calling for the establishment of a data exclusivity regime to protect clinical trial data submitted during regulatory approval processes; the linkage of pharmaceutical product registration to patent status; the requirement that patents be granted for 'new uses', or second indications, of known compounds; the ban on parallel importation of cheap, generic drugs; and the use of dispute settlement processes that are different from the one mandated by the WTO.[38] Although the WTO prohibits member states from taking retaliatory measures before exhausting all of the actions permissible under its rules,[39] TRIPS-extra provisions are likely to rejuvenate the Section 301 process and may lead to greater use of trade threats and unilateral sanctions, as the provisions cover issues outside of the TRIPS Agreement.

Finally, TRIPS-restrictive provisions neither increase the protection under the TRIPS Agreement nor cover a new area of protection outside the Agreement. Instead, they enclose the innovation space of less developed countries by restricting the interpretation of the Agreement. A textbook example of such provisions is one that requires less developed countries to protect plant varieties by introducing the 1991 Act of UPOV (International Union for the Protection of New Varieties of Plants), notwithstanding the fact that the TRIPS Agreement allows each member state to decide whether it wants to offer protection through patents, sui generis protection or a combination of both.[40]

Taken together, these three types of provisions in TRIPS-plus trade and investment agreements have greatly enclosed the already very limited innovation space less developed countries have under the TRIPS Agreement. As noted development economist Chang Ha-joon observed, the existing international system has enabled developed countries to '"kick

---

[37]   Yu, supra note 18, at 868.
[38]   *Ibid.* at 868–69.
[39]   World Trade Organization, 'United States – Sections 301–310 of the Trade Act of 1974', WT/DS152/R, 22 December 1999.
[40]   Yu, supra note 18, at 869.

away the ladder" by which they have climbed to the top'.[41] These efforts have prevented less developed countries from adopting policies and institutions developed countries themselves have used during their formative period of development. Similarly, international relations scholar Kevin Gallagher lamented how developed countries, such as the United States and members of the European Union, have used trade and investment agreements to induce less developed countries to 'trade away' their ladder.[42]

5. PLURILATERAL CLUBS

Although large developing countries, including China, have sought to respond to these TRIPS-plus agreements by establishing development agendas,[43] moving activities to other international fora and establishing their own versions of bilateral, plurilateral or regional trade agreements, they have had very limited success thus far. For instance, although China has successfully negotiated FTAs with Pakistan, Chile, New Zealand, Singapore, Peru, Costa Rica, Iceland, Switzerland and members of the Association of Southeast Asian Nations (ASEAN),[44] these agreements have no or very limited substantive provisions on the protection of intellectual property rights.[45] As a result, the agreements do not allow China to reclaim its lost innovation space.

---

[41] Ha-joon Chang, *Kicking Away the Ladder: Development Strategy in Historical Perspective*, London: Anthem, 2002, p. 129.

[42] Kevin P. Gallagher, 'Trading Away the Ladder? Trade Politics and Economic Development in the Americas', *New Political Economy*, 2008, vol. 13, pp. 37–59.

[43] Yu, supra note 13, at 511–40.

[44] On China's free trade agreements, or what I have termed 'Sinic trade agreements', see Henry Gao, 'The RTA Strategy of China: A Critical Visit', in Ross Buckley, Vai Io Lo and Laurence Boulle (eds), *Challenges to Multilateral Trade: The Impact of Bilateral, Preferential and Regional Agreements*, Alphen aan den Rijn: Kluwer Law International, 2008, pp. 53–64; Marc Lanteigne, 'Northern Exposure: Cross-Regionalism and the China-Iceland Preferential Trade Negotiations', *China Quarterly*, 2010, vol. 202, pp. 362–80; Peter K. Yu, 'Sinic Trade Agreements', *U.C. Davis Law Review*, 2011, vol. 44, pp. 953–1028.

[45] Peter K. Yu, 'Sinic Trade Agreements and China's Global Intellectual Property Strategy', in Christoph Antons and Reto M. Hilty (eds), *IP Aspects of Free Trade Agreements in the Asia Pacific Region*, Guildford: Springer, 2014, forthcoming.

To complicate matters, just as less developed countries were actively exploring policy responses and countervailing strategies, developed countries doubled down by launching new efforts to develop club-based treaties outside the multilateral trading system. Examples of these non-multilateral efforts include the development of the controversial ACTA and the equally problematic TPP. Although both agreements technically are plurilateral agreements, similar to those FTAs and EPAs discussed earlier, their aspiration to use a 'country club' approach to set alternative international intellectual property norms deserves our greater attention.

In October 2007 the United States, Japan, the European Union and other like-minded countries announced their intention to negotiate the Anti-Counterfeiting Trade Agreement in October 2007.[46] The Agreement aims to set higher standards for international intellectual property enforcement, responding to the frustration they had over the limited success in pushing for higher standards at both the WTO and WIPO. As Susan Schwab, the former USTR, formally declared when announcing the launch of the ACTA negotiations:

> The goal [of the Agreement] is to set a new, higher benchmark for enforcement that countries can join on a voluntary basis. ... The envisioned ACTA will include commitments in three areas: (1) strengthening international cooperation, (2) improving enforcement practices, and (3) providing a strong legal framework for [intellectual property] enforcement.[47]

Since the announcement, 11 rounds of negotiations have been held, and 37 countries participated in the negotiations for close to three years (with Jordan and the United Arab Emirates also joining them initially in the first round of negotiations[48]). The final text of ACTA contains six different chapters: (1) initial provisions and definitions; (2) legal framework for enforcement of intellectual property rights; (3) enforcement

---

[46] On ACTA, see Michael Blakeney, *Intellectual Property Enforcement: A Commentary on the Anti-Counterfeiting Trade Agreement (ACTA)*, Cheltenham: Edward Elgar Publishing, 2012; Peter K. Yu, 'ACTA and Its Complex Politics', *WIPO Journal*, 2011, vol. 3, pp. 1–16; Peter K. Yu, 'Enforcement, Enforcement, What Enforcement?', *IDEA*, 2012, vol. 52, 241–86; Peter K. Yu, 'Six Secret (and Now Open) Fears of ACTA', *SMU Law Review*, 2011, vol. 64, pp. 975–1094 (Yu, 'Six Secret Fears').

[47] USTR, 'Ambassador Schwab Announces U.S. Will Seek New Trade Agreement to Fight Fakes', http://www.ustr.gov/ambassador-schwab-announces-us-will-seek-new-trade-agreement-fight-fakes.

[48] Yu, 'Six Secret Fears', supra note 46, at 1075.

practices; (4) international cooperation; (5) institutional arrangements; and (6) final provisions. Chapter II, which is the most controversial and longest part of the agreement, is subdivided into five different sections: (a) general obligations; (b) civil enforcement; (c) border measures; (d) criminal enforcement; and (e) enforcement of intellectual property rights in the digital environment.

On 15 April 2011 ACTA was finally adopted, after more than five years of negotiations, pre-negotiations, debate and planning.[49] A few months later, eight countries – Australia, Canada, Japan, Morocco, New Zealand, Singapore, South Korea and the United States – signed the Agreement in a ceremony in Japan. As Mexico prepared to join the TPP negotiations, it also signed the Agreement in July 2012. As of this writing, Switzerland and five members of the European Union (the Netherlands, Cyprus, Germany, Slovakia and Estonia) are the only negotiating parties that have refrained from signing the Agreement. Because ACTA will not enter into force until six parties have deposited their instruments of ratification, as opposed to merely signing the agreement, it remains interesting to see if and when the Agreement will enter into force.

While developed countries and their like-minded partners were actively completing the ACTA negotiations, the United States also began the TPP negotiations with Australia, Brunei Darussalam, Chile, Malaysia, New Zealand, Peru, Singapore and Vietnam.[50] (Canada, Mexico and Japan have since joined the negotiations.) It is anticipated that the TPP Agreement will include an intellectual property chapter, similar to those intellectual property chapters found in existing US FTAs. As the USTR stated in his recent update on the TPP negotiations:

> TPP countries have agreed to reinforce and develop existing [TRIPS] rights and obligations to ensure an effective and balanced approach to intellectual property rights among the TPP countries. Proposals are under discussion on many forms of intellectual property, including trademarks, geographical indications, copyright and related rights, patents, trade secrets, data required for the approval of certain regulated products, as well as intellectual property enforcement and genetic resources and traditional knowledge. TPP countries

---

[49] Peter K. Yu, 'The Alphabet Soup of Transborder Intellectual Property Enforcement', *Drake Law Review Discourse*, 2012, vol. 60, pp. 16–33, 23.
[50] *Ibid.* at 24.

have agreed to reflect in the text a shared commitment to the Doha Declaration on TRIPS and Public Health.[51]

Due to the secretive and dynamic nature of the negotiation process, it remains unclear what provisions would find their way into the final text of the agreement. It is also unclear whether the agreement would be completed (as with ACTA) or whether the negotiation would fail in the end (as with the negotiation of the Free Trade Area of the Americas). Regardless of the outcome of the negotiations, however, leaked documents and expert commentaries suggest that the TPP, if adopted, will likely be more dangerous than ACTA from a public interest standpoint.[52] This is particularly true considering that the United States has more and better items to offer to trading partners in the TPP negotiations.[53]

In sum, both ACTA and the TPP help continue the developed countries' trend in using TRIPS-plus agreements to establish higher standards of intellectual property protection and enforcement. Although China is not a party to either agreement, the TRIPS-plus norms set in these agreements are likely to have a strong impact on the country's continued ability to innovate. For example, the USTR could take ACTA and the TPP into consideration in the Section 301 process once the agreements enter into effect.[54] Indeed, failures to ratify new treaties have been considered as shortcomings within the process in the past. Canada was put on the Section 301 Watch List repeatedly because of its failure to ratify the WIPO Internet Treaties, among other reasons.[55] Likewise, before China acceded to the WIPO Internet Treaties, the USTR noted in the *2005 National Trade Estimate Report on Foreign Trade Barriers* that 'the United States considers the WIPO treaties to reflect many key international norms for providing copyright protection over the Internet'.[56] That report further stated that 'China's accession to the WIPO treaties is an increasingly important priority for the United States'.

---

[51]   USTR, 'Outlines of the Trans-Pacific Partnership Agreement', http://www. ustr.gov/about-us/press-office/fact-sheets/2011/november/outlines-trans-pacific-partnership-agreement.

[52]   Yu, supra note 49, at 24–33.

[53]   *Ibid.* at 26.

[54]   Yu, 'Six Secret Fears', supra note 46, at 1040–42.

[55]   *Ibid.* at 1041–42.

[56]   Office of the United States Trade Representative, *2005 National Trade Estimate Report on Foreign Trade Barriers*, Washington, 2005, p. 96.

6. CHINA'S EMERGENCE AS AN INNOVATIVE POWER

Interestingly, and perhaps coincidentally, just as developed countries used TRIPS-plus agreements and plurilateral clubs aggressively to further enclose the innovation space of less developed countries, China has been slowly emerging as an innovative power. Although China joined the WTO in December 2001, it did not begin paying greater attention to the development of an innovation- and knowledge-based economy until the mid-2000s.

In February 2006, the State Council released the National Long-term Scientific and Technological Development Program, formally declaring its commitment to turn China into an innovation-based economy within 15 years.[57] Since then, top Chinese leaders have increasingly recognized the economic and strategic importance of a well-functioning intellectual property system. For example, President Hu Jintao remarked in the Group Study of the Political Bureau of the Central Committee of the Chinese Communist Party in May 2006: 'Strengthening the building of China's system of intellectual property right and vigorously upgrading the capacity of creation, management, protection and application regarding intellectual property are our urgent need for the purpose of enhancing independent and self-driven innovation capabilities and building an innovation-oriented country.'[58] Likewise, Premier Wen Jiabo observed: 'One thing necessary to stress is the need to concretely strengthen IP protection. In the new era, global science and technology competition, as well as economic competition, is primarily a competition of IP rights. Promoting IP protection therefore promotes and inspires innovation.'[59]

Taking the lead of these Chinese leaders, the State Intellectual Property Office (SIPO) set very ambitious goals for its National Patent Development Strategy (2011–2020). Included in the 2015 targets were the following goals:

---

[57] Feng Xiaoqing, 'The Interaction between Enhancing the Capacity for Independent Innovation and Patent Protection: A Perspective on the Third Amendment to the Patent Law of the P.R. China', *Pittsburgh Journal of Technology Law and Policy*, 2008, vol. 9, para. 7.

[58] Wu Handong, 'One Hundred Years of Progress: The Development of the Intellectual Property System in China' *WIPO Journal*, 2009, vol. 1, pp. 117–24, 120.

[59] State Intellectual Property Office, 'China's Intellectual Property Protection in 2008', http://english.sipo.gov.cn/laws/whitepapers/200904/t20090427_457167.html.

The annual quantity of applying for patents for inventions, utility models and designs will reach 2 million. China will rank among the top two in the world in terms of the annual number of patents for inventions granted to the domestic applicants, and the quality of patents filed will further improve. The number of owning patents every one million people and the number of overseas patent applications filed by Chinese applicants will double. The proportion of patent applications in industrial enterprises above designated size will reach 8% and the quantity of owning patent rights will significantly rise. ... The patent transaction services will be established in major cities of China with annual patent transaction amounts reaching 100 billion yuan. ... The patent examiner[s] will reach 9,000. ... The talents in the patent service industry will be greater and the professional categories will be more complete, with certified patent agents reaching 10,000.

In addition, SIPO has been very active in developing professional ties with patent offices around the world. In 2007, for example, its officials met with their counterparts from the European Patent Office, the Japanese Patent office, the Korean Intellectual Property Office and the United States Patent and Trademark Office to discuss ways to 'improv[e] the efficiency of their examination systems and to harmonize their office systems'.[60] These so-called 'IP5' discussions, which are ongoing, further strengthen SIPO's status as 'a player in the top tier of patent offices that will dominate the emerging system of global patent administration'.[61]

While questions remain concerning what a country could do with two million patents per year and whether such ambitious goals would result in low patent quality,[62] it is hard not to be amazed by the quick turnaround China has experienced in the intellectual property arena in less than three decades. Although the country did not have any modern patent system before 1984, it is now on track to become the world's leader in both domestic and international patent applications. When interviewed by *The New York Times* about SIPO's 2015 targets, David

---

[60]   Peter Drahos, *The Global Governance of Knowledge: Patent Offices and Their Clients*, Cambridge: Cambridge University Press, 2010, p. 236.

[61]   *Ibid.* at 233.

[62]   Mark Liang, 'Chinese Patent Quality: Running the Numbers and Possible Remedies', *John Marshall Review of Intellectual Property Law*, 2012, vol. 11, pp. 478–522; Dan Prud'homme, *Dulling the Cutting-Edge: How Patent-Related Policies and Practices Hamper Innovation in China*, Shanghai: European Union Chamber of Commerce, 2012; Peter K. Yu, 'Five Oft-repeated Questions about China's Recent Rise as a Patent Power', 2013, *Cardozo Law Review De Novo*, pp. 78–113, 81–88.

Kappos, the former director of the United States Patent and Trademark Office, could not help but describe those numbers as 'mind-blowing'.[63]

Today, China is already among the top five countries filing patent applications through the Patent Cooperation Treaty (PCT). In 2013 the number of PCT applications increased by 15.6 per cent to 21,516, earning China the third spot, behind only the United States and Japan.[64] Among all the applicants, ZTE Corp. (formerly Zhongxing Tele-communication Equipment Corp.) and Huawei Technologies, respectively, had the second and third largest number of PCT applications. With significant backing from the Chinese government and the anticipated involvement of the world's largest public sector, China will likely catch up with the existing intellectual property powers more quickly than many have anticipated.

Moreover, as John Orcutt and Shen Hong observed, China has made many notable achievements in space technology, biotechnology (including genomics and stem cell research), information technology, nanotechnology and advanced energy technology:

- China is one of only three countries to put a person in space with its own rockets (and China recently conducted its first spacewalk).
- Chinese research teams helped to map the genome for rice and have since helped to extend genomic sequencing to other plants, as well as a variety of insects and parasites.
- China passed the United States as the leading exporter of information-technology goods in 2004.
- China has become a world leader in the field of nanotechnology – producing major nanotechnology breakthroughs (e.g., improved production of carbon nano-tubes) and generating a significant portion of the world's nanotechnology publications and patents and new nanotechnology firms.
- China has long been a leader in nuclear technology and is positioned to become a leader in a number of other energy fields, including clean coal and hydropower.[65]

63   Steve Lohr, 'When Innovation, Too, Is Made in China', *New York Times*, 2 January 2011, p. 3.
64   WIPO, 'US and China Drive International Patent Filing Growth in Record-Setting Year', http://www.wipo.int/pressroom/en/articles/2014/article_0002.html.
65   John L. Orcutt and Shen Hong, *Shaping China's Innovation Future: University Technology Transfer in Transition*, Cheltenham: Edward Elgar Publishing, 2011, pp. vii–ix.

In sum, although developed countries have used bilateral, plurilateral and regional trade, investment and intellectual property agreements aggressively to further enclose the innovation space of less developed countries, China may have successfully emerged as a country that will receive *some* benefits from such enclosure. It therefore remains to be seen how the developed countries' recent efforts will affect China's ability to innovate and to play catch-up with countries in the developed world. It is also unclear whether China will follow the footsteps of these countries to enclose the innovation space of other less developed countries.

7. FOUR FUTURE CHALLENGES

In the future, the international intellectual property regime is likely to pose four sets of challenges to China's effort to strengthen its innovative capacity. The first challenge concerns the 'international enclosure movement' described throughout this chapter.[66] Although recent intellectual property literature focuses mostly on the enclosure of the public domain and the upward ratcheting of intellectual property protection, this international movement encloses the policy space – or, in this context, the innovation space – of individual countries in the name of international harmonization.

As a result of this enclosure, countries, especially those in the less developed world, are increasingly forced to adopt one-size-fits-all – or more precisely, super-size-fits-all – legal standards that ignore local needs, national interests, technological capabilities, institutional capacities and public health conditions. Whether it is for greater protection (in the area of traditional knowledge, traditional cultural expressions or genetic resources) or weaker protection (in the area of limitations, exceptions or safeguards), countries now have very limited 'wiggle room' to implement the type of intellectual property policy they need and prefer.

The second challenge concerns the emergence of a non-multilateral era. Although the establishment of TRIPS-plus trade, investment and intellectual property agreements could potentially lead to further consolidation, resulting in what commentators have referred to as 'TRIPS II',[67]

---

[66] The term 'international enclosure movement' was coined in Yu, supra note 18.

[67] Graeme B. Dinwoodie, 'The International Intellectual Property Law System: New Actors, New Institutions, New Sources', *American Society of International Law Proceedings*, 2004, vol. 98, pp. 213–22, 217; Rochelle Cooper

these myriad agreements could also spark a race among the major trading powers, precipitating an undesirable 'battle of the FTAs'.[68] Indeed, the rapid proliferation of these new agreements seems to have already ushered in a new era of non-multilateralism. This era has raised new and difficult questions concerning not only the appropriate policy responses, but also the future of the international intellectual property regime and the interrelationship between this regime and other international regimes.[69]

The acceleration of non-multilateral activities, however, does not mean that countries will abandon the use of multilateral fora. China, for example, has been increasingly assertive in the international intellectual property regime.[70] Its hosting of the WIPO diplomatic conference in June 2012 has undoubtedly contributed to the successful negotiation of the Beijing Treaty on Audiovisual Performances, which was signed by close to 50 WIPO members. A year later, WIPO adopted the Marrakesh Treaty to Facilitate Access to Published Works for Persons Who Are Blind, Visually Impaired, or Otherwise Print Disabled. Taken together, these two new agreements seem to suggest that both multilateralism and non-multilateralism will be developing in a parallel fashion – at the same time and perhaps even at the same pace.[71]

The third challenge concerns the increased fragmentation of the international intellectual property regime. While international intellectual property standards have been set at the WTO and WIPO in the past, there have been growing developments in other international regimes, such as those governing public health, human rights, biological diversity, food and agriculture, and information and communications.[72] These developments have resulted in the creation of what I have described as the 'international intellectual property regime complex' – a non-hierarchical, decentralized conglomerate regime that includes not only the traditional

---

Dreyfuss, 'TRIPS-Round II: Should Users Strike Back?', *University of Chicago Law Review*, 2004, vol. 71, pp. 21–35; Gervais, supra note 17, at 48.

[68] Yu, supra note 44, at 1018–27.
[69] Yu, 'ACTA and Its Complex Politics', supra note 46, at 9–12.
[70] Yu, supra note 2, at 237–58.
[71] Peter K. Yu, 'The Non-multilateral Approach to International Intellectual Property Norm-setting', in Daniel J. Gervais (ed.), *Research Handbook on International Intellectual Property Law*, Cheltenham: Edward Elgar Publishing, 2014, forthcoming.
[72] Yu, supra note 13, at 522–40.

area of intellectual property laws and policies, but also the overlapping areas in related international regimes or fora.[73]

To date, it remains unclear whether these forum-manipulative activities will benefit primarily developed or less developed countries.[74] On the one hand, these activities will allow weaker countries to better protect their interests by mobilizing in favourable fora, developing the needed political and diplomatic groundwork, and establishing new 'counter-regime norms' that help restore the balance of the international intellectual property system.[75] The existence of multiple fora will also help promote 'norm competition across different fora as well as ... inter-agency competition and collaboration'.[76] On the other hand, a proliferation of fora will benefit more powerful countries by raising the transaction costs for policy negotiation and co-ordination and thereby helping these countries to retain the status quo.[77] Such higher costs, along with the increased incoherence, fragmentation and complexity in the international intellectual property regime complex, will be particularly damaging to less developed countries, as these countries tend to lack resources, expertise, leadership, negotiation sophistication and bargaining power.

The final challenge concerns the changing governance within the international intellectual property regime. From the Paris Convention to the TRIPS Agreement, the international intellectual property regime was built upon a state-centric international legal system. This system 'historically deferred to states as the guardians of domestic welfare, with the assumption that the appropriate exercise of sovereign power for domestic

---

[73]   Yu, supra note 43, at 13–21.

[74]   On forum-manipulative activities, see John Braithwaite and Peter Drahos, *Global Business Regulation*, Cambridge: Cambridge University Press, 2000, pp. 564–71; Laurence R. Helfer, 'Regime Shifting: The TRIPS Agreement and New Dynamics of International Intellectual Property Lawmaking', *Yale Journal of International Law*, 2004, vol. 29, pp. 1–83; Christopher May, *The World Intellectual Property Organization: Resurgence and the Development Agenda*, London: Routledge, 2007, p. 66.

[75]   Helfer, supra note 74, at 14; Donald J. Puchala and Raymond F. Hopkins, 'International Regimes: Lessons from Inductive Analysis', in Stephen D. Krasner (ed.), *International Regimes*, Ithaca: Cornell University Press, 1983, pp. 61–91, 66.

[76]   P. Bernt Hugenholtz and Ruth L. Okediji, *Conceiving an International Instrument on Limitations and Exceptions to Copyright: Final Report*, New York: Open Society Institute, 2008, p. 41.

[77]   Eyal Benvenisti and George W. Downs, 'The Empire's New Clothes: Political Economy and the Fragmentation of International Law', *Stanford Law Review*, 2007, vol. 60, pp. 595–631; Yu, supra note 13, at 556.

public interest would inure inevitably to the benefit of the global community'.[78] To the extent that non-state actors are involved, their interests are usually reflected through state actors who represent them.

Since the adoption of the TRIPS Agreement, however, civil society organizations have become much more active in the intellectual property arena. Consider their recent activism for example. From the widespread protests in Europe against the signing of ACTA to the massive internet service blackout in the run-up to the deliberation of the US SOPA/PIPA legislation, civil society organizations and internet user communities have played important roles in preventing the further enclosure of innovation space at both the domestic and international levels. As Sisule Musungu and Graham Dutfield observed, '[c]ivil society groups have been the single most important factor in raising the issue of the impact of the international intellectual property standards, especially TRIPS standards, on development issues such as health, food and agriculture'.[79]

Notwithstanding the many benefits provided by civil society organizations, China continues to have an uneasy relationship with these organizations.[80] Thus, if new fora were to be developed in the international intellectual property regime to better accommodate their positions and interests, such as the 'multilateral, multi-stakeholder, democratic and transparent' policy dialogue advocated in the World Summit on the Information Society and implemented through the Internet Governance Forum,[81] it is unclear how China would actively embrace this effort. It also remains to be seen whether China would take full advantage of these non-state-based dialogues to claw back some of the innovation space it has lost through the international enclosure movement.

---

[78]   Ruth L. Okediji, *The International Copyright System: Limitations, Exceptions and Public Interest Considerations for Developing Countries*, Geneva: UNCTAD-ICTSD Project on IPRs and Sustainable Development, 2006, p. ix.

[79]   Sisule F. Musungu and Graham Dutfield, *Multilateral Agreements and a TRIPS-plus World: The World Intellectual Property Organisation (WIPO)*, Geneva: Quaker United Nations Office, 2003, p. 22.

[80]   On the development of civil society organizations in China, see Karla W. Simon, *Civil Society in China: The Legal Framework from Ancient Times to the 'New Reform Era'*, Oxford: Oxford University Press, 2013.

[81]   Peter K. Yu, 'Intellectual Property and Human Rights in the Nonmultilateral Era', *Florida Law Review*, 2012, vol. 64, pp. 1045–100, 1079–80.

CONCLUSION

This chapter has painted a rather gloomy picture of the growing enclosure of innovation space within the international intellectual property regime. It shows how such enclosure could make it more difficult for China and other less developed countries to experiment with new, alternative forms of innovation[82] and to set standards that are tailored to their local needs, national interests, technological capabilities, institutional capacities and public health conditions.

Although China will certainly have more political and economic leverage than many poorer and smaller countries, the ongoing development of the existing international intellectual property regime will likely provide significant constraints on the country's ability to design new policies that are tailored to its specific needs, interests, conditions and priorities. Nevertheless, the recent emergence of China as an innovative power suggests that these constraints, while significant, may not affect China as much as other less developed countries. In many areas, China's developments are closer to those in developed countries than in other less developed countries, even though it continued to identify itself as the world's largest developing country and accrued strategic benefits by playing a leading role in the less developed world.

In addition, it is important to remember that the development of the international intellectual property regime remains highly dynamic. Indeed, the shape and size of this regime are likely to change as China becomes more assertive in setting international intellectual property standards. As I have noted elsewhere, the country may prefer a very different regime than the one existing today as its leverage and power continue to strengthen in the intellectual property arena.[83] Instead of following a well-trodden path set in the 19th century by today's developed countries, as discussed at the beginning of this chapter, China may want to become an innovator in not only the field of technologies, but also the field of intellectual property standards. Only time will tell whether China will succeed in building a new international intellectual property regime that aligns with its historical traditions, cultural backgrounds, socio-economic conditions, ideological values and policy preferences.

---

[82]   On the emergence of alternative forms of innovation in China, see Peter K. Yu, 'Intellectual Property and Asian Values', *Marquette Intellectual Property Law Review*, 2012, vol. 16, pp. 329–99, 389–92.

[83]   Peter K. Yu, 'The Global Intellectual Property Order and Its Undetermined Future', *WIPO Journal*, 2009, vol. 1, pp. 1–15, 13.

Index